BALANCING

REVISED
EDITION

ACT

A Canadian Woman's Financial Success Guide

D0191224

JOANNE THOMAS YACCATO

Prentice Hall Canada Inc.
Scarborough, Ontario

Canadian Cataloguing in Publication Data

Thomas Yaccato, Joanne, 1957–
     Balancing act: a Canadian woman's financial success guide

Rev. ed.
ISBN: 0-13-399627-1

1. Women – Canada – Finance, Personal. I. Title.

HG 179.T56   1996   332.024'042   C95-931893-3

Prentice-Hall, Inc., Englewood Cliffs, New Jersey
Prentice-Hall International (UK) Limited, London
Prentice-Hall of Australia, Pty. Limited, Sydney
Prentice-Hall Hispanoamericana, S.A., Mexico City
Prentice-Hall of India Private Limited, New Delhi
Prentice-Hall of Japan, Inc., Tokyo
Simon & Schuster Asia Private Limited, Singapore
Editora Prentice-Hall do Brasil, Ltda., Rio de Janeiro

ISBN 0-13-399627-1

Production Editor: Avivah Wargon
Production Coordinator: Anita Boyle-Evans
Copy Editor: Tanya Long
Cover and Interior Design: Olena Serbyn
Cover Photo: Neil Graham
Page Layout: Hermia Chung

2 3 4 5   00 99 98 97 96

Printed and bound in Canada.

Hair: Alan Davis of Alan Davis Salon
Dress: Holt Renfrew
Esthetics: Toula of Allazo Skin Care

Readers wishing further information on data provided through the cooperation
of Statistics Canada may obtain copies of related publications by mail from:
Publications Sales, Statistics Canada, Ottawa, Ontario, K1A 0T6, by calling
1-613-951-7277 or toll-free 1-800-267-6677. Readers may also facsimile
their order by dialing 1-613-951-1584.

DEDICATION

TO

DIANNE KATHLEEN THOMAS YACCATO
MY MOTHER AND BEST FRIEND

SHE MAKES THE ACT OF
BALANCING LIFE AN ART FORM.

CONTENTS

FIGURES

TABLES

AUTHOR'S NOTE

Those with an astute eye for detail will notice my waistline, evident on the cover of the first book, has for all intents and purposes disappeared in the photograph on this edition's cover. This should provide something of a clue to how life has progressed since the first edition of *Balancing Act* came out.

Curious? Read on, dear readers. The answer awaits you somewhere within these pages.

Joanne Thomas Yaccato
September 1995

FOREWORD

A married woman visits a financial advisor. She has just inherited $50,000 and wonders whether to pay down the mortgage on the family home or invest it. "Think carefully," the advisor says. If you pay down the mortgage and later split up with your husband, he gets half the house. If the money is invested, you keep it all in a divorce, since inheritances don't fall under the *Family Law Act.* "Be realistic," the advisor says. "One in three marriages ends in divorce. Protect yourself in case yours breaks up too."

The advisor was Joanne Thomas Yaccato, and she told this story to a focus group she had organized before writing this book. I was there and thought, "Hey, she's onto something." Women need independent financial advice from someone who understands their special status. The course of action that's right for a man may not be appropriate for a woman in the same position. It all depends.

As someone who encouraged Joanne to take on this project and saw her through it, I think her message is important and needs to reach a wider audience. Her strongly personal tone—and her unflinching honesty in admitting mistakes—should strike a chord in many readers.

Women are generally very good money managers. We're good at budgeting and comparison shopping and making our dollars stretch further. Where we've lagged behind is in long-term financial planning and investing. We've left it to the men in our lives, or skipped over it because it can be dull and technical—some of us fear math.

I've been writing about money for 20 years, first as a consumer advocate and later as a personal finance specialist. When I switched from news to business in 1987, I found my female readership dropped off dramatically. Many women asked if I had left *The Globe and Mail.* The readership of *Report on Business* is about 80 percent men and 20 percent women. That's a shame because business and economic events affect all of us, no matter which way we button our shirts, and we all need to keep a watchful eye on what's happening.

x

When I started reading financial books, I noticed many of them were written by male accountants and lawyers for male readers. Women did not figure prominently except as a tax deduction. Few authors acknowledged the new economic realities—that women were earning money (often more than their spouses), saving and investing, and looking after their own financial futures. At the same time, women were discriminated against by a male-oriented tax and pension system, coping with divorce and custody laws that could leave them destitute and messy estate procedures after their husbands died.

In her work with the Women's Financial Planning Centre, Joanne has seen it all. She knows where women are coming from and where they should be going. This book describes her own financial journey from recklessness to self-awareness and should help others who are beginning the same arduous route.

Joanne is energetic, lively, funny and earthy. An entertaining speaker, she will be tireless in spreading the word to Canadian women. She is just what we need to get us off our butts and into action. So sit back and enjoy it. You're in for a treat.

Ellen Roseman
Associate Managing Editor
The Globe and Mail

ACKNOWLEDGMENTS

Financial services is a tough business but writing a book is even tougher. Having someone to guide you through the interminable maze and console you when you think you are about to go off the edge is a real blessing. Well, God was sure smiling on me. I have not one, but a cast of thousands who lived, breathed and supported this project with me. My dear friend and mentor, David Chilton, planted the seed in my brain about writing a book on personal finance for Canadian women. He continually urged me to rise to this challenge, believing I was capable even though, at times, I may not have been so sure. David's unfailing moral support, steady input and really bad jokes throughout this process made the whole thing not only possible, but palatable. Ellen Roseman and Peter Volpé are two of the most generous and patient people I have ever met. Though ultimately my complete responsibility, Ellen and Peter were my technical advisors and combed the manuscript to ensure accuracy. Their contributions guaranteed high quality content. But more importantly, Ellen and Peter were steadfast supporters. In a nutshell, I drove them crazy. It was a true test of friendship as they good-naturedly welcomed my almost daily barrage of questions and calmed my frazzled nerves when the pressure became too much. We weathered a lot together.

Murray Oxby, Eleanor Whyte and Hubert Frenken spent much of their free time reviewing the manuscript and astounded me with their generous spirit. Without exception, every idea and suggestion they had was incorporated in the book.

My family couldn't be more excited if I had become Canada's second woman Prime Minister. My mother was my strongest ally and most sensible critic. I trusted and depended entirely on her for everything from actual book content to editing the manuscript. My father is a man of few, but usually well-chosen, words. He didn't say much, but he made sure I felt what I needed to.

Kim Speers started out as my research assistant and quickly became a friend and confidante. We experienced a great deal of frustration researching this book, but after every 12-hour day, we would end up laughing uproariously at something or other.

Her sense of the absurd and wonderful humour made the experience so much more joyful.

Linda, Marion and Clarence Arthur are truly remarkable people. They generously opened their hearts, their home and their tractor to me when I decided I needed the contemplative surroundings of the country in which to write. I spent close to a year living on their farm, completely unplugged from the usual distractions of the city. I firmly believe this book could never have been written had I not had access to the peace and tranquillity of rural Ontario and their unflagging moral support. I also want to thank the good people of Everett and Alliston and the staff of the Globe Restaurant in Rosemont who warmly welcomed me into their community.

Children had the greatest impact on my mental health through this project. The time I spent with my brilliant and talented twin five-year-old nieces, Krystal and Vanessa Yaccato, did more to ground me than just about anything else. They constantly reminded me of what was really important in life: eating, sleeping and unconditional love. It's not a whole lot more complicated than that.

Two very special friends worked tirelessly through every technological disaster and nightmare I experienced while writing this book. Ruth Gastle and Sheldon Waters of Data Systems Marketing endured phones calls at all times of the day and night and always laughed at the fact that my crisis of the day would invariably be "operator error."

There were many people who read the manuscript and offered wonderful feedback that I truly appreciated and most often incorporated into the book. My heartfelt thanks to all of you who spent time and energy reading the manuscript. I also want to thank the countless people from the financial services industry and periphery who opened their files and research to me and Kim to use in this book. There were so many that it would be impossible to name everyone. When all was said and done, Kim and I both agreed that our faith in the financial services community, for the most part, was restored.

A note of appreciation to all those folks who stayed in touch, just to be sure I hadn't run off with the farmer next door. And a special thanks to a fellow I have nick-named my "guardian angel."

Paul McKinstry went a long way to help smooth out the rough spots over the last year.

I agonized for months over what to name the first edition of this book. My good friend, Pat Toms, a nurse and eight months pregnant with her third child, came up with *Balancing Act* over dinner one night. How appropriate. Of course, she would know.

A special thank you to Michelle MacIsaac, General Manager of Women and Money Inc., for showing me the *real* value of a dedicated employee. I couldn't have done any of this without her.

Richard Wessell and *The Globe and Mail*'s Brian Gable are the two talented cartoonists who greatly livened up the pages of this new edition.

Lastly, but only chronologically, is my dear friend, Barbara Sampson. Barbara opened the door for me into a whole new world. She took a chance on a complete unknown, and that chance changed my life.

MY STORY

"Please know that I am aware of the hazards. I want to do it because I want to do it. Women must try to do things as men have tried. When they fail, their failure must be but a challenge to others."

Amelia Earhart (1898-1937) in a letter to her husband, before her last flight

The memory is vivid. I close my eyes and allow the images to shimmer to life. I can see the surroundings and experience the feelings, even though this event happened over 30 years ago. I was one of the first of 29 grandchildren in a large Irish-Italian family. For four years, my status remained unchallenged and I revelled in the numero uno spot. Queen of the castle, as it were. But then this all changed.

The arrival of my brother Jeff motivated my mother to introduce me to my first adult concept: *allowance*. It was Saturday morning. Mom helped me bathe and change my new brother Jeff. Afterward, she invited me to sit with her on my bed for one of our talks. As I followed her into my room, a stab of fear went through me. I had a finely tuned sense of guilt even at five. "Joanne," she began, "you have been such a big help to mommy with Jeff, I think it's time to start giving you an allowance." I let out a sigh of relief.

She continued, "Honey, do you understand what I am saying?" This was a poignant moment between mother and daughter. I was curious and impatient. I sensed that my mother was talking about something very important, though I had no idea what an allowance was.

"Daddy and I think you are big enough to have your own money. You can do whatever you want with it."

My mother went on. "An allowance is money you earn by doing extra things around the house. We are going to give you ten cents a week." She pressed a shiny, thin dime into my tiny palm and gently closed my fingers around it. Her tone grew more serious. "We trust you with this responsibility, sweetheart. If you spend it all at once, you will have to wait until next Saturday before you get any more money. Try to budget and spend one or two cents each day for your special treats."

I looked up at my mother's face and saw a very special pride. Her little girl was growing up. I nodded gravely as the implications began to register. Then I did what any self-respecting, budding contrarian would do.

I promptly went out and dropped the whole bundle.

That behaviour pattern repeated itself in varying degrees for the better part of 25 years. There isn't a financial mistake that I, or a member of my family, has not made. I used to describe myself as being one of the "financially challenged." When they pick up this book and see my name on the cover, people who knew me years ago will react in one of two ways: they will either gasp in total disbelief or laugh uproariously.

Laugh on, McDuff! I'm what you call born-again, a recovering spender. I put away childish notions that "he" will come and relieve me of this tiresome burden of money and all that it entails. I've buried the knight in shining armour. I went from being diagnosed as hopeless and thrown out of grade 11 math to doing tax and estate planning for a living.

Prior to "crossing over," my eyes would glaze over or I would fall asleep at any talk of money or investing. I now endeavour to keep thousands of people awake each year giving speeches on this very same topic. In my early 20s, I managed to get in trouble with credit cards, so much so that I needed the services of the Credit Counselling Service of Metropolitan Toronto. Today, I sit on their Board of Directors. How did this amazing transformation take place? What deep, profound experience provoked such a change?

I turned 30.

On the morning of my 30th birthday I woke up and mentally looked about. This was not what I had envisioned for myself as I was growing up. I awoke that morning in a rented house with a leased car in the driveway. My closet boasted the finest quality clothing money could buy but a family of moths had taken up permanent residence in my bank account. If an emergency happened that cost more than $24, I was in deep trouble. I used to joke that I had all the money I needed...if I died by four o'clock. It was a "live for the moment" type of existence. It wasn't money that was my problem. It was my attitude toward it that needed adjusting.

It was the booming '80s. The computer industry was exploding. I had a very successful career as a senior account executive for a major computer company selling office automation and networks to Fortune 500 companies. There was a certain irony in the fact that I was responsible for sales and marketing to banks, large brokerage houses and insurance companies. There was a group of us in our late 20s earning absurd amounts of money. Like that five-year-old with her allowance, I was spending it as fast as I made it. Bills got paid but inconsistently. Credit card bills waited sometimes two or three months before I'd take care of them. Rent and car payments were always on time but only because of post-dated cheques. Savings consisted of the odd Canada Savings Bond deducted at source from work, but invariably it would be cashed before the year was out, usually to pay a bill. If the bond made it to maturity, I would use it to buy my family or that special someone a ridiculously expensive Christmas present. My money disappeared like a snowflake on a hot stove.

I had always wanted to own my own home but never gave it very serious thought because it seemed completely out of my financial reach. I wasn't about to alter my lifestyle to try to save for a down payment. Underneath this high-spending lifestyle, I was living with that low-level anxiety that creeps into the base of your neck and shoulders. It was there all the time but I worked hard not to notice it. I would think about money only when absolutely necessary. That was usually when correspondence from the bank highlighted with red ink arrived via priority post. I lurched from one financial crisis to another.

My career was a double-edged sword. Income did not determine my lifestyle. On the contrary, lifestyle determined my income. Because I was very good in sales and marketing and was paid commission, I could "write my own paycheque." If I needed more money, I was able to go out and earn more. Although I made a lot of money, my attitude toward it was the same as when I was an impoverished university student. The concepts of budgeting, saving and self-restraint were as foreign to me as cuneiform. I came to depend on my earning power for financial stability. It was a harrowing way to live.

I should have become aware of a burgeoning budgeting problem when I found myself giving the woman in charge of our payroll an expensive bottle of wine and a thank you card for Christmas one year. She and I got to know each other reasonably well as a result of my frequent visits requesting advances until payday. Sales has a way of being cyclical, even at the best of times. At the worst of times, there were months when the money simply wasn't there.

In my early 20s, I discovered the seductive power of credit cards. The banks were pushing their wares at the university I attended. Like many, I jumped on the bandwagon with reckless abandon and passed through the portals of adulthood. I became the proud owner of my first Visa card. But I was not equipped to understand the dark side of credit. However, it quickly reared its head. It began when I broke my ankle in three places and subsequently lost my job. I was a commissioned salesperson. If you can't walk, you can't work. If you can't work, you can't sell. If you can't sell, you can't keep your job. No job, no income. Enter Ms. Visa and her trusty sidekick, Mary Mastercard. These proved to be a very expensive source of emergency funds. They were also the instrument of the beginning of an insidious downward spiral into debt. For me, using credit cards wasn't like spending real money. They were simply pieces of plastic that allowed unnecessary indulgences on a whim. I was able to continue my lifestyle uninterrupted especially during those lean periods commonplace in sales. At the time I believed credit cards saved my life.

I lived in the shadow of debt for five years before I finally cried "uncle." On two credit cards alone, I carried balances that were anywhere from one to two thousand dollars monthly but often I would pay only the minimum required each month. If you miss a month or two, that minimum really adds up, not to mention what it does to your credit rating. In addition, there were other minor annoyances such as rent, car payments, student loan and so on.

The irony was that I hated debt. As a teenager, I had witnessed first hand the destructive power of unmanaged debt. The recession of the '70s saw my father get caught in the dying economy. That, combined with his "money is for making and spending, not keeping" philosophy, forced him to file for personal bankruptcy. I was 19 when we lost everything. The memory of this experience did much to intensify the fear I had deep inside that I would end up a bag lady—old, alone and broke. It was a terrifying image to break from but I had to try. I decided that, if nothing else, I had to get out of debt. I was beginning to see how easily one could lose control. By the age of 28, with the help of a credit counselling agency, I had managed to wrestle the debt monster to the ground. I was debt free, but I had unknowingly destroyed my credit rating. I couldn't even get a Zeller's credit card.

RRSPs? Mutual funds? Emergency fund? Insurance? Consider the odds! Money was something you spent. Invest? The thought never occurred to me. On that wintry, gray March morning that I turned 30, I had an epiphany. Well, more like a bash on the head with a large, blunt object. Just where was that house with the white picket fence? The 2.5 children in Montessori school? The golden lab? What about Mr. Right? He turned into Mr. Left. All there was, quite simply, was me.

And yet, I reasoned, things could be worse. I could have the house with forest green trim and matching shutters, the twin son and daughter, the golden lab, be married to Mel Gibson and still be a financial illiterate when I ended up in divorce court. Too many weddings I have attended have ended up in the hands of divorce lawyers. The statisticians say that one in three marriages fails. "At least," I thought, "I'm still on the youthful side of adult and have only myself to worry about." I looked at myself in the mirror with a very critical eye, examining the inside as well as the outside.

The outside. That was something else again.

I had quit smoking five years earlier. I turned around slowly, looking in the mirror gasping in amazement. The 115-pound body I had always taken for granted had gone into hiding. Deep hiding. It looked as though the good old days were over. I couldn't disguise the alarming fact that I had jumped up two sizes. "Fat and broke," I thought miserably. The urge to go back to bed with a lifetime supply of M&Ms was overwhelming. I felt as though I had hit rock bottom. I began to wonder why, since I had discipline in other areas of my life, I wasn't able to tackle these two thorns in my side. I decided this was the time to take financial control. If I was able to have a decent and fulfilling personal life, why couldn't I have a decent and fulfilling financial life? The two, I decided, were not necessarily mutually exclusive.

There was only one thing stopping me. Pure unadulterated fear.

The task seemed huge. Though I had managed to pay off the National Debt, credit was an integral part of life and I was unable to get it. There was advanced mathematics to learn, the *Income Tax Act* to master, banks to rob to acquire enough money to invest, and the care and feeding of the stock market. The list went on and on. Not surprisingly, by my second cup of coffee, I had convinced myself I was still much too young to be concerned about financial security. Strains of "Live for today! Tomorrow will take care of itself!" reverberated through my head. I found myself wondering how I had gotten to this place. What do I do now? How does one get good with money? Isn't that something you're born with? The accepted conventional wisdom I had always been bombarded with suggested clearly that men came out of the womb with inherent knowledge about finances and how to fix cars. Women, on the other hand, knew all about babies and how to cook. "Good news!" I thought dismally. "I'm 0 for 2."

However, it's like coming out of a long coma; as much as I might have wanted to, I couldn't go back to blissful oblivion. I realized that through the simple act of waking up, I had put an end to my old financial habits. There was no turning back.

I also realized that it was virtually impossible for me to change my behaviour around money until I knew *why* I behaved the way I did. I had tried countless times to get my money life on track, only to have it derailed after a credit-card-induced impulse purchase. I had spent 30 years trying to will myself to change and develop this elusive discipline. All it did was reinforce my belief that I wasn't any good in this area. I slowly began to see that beliefs about money are based on emotional responses to certain life experiences. I began to challenge my beliefs. I stopped caring whether they made sense or were true. They were there and had to be recognized. I was getting pretty tired of the huge gap between what was supposed to happen in my money life and what really went on.

I stopped the perpetual questioning: "Why can't I control my spending? Why can't I be more disciplined? Why can't I get rid of this stupid fear around money? Why can't I get this math thing? Why can't I....Why can't I...." I began to change my language. Instead of "why can't I," the drill became "why not." I deleted the phrases "I shouldn't have to," "I don't want to" and "I can't" from my vocabulary. I found myself beginning to question all the conventions I had accepted at face value. I was appalled at how little I was taught or how little I was expected to know about looking after myself financially. And I don't mean my parents. All institutions had a hand in it: school, religion, media, government. But criticizing myself and the world around me was a waste of valuable energy. I needed to channel this energy correctly. I decided to keep things simple. There was absolutely no risk here for me. It's hard to fall off the bottom.

And so I began the arduous journey to physical and financial fitness. I had to take steps to ease my fears around money. Admitting I needed to do something and beginning to talk about money was a good first step. I found myself talking with others who had surprisingly similar experiences. Seeing the similarities helped to rid me of the shame of my youthful indulgences. There were few resources readily available. In those days, personal finance sections in bookstores didn't exist. Bank managers, stock brokers and insurance agents didn't fall over themselves to knock on your door if you were a woman. Their advice wouldn't have meant much to me anyway until I understood what the crux of my financial problem was. I demonstrated discipline and skill in many areas of my life but I couldn't figure out why I had none (or so I thought) with money. I finally figured it out.

I had no training about money and no *expectations* except, perhaps subconsciously, those of the man I was going to marry. With no appropriate training and with conflicting role models, how could I expect myself to have appropriate behaviour? With so little understanding of my behaviour around money, it was no small wonder that my attempts at budgeting and planning had failed so miserably in the past. It was a huge relief to realize there was absolutely nothing wrong with me. I just had to concern myself with the minor business of completely unlearning what I had been taught and of learning what I hadn't been taught, which was workable money behaviour. A crucial element in the success of my financial recovery was recognizing that the solution to becoming financially secure was not to be found outside of myself. The government was broke and men had enough to contend with in their own lives. I had to unlearn that I didn't need to worry about paying my bills. I had to unlearn that I didn't need to know the rules of the credit game. I had to unlearn that someone else was going to come along with a house or at least the money to buy one. Unlearning that putting off paying taxes is not really wise and unlearning that someone else will look after me in old age was a painful process. The most important unlearning meant dismissing the messages everywhere that I didn't need to worry about being successful, financially or otherwise, as long as the man I married was.

I was afraid that learning new behaviour around money was going to be unbelievably hard. The idea filled me with tremendous fear until I realized it was going to be a cakewalk compared to the way I was living. So it was first things first. I grappled with my weight by eliminating red meat, sugar and alcohol. I began to exercise in earnest. One year later, I was 25 pounds and two suit sizes lighter. It was a remarkably freeing experience. As easy as it was to get caught in the downward spiral, I discovered the reverse was also true. I joyfully embarked on a positive spiral. Physically fit, I was now committed to getting on my way to financial health.

Though my debt was under control, I still had no savings or investments of any sort. I didn't understand what an RRSP was.

Though I was willing to talk to certain people I trusted, I wasn't about to walk up to a bank teller and admit total ignorance. I was still caught in the old paycheque to paycheque regime. In short, I had no long-term financial goals. Long-term to me meant, at the outside, the following month. As fate would have it, the solution fell right into my lap.

A year after my "financial epiphany," I closed a deal to provide laptop computers to a major insurance company for their agents in the field. This same company had developed a marketing concept that offered a financial planning centre specifically targeting their financial services to women. When I heard about this centre, I was intrigued. One of my biggest goals was to find a place that could give me what I needed—education. I wanted a place that would treat me seriously and take the time to teach me the most basic elements of financial planning. I wanted to talk with someone to whom I wouldn't be embarrassed to admit that the only thing I knew about an RRSP was how to spell it.

I gritted my teeth and plunged headlong into the world of financial planning. I understood instinctively that if women were to achieve real freedom, it had to start with financial independence. Talking to an advisor was the beginning of a journey that would become one of financial and personal self-discovery. It was an evolving process fraught with pain and much laughter. The hardest part of getting my financial house in order was developing realistic expectations. It was 20 miles into the woods. I wasn't going to get out in two.

As I was slowly getting my financial act together, there were several attempts to recruit me at this centre. My reaction was always a light-hearted and jokingly pompous, "You couldn't afford me." The reality was I would have felt like an impostor. I knew how to make money. But although I was slowly learning, I still didn't know what to do with it or how to keep it. I became friends with my financial advisor, Elaine, who was also the manager of this centre. One day over lunch she pinned me down with a formal job offer. Elaine started by saying that she thought I would be a tremendous asset in helping educate women to become financially knowledgeable. After all, I was a successful and independent career woman. I would be a terrific role model. I was committed to women's and men's equality in all facets of life so why not consider helping women take financial control.

I have always been very involved in helping others through volunteer work or paid jobs. I have worked at crisis intervention centres, I've designed programs for seniors that allowed them to stay in their own homes instead of being institutionalized and I've worked with aboriginal groups and low-income families. The idea of being of service by helping women take financial control of their destiny was almost too good to be true. This woman had struck a chord.

Elaine went on. Sure, I would have to "go back to school" to learn everything I needed to. She threw around terms like mutual funds licence, life and disability insurance licence, Chartered Financial Consultant, Chartered Financial Planner, Registered Financial Planner and Chartered Life Underwriter. I looked at her with considerable skepticism. One thing kept echoing in my mind, "This is absurd, you can't do this! You're a no-brainer in math." There was little encouragement for young women to go into math or science at my high school. There were significantly fewer females than males in these areas of study. The girls who did go into science and math were in a league of their own. They were called the "brainers" and were decidedly uncool. Most of us followed the more traditional female route of social sciences, languages or the humanities. In grade 11, I found myself face to face with a formidable challenge—algebra. To say I hated it would be a grave understatement. I stood firm in my refusal to remain conscious during the class. I was convinced in real life there was no such thing as algebra. I remember my algebra teacher calling my mother to the school for a meeting to discuss my difficulties. He informed us that it was not unusual for "girls" to struggle with math. He had seen it over and over again in his career. It would likely be in my best interest to get out of math and concentrate on what I had shown an aptitude for—English. We all agreed, I most enthusiastically. After all he was the teacher and should know. At that moment, I came to believe what so many young girls are socialized to believe, that I was useless in math. This incident changed the course of my life. Instead of being encouraged in an area where I experienced a certain conceptual difficulty, I was pulled out of it completely. I was left with the impression that I wasn't any good with numbers.

I went on to get my Arts degree in psychology, which I chose specifically for its alleged lack of math. I was in for another of life's many rude awakenings as I discovered too late that quantitative statistics was a compulsory course. One of my professors told me this in passing one day and nothing could have prepared him for my reaction. We were sitting in the cafeteria at lunch time. The silence hung heavily between us for about ten seconds as I processed this news. I was now in the enviable position of having to draw on grade 11 math to help master the elements of university-level statistics. I blinked once and began to laugh. Not a casual titter or giggle, but an actual howl, with a notable edge of hysteria. The laugh gathered momentum and volume as I began to sputter and gasp for breath. By the time my professor had leaped to his feet to calm me down, the cafeteria had become completely silent. Every pair of eyes was riveted to my now crimson face.

I would be lying if I said that thoughts of putting that algebra teacher to death hadn't crossed my mind. Interestingly enough, as a result of countless sleepless nights and fierce, stubborn determination, I passed the statistics course. I sometimes wonder how different things might have been had my math teacher encouraged me to tough it out. My disdain for anything mathematical might not have been so pronounced. At the very least, I would have slept more during that statistics course.

As Elaine continued to talk about the rewards of this new career she was offering me, my thoughts wandered to the strangeness of it all. It was evident that my image was pretty convincing. The outside package reflected a highly competent woman. I was, in fact, very competent except in the vital area of managing my personal finances. I made my living at managing national accounts and conducted and negotiated financial transactions in the hundreds of thousands of dollars as a matter of course. Yet my own finances had been a shambles. So, if I were to consider seriously this career change, I would have to deal with the Impostor Syndrome. Money was about power and I certainly didn't feel powerful in that area. And what about the math? All those designations required courses in accounting. Hadn't I already been told I couldn't do this?

And there was another matter: Surely someone with my financial past couldn't possibly begin to advise others on financial matters. Or could they? It has always been my experience that the best teachers were the ones who "walked the walk."

Anyone could "talk the talk." Maybe I was as good a candidate as anyone. Maybe better. I began to wonder why I was being asked to consider doing something for a living that involved the number-one nemesis in my life. The possibility of helping women become financially literate would force me to turn and look full in the face my fear about money and everything it stood for. I decided to come clean and tell Elaine my story. All of it.

"…So there you have it," I finished. I was spent, as though I had run an ironwoman triathlon. Being rigorously honest is an exhausting experience. After listening to me for over an hour, this wonderful woman looked at me evenly and in a confident voice said, "You're hired." And that, as they say, was that. I ended a lucrative career in the computer industry, took the next six months off and studied hard to become a licensed financial advisor. It was over the course of my time with Elaine that I became financially literate. Each session offered new insights and information that proved invaluable. I was astounded at how quickly the fear disappeared. I ended up demystifying the process by becoming part of it.

Over the next few years, I counselled thousands of women and men on the importance of financial planning. I often shared my experiences, which broke the ice and eased people's angst around this topic. I became fascinated by women's wide-ranging attitudes on money and what it represents. Men's attitudes toward women's attitudes on money was even more compelling. As part of my ongoing research, I conducted regular focus groups for women, each concentrating on a different aspect of the subject. The men's groups, where we discussed men's views of women and money, were of particular interest. Especially to the women. They tried to coerce me into playing the taped men's sessions at their focus group. I graciously declined. I did discover, however, that little has changed in spite of appearances.

The focus groups clearly illustrated that the families of many women didn't take their goals and dreams seriously. It was also my experience that my career and financial contribution was often disregarded. I can remember on several occasions trying to discuss money matters with one particular partner. As we attempted to plan financially for a house and children, I noticed he never factored in or even acknowledged my income. Everything was based entirely on his. It was my intention to continue my career, which would have been possible if he were willing to assume 50 percent of the work at home. I brought this to his attention often but he would fall silent. Occasionally he would grunt an enthusiastic, "Oh, yeah." The next time we talked about money, the same thing would happen. It was as if I didn't financially exist. I finally figured it out. Besides his full repertoire of prehistoric beliefs, it was probably tough to take seriously someone who continually blew money the way I did. I was fiercely independent in all spheres of my life, but had done nothing to financially ensure this independence. Even though it was clear I was trying to mend my ways, my history spoke for itself.

Some women are passive in their attitudes toward money, as I was, because we had been taught nothing about it or that our partners would look after it. If I, and thousands of women like me, were to move forward, we needed to put the proverbial knight in shining armour to rest. In my capacity as a financial advisor for women, I take great pride in the fact that I have been instrumental in the assassination of countless Knight-in-Shining-Armour Syndromes (not the knight himself). There are now many more women who are comfortable with having themselves to count on financially. It is easier to deal with life on life's terms when you finally realize that Prince Charming doesn't come on a white horse anymore. He comes in a Ford and needs help with the payments.

Financial planning is not, in and of itself, a gender issue. A stock is oblivious to the chromosomes of its owner. However, there are differences in what motivates each sex on the topic of money. These differences are the direct result of how women and men are socialized. Having said that, I must also say that trying to put a segment of the population as large and as diverse as "women" into one special interest group is not only inaccurate, it's downright idiotic. Women are not a homogeneous group that think, feel, act and dream the same way. Economic class, race, sexual orientation, age, geographic location and a host of other characteristics all help to diversify women's identity. To try to make general statements about all women and their financial practices is irresponsible. Not all women are spendthrifts, conservative investors or afraid of risk. A financial plan needs to be as individual as the person who has it. Women in their 20s have dramatically different financial goals than women in their 50s and 60s. This is the result not only of age, but of differing experiences and expectations.

There are, however, some noteworthy similarities in women's attitudes about money that derive from our socialized role. There is also the matter of biology. Being the child bearers of the species has serious financial ramifications that contribute to women's "financial alikeness." In my research I discovered that many women don't use the male standard to measure success. Women are often motivated by variables that include but go beyond money and power. This is certainly the case for me. I didn't think in terms of "money and power." I was more interested in independence, being of use and service to others, liking my work and receiving recognition from my peers. Pursuing these goals subsequently brought money and then power. This is not to suggest men aren't also motivated by such things as a desire for independence and being of service. But if you ask a man and a woman (as I often do) to compile a list of what motivates them and what constitutes success, both lists most often include the same things. Money, power, adequate family time, financial freedom to travel or stay at home, secure retirement, material possessions and peace of mind are just a few of the items frequently mentioned. It's the order of importance in which they are listed that separates the sexes. To prove the point, I conducted an experiment with several women who were ardently against the notion that there were any differences between men and women on the issue of money. They did this simple exercise of listing their priorities, with their mates. After we reviewed the results, I couldn't help myself. I smugly sat back and levelled them with my best "I told you so" gaze. Most of them were astonished by the results. What headed many of their lists often sat at the bottom of their partners' lists. Certainly not in all cases, but in enough cases to catch one's attention.

Frankly, the majority of people are still not used to the idea of women having money and power. There are deeply pervasive attitudes that women have no place in or no head for business and finance. These are historically a man's domain. In most cases, the thought that women are out of their realm in business or finance is not even a conscious one, but more a deeply inbred expectation that has been passed on by generations.

I remember an incident that happened in my health club one morning. It was customary for me as a Stairmaster enthusiast to climb these stairs to nowhere and read the newspaper. As a financial advisor, naturally the first section I turned to was the business section. As I read each section, I would discard it in a pile beside me. A gentleman in his early 50s approached me politely and asked if he might read some of my paper. Before I could answer affirmatively, he bent over and picked up the just discarded business section. He innocently said, "Oh terrific, I'll read this. It's business, you won't want it." I was dumbfounded. "Why might that be?" I quietly inquired. He started to stutter and stammer some kind of reply. I was then witness to his dawning realization that he had made this assumption because I was a woman. He was horrified. He fell over his feet apologizing, trying to offer some kind of explanation. He couldn't get away from me fast enough. What was most interesting was not so much my reaction to his remark, but his own reaction to it. It shocked him that he had made such a remark, but even more so that he had thought it. Attitudes can be so deeply ingrained we don't even know we hold them much of the time. Every year I had been in the financial planning business, I had qualified for the insurance industry's Million Dollar Round Table. This is a designation that less than two percent of the industry worldwide attained and was based on service and sales performance. Even though I had earned the right to be part of this so-called "elite," predominantly male club, I still had to deal with being called "babe" and "honey" by a few of my older male colleagues.

In 1992, I qualified to attend my company's U.K. division's conference in Paris as one of Canada's top representatives. I was excited beyond all imagination, as it was my first trip to "the continent." Once over there, I had the most eye-opening experience. Out of over three hundred delegates, I was one of only three women attending who wasn't married to a qualifier, and the *only* one from this side of the pond. My then partner, whom I had invited along, was totally amused by the fact that everyone who came up to us thrust out their hand to shake *his* hand and congratulate *him* on getting to Paris. He would smile and quickly retort, "Wrong person, chap! Joanne's the one you should be congratulating." This was invariably met with surprise and the look of wide-eyed curiosity one generally experiences when seeing snow for the first time. Even the president's wife, over dinner one night, had the audacity to ask what my position was with the human resources department. My partner overheard this comment and quickly excused himself from the table. You could hear him howling all the way to the washroom. The comment from his wife prompted the company president to make an announcement the next day that it was I, not my partner, who had qualified to be in Paris. This experience drove home something that I didn't really want to ever acknowledge, and that was that both *women* and *men* are still not used to seeing women in positions of power and prestige.

Thankfully, these definitions, roles and labels we put ourselves into are starting to break down and men and women are crossing over into each other's traditional territories. However, it's impossible to change overnight something so fundamentally ingrained, which may explain why many of these traditional attitudes persist even with today's generation. The experiences I had did little to help combat the "Impostor Syndrome" I fought with almost every day of my adult life. They reinforced the "you don't belong here" feeling. No matter what job I was in, as I got higher up the echelon I would think how "lucky" I was. Seldom did I think "you deserve this because you worked your tail off!" At the same time, I was terrified at the prospect of being successful. My mind would race at a dizzying pace: "What happens if I can't continue at this level of success? What do I do for my next trick? Do I really belong here or is this a weird accident or twist of fate?" It was only after realizing and admitting that this was a self-esteem issue and not a capability issue that I started to feel less and less the impostor. The words of Eleanor Roosevelt rang very true for me at this point: "No one can make you feel inferior without your consent."

There is no question the best thing I ever did for myself was to change my career path into financial planning. The more I learned, the more I realized how little the financial services industry knew about women and their money behaviour and potential. I knew because I worked at the grassroots level teaching women and men proper financial planning based on the realities of women's lives. The demand for information was growing at a monumental rate. I started to preach the edict, "never confuse lack of education with lack of ability." Both women and men *both* in the financial services area and outside of it needed to be educated on women and money. This was my calling. I eventually decided to stretch my wings and start my own company, Women and Money Inc., which specializes in educating women about money and educating the financial services industry about women. We teach the teachers.

During the course of our research, we uncovered government and United Nations statistics that determined several things that women need to pay attention to.

The 1995 UN Human Development Report says that in every region of the world, women placed a distant second to men in terms of wages, leisure time, political power, legal rights and business opportunities. John Stackhouse of *The Globe and Mail* reported, "In no society do women enjoy the same opportunities as men."[1]

The United Nations survey ranks Canada first among nations in terms of overall human development such as literacy and life expectancy but only ninth when the gap between men and women is considered. Since 1970, Canada's ranking on gender equality—once second to the United States—has fallen seven places, mainly because Canada has made less progress than other industrial nations in closing the wage gap between women and men. The report states that in non-agricultural sectors Canadian women earn only 63 percent of what men earned, as compared to the global average of 74.9 percent. This puts Canada in 47th place out of 55 countries and last among members of the Organization for Economic Cooperation and Development (OECD).

As reported in *The Globe and Mail*, the findings are "a major indictment of the continuing discrimination against women in most societies," said James Gustave Speth, administrator of the UN Development program.[2] The report goes on to say that on every continent women work longer hours, earn less money and are more likely to live in poverty than are men. It estimates that a full 70 percent of the world's 1.3 billion poor are women. The UN says the formal economy fails to account for $11 trillion a year of economic goods and services—from home care in Canada to firewood collection in Kenya—produced by women. Incidentally, the UN itself does not hold itself in great stead—only 30 percent of all professional jobs and 11.3 percent of senior management jobs in its various agencies are held by women. Statistics Canada supports these findings with its own research.

For example, 60 percent of women aged 60 to 65 are at the poverty line or lower. Single mothers make up a disproportionate number of Canada's poor. To make matters worse, women earn one-third less than men but live on average six years longer.

Living longer on less money makes women financially vulnerable. It's astounding to me that even women with the same education levels as men still earn so much less than men. The chart below from Statistics Canada shows that a university educated woman does somewhat better than a woman with a high school diploma but still gets paid only 75 percent of what her male counterpart receives. What *is* particularly compelling to note is the impact of marital status on women's earnings. Statistics Canada reports that in 1993 *single* women employed full-time for a full year earned *96 percent* of what men earned whereas the earnings of both married and other women were only about 70 percent. I'll let you draw your own conclusion.

Women generally have lower incomes than do men, regardless of their station in life. In 1993, StatsCan reported the average annual pre-tax income of women aged 15 and over from all sources was $16,500, just 58 percent the average income of men ($28,600).

TABLE 1.1 GENDER GAP IN PAY

Women working full-time earned less than men in 1993 despite same level of education.

	Women	Men	Women's earnings as a % of men's
Educational attainment			
Less than Grade 9	$20,024	$29,127	68.7
Some secondary school	21,124	34,165	61.8
Secondary school graduate	24,873	34,703	71.7
Some postsecondary	24,470	37,995	64.4
Postsecondary certificate/diploma	28,183	38,174	73.8
University degree	40,669	54,152	75.1
Total	28,392	39,433	72.0

Source: Statistics Canada.

FIGURE 1.1 PERCENTAGE OF WOMEN EMPLOYED PART-TIME WHO WANT FULL-TIME EMPLOYMENT, 1976–1994

Women represent 45 percent of the Canadian paid labour force, yet 57 percent of the women work in jobs that don't provide pensions. Women make up almost two-thirds of the part-time workforce, which provides no benefits of any sort. As indicated by Figure 1.1, a growing number (34 percent) of this part-time labour force is women who cannot find full-time work. As child bearers, women lose the ability, or have that ability seriously diminished, to make RRSP, Canada Pension Plan and private pension plan contributions while on maternity leave. And what about women who choose to work full time unpaid in the home? They can't benefit from any of the above.

The professional world is another telling story. According to Statistics Canada, women represent close to 50 percent of the students graduating from the legal and medical faculties at the universities. Yet, they leave the professions in disproportionately higher numbers than men largely because of the stress of having to handle two jobs, the unpaid one at home and the one at the office. The corporate world offers its own set of challenges with its "glass ceiling" and often inflexible attitudes toward women and men juggling career and child care. StatsCan states that even when employed, women are still largely responsible for look ing after their homes and families. In 1992, employed women with a spouse and at least one child under the age of five spent 5.3 hours a day on household activities, including domestic work, primary child care and shopping. This was about two hours more per day than their male counterparts spent on unpaid housework. Broken down, it looks like this: women in Canada prepare 76 percent of the meals, are responsible for 71 percent of the child care and perform 59 percent of the shopping and other housework. Check out Table 1.2 to see exactly what women and men do at home. I also find it astounding that men are never asked how they are going to manage combining career and family.

We also discovered a wide range of studies[3] which showed that in North America, women's standard of living dropped anywhere from 41 to 73 percent after divorce, while men's standard increased anywhere from 7 to 42 percent. The numbers vary dramatically, but one thing is certain: Regardless of the study, the numbers for women went down and the numbers for men went up. What is particularly sobering about this is StatsCan says there is a 28 percent chance that divorce will occur for each marriage in Canada. Women cannot wait until disaster strikes before becoming motivated to get financially organized. It is time for the right message to get out.

Clearly, there is no doubt women face greater challenges than do men. But we must never lose heart. Women are firmly entrenched in middle management and are very successful entrepreneurs; they have also begun to buy their own homes at a significant rate. I do want to make the point, however, that we should not buy into the message that women have arrived and are finally equal to men in Canadian society. In fact, there is a backlash occurring as women *begin* to make significant inroads into positions of power. This is evidenced everywhere. Take Ontario, for example. The provincial government has eliminated employment equity programs and drastically reduced funding for pay equity programs and day care in the name of balancing the budget. Programs affecting women and children are invariably the first on the government's chopping block. As the studies suggest, there is much work left to do so we cannot afford to be complacent. Never before has it been so essential for women to have their wits about them. This means taking financial control of

TABLE 1.2 AVERAGE TIME SPENT ON SELECTED ACTIVITIES BY EMPLOYED WOMEN AND MEN, BY FAMILY STATUS, 1992

	Total productive activity[1]	Paid work/ education	Total unpaid work[2]	Domestic work	Primary child care	Shopping/ services	Personal care	Free time
			Hours per day[3]					
Those w/children under age 5[4]								
Female lone parents	9.3	4.8	4.5	1.6	1.8	0.8	10.0	4.8
Women w/spouse	10.6	5.4	5.3	2.4	2.2	0.6	10.0	3.4
Men w/spouse	10.2	6.8	3.4	1.4	1.2	0.6	9.6	4.1
Those w/children age 5 and over[5]								
Female lone parents	9.6	5.6	3.9	2.0	0.7	1.0	10.2	4.2
Women w/spouse	9.96	5.4	4.4	2.6	0.7	0.8	0.2	4.0
Men w/spouse	99.3	5.6	2.8	1.5	0.3	0.6	9.9	4.8
Those w/o children								
Women w/spouse	9.9	6.3	3.7	2.6	0.1	0.9	10.3	3.8
Men w/spouse	8.9	7.3	1.6	1.0	0.0	0.6	10.0	5.1

1 Includes paid work, education and unpaid work; sub-totals may not add due to rounding.
2 Includes domestic work, primary child care, and shopping and services.
3 Figures averaged over a seven-day week.
4 At least one child under age 5.
5 Youngest child aged 5 and over.

Source: Statistics Canada, *General Social Survey* 1992.

their lives. I've figured out that this is why I was put on this earth. To help show people the way.

As Women and Money Inc. grew in scope and perspective, I never lost sight of the elements that gave me the confidence and knowledge to pursue this passion. This was, quite simply, getting my own financial house in order. Many of the seminars I give show how I achieved this and the ease with which it can be done. One of the key ingredients is to give women an understanding of the language used in the money world. Another is to provide concrete direction. When I first went to the centre to get a grip on the money scene, my advisor Elaine showed me a tool that simplified and took the mystery and confusion out of this fearful topic. The priority pyramid is used in some form by most financial advisors and provides an easy-to-understand road map to successful financial planning. One of the main reasons I had waited so long to get started was that I didn't have a clue what, how and in what order things needed to get done. I wanted to go right to the razzle dazzle. This concept saw that I stuck to "first things first." The pyramid is idiot proof, which meant I had a fighting chance. I subsequently taught the priority pyramid to thousands of women and men who all appreciated its simplicity.

I have a standard procedure at my seminars. I stand inconspicuously off to one side as the crowd files in. I listen carefully (OK, so I eavesdrop) as the women chat amongst themselves. I am never disappointed. Invariably, there are *always* one or two who comment: "I don't know what I'm doing here. I don't have any money to financially plan with!" "Aha!" I exclaim as I pounce on the poor, unsuspecting victim. "You will never have any money unless you financially plan." It seems to me that most of the world has this backwards. There is a common misconception that you need to be wealthy or a reasonable facsimile thereof to get involved in financial planning. Absolutely not so. For people just getting started, financial planning can mean something as simple as getting organized. That's financial planning. Paying your bills on time or taking your receipts out of the shoe box and putting them into a proper filing system is financial planning. Reading books like this one or attending a free seminar, that's financial planning. Any step you take toward financial literacy is part of the process. And it doesn't have to cost you a cent. Eventually, however, you are going to have to start organizing the actual dollars you spend and siphon some off to build your financial base. I had to re-orient my thinking to realize that the money I was putting into retirement savings and mutual funds was not money "spent." In fact, it was money that would eventually come back to me, with interest. I had to let go of the idea that this money was "gone."

The first thing to do is to build a financial base. There is no sense in having Jacuzzis and fancy chandeliers in your house if the foundation is cracked and leaking water. I was told that my foundation was in grave disrepair. I needed to fix it so that I could have a safe and secure base to work from. Then, and only then, would I be allowed to wander off and play in the big sandbox.

FIGURE 1.2 THE PRIORITY PYRAMID

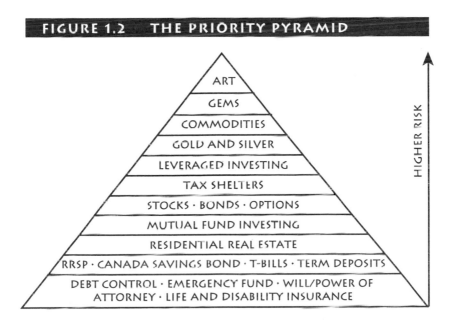

The pyramid is built up according to risk, the base being safe and virtually risk free with the riskiest investment at the top. This pyramid isn't suggesting that the first thing to do is pay off your debts and then, just before you die, you run out and buy a painting. It simply allows you to pick and choose the type of investments that are in your particular comfort zone while minimizing the risk to your complete portfolio. You may never invest in gold or art. But if you choose to, at least you will have the security of your financial base to fall back on should your brilliant investment scheme turn into a turkey. The base of your pyramid should provide adequate money in the event of emergency, disability or death. This is after your non-deductible debt load is paid off or at least manageable.

Though I had not had any debt for several years when I went to the centre, there was still the mangled credit rating to fix. In fact, I was completely in the dark about the inner workings of the world of credit. My experience with it had not been a warm one, so I made it my business to understand it. Understanding how credit works and the different forms available to use and abuse is a wonderful place to start your financial journey. I needed to complete this task myself and understanding credit is exactly where I had to begin.

GETTING STARTED:
UNDERSTANDING THE VOLATILE
WORLD OF CREDIT

> *"All the perplexities, confusions and distresses in America arise, not from defects in their constitution or confederation, not from want of honour or virtue, so much as the ignorance of the nature of coin, credit and circulation."*
>
> John Adams, in a letter to Thomas Jefferson, 1787

It was one of thousands of business lunches I had attended while in the computer industry, but this one was to be the most memorable. The deal had taken over two years of intense negotiating and hand-holding. A major financial institution had finally agreed to go with my company for their national software and hardware requirements. This was very big. It was May and I had just made my year's quota. After the contracts were signed and safely tucked inside my briefcase, I whisked the three executives, including the company president, to an elegant restaurant in Toronto's King and Bay district for a celebratory lunch.

It was a festive occasion with the wine flowing and food in abundance. This was a stellar moment for me. I had faced fierce competition from the best in the business. The deal was almost

25

lost a couple of times. Part of me stood up and cheered inside because I was the only woman in the game out of seven vendors. As I basked in the glow of this significant achievement, the bill arrived, which I promptly scooped up. I didn't even give the bill a token glance. The waitress took away one very seasoned credit card. We continued our lively conversation, the three gentlemen congratulating me on a job well done. The waitress approached the table. Now, I could have endured, "I'm sorry, your card is over its limit." I would have been embarrassed, but it does happen. Instead, the waitress, in a brusque tone and with a complete absence of tact announced, "Madam, not only has your card been refused, but the credit card company has asked me to confiscate it. How do you propose to pay this bill?"

I thought I would faint.

I knew these gentlemen quite well as a result of our frequent meetings over the course of two years. They completely fell apart. As the room filled with peals of laughter, I, red-faced, spoke with the owner of the restaurant and finally persuaded him to take a personal cheque. Apparently this is what happens if you constantly park at your credit limit and have only a semi-consistent payment pattern. I'd receive a bill, throw it on the pile and promptly forget it until a couple of months later. My debt had been slowly accumulating over the years and was now reaching critical proportions.

There was one other event that had to happen before I finally admitted defeat.

A word of advice to all of you who take the repayment of your student loan lightly. Don't.

I had moved to Vancouver a few years after graduating from university and the student loan people and I kind of lost track of each other. After I had destroyed my ankle and lost my job, there was little money for items such as student loans. So I stopped paying it. Mind you, my intention was that this was only until I started to work again. Since I hadn't heard a word or received a single notice, I easily dismissed the loan from my memory. Around the same time as the business luncheon fiasco, the government and I had a reunion. It came in the guise of a collection agency. Collection agents, I'm convinced, are graduates of the Mike Tyson School of Charm. Murray Oxby, a writer with Canadian Press, described them in an article on how to deal with bill collectors as "the pit bulls of the financial world." People come to me in a state of panic and anxiety after receiving threatening and abusive phone calls from an agency. Provincial law prohibits collectors from harassing or making unreasonable threats. But many cross over the line and use humiliation tactics. Now, in the collection agencies' defence, they save companies millions of dollars each year collecting money from so-called deadbeats. But, I can tell you, not all people who have tough times paying bills are deadbeats. Far from it. Yet, many bill collectors are remarkably adept at making people feel like one.

When I received that brutish phone call from the agency, I didn't get scared. I got angry. I had every intention of paying the student loan back in a short period of time and informed the man of that. It didn't matter. The balance was due in full within 48 hours or they were going to garnishee my wages and take me to court. What angered me the most was that the guy seemed to really enjoy his job. I could actually hear him smiling over the phone. I was curious as to why there hadn't been any warning before such drastic action was taken. Apparently, once the computer sends you a certain number of notices, you automatically get to enjoy deadbeat status whether you received them or not. I have since come to realize that debtors have rights. The right not to be threatened, distressed and humiliated is one of them. These people are supposed to be businesslike and polite. If you are being harassed, be sure to contact the appropriate provincial government agency.

Had I contacted the bank and told them of my financial difficulty, the chances are reasonably good it would never have come to this. One of the many lessons I learned during this period was to be honest with your creditors when you are in trouble. This is especially true in this day and age when so many people are finding it tough to manage. The traditional intimidating attitude among financial institutions toward bad debt is beginning to soften somewhat. Though it is substantially harder to get credit these days, most banks are evolving to a more sympathetic role. One Canadian bank claims to enjoy one of the lowest delinquency rates because of this "friendly factor." If you are having financial difficulty and are missing your mortgage or loan payments, a video is sent to you featuring a man dressed in a cardigan sitting in the warmth of his living room. He smiles at you and asks you to come in and talk about your financial troubles.

The idea is to invite the client to rid themselves of their fear and work together with the bank to find a solution. This is much easier to do if you are only five days late with a payment. I can personally vouch for how much more difficult it becomes after that. If I had called the bank when I was in trouble, I may have been able to take advantage of a variety of options, from a no-payment period to a renegotiation of the loan. Hindsight has 20/20 vision.

Humiliation can be a powerful motivator. After that memorable lunch, I took myself off to the bank to secure a bill consolidation loan. It made sense to me that my first step to sleeping more soundly at night might be to find a way to manage this debt albatross around my neck. I was paying over 22 percent on my credit cards at the time. I knew I could do a darned sight better with a bank loan. In fact, I could cut the interest rate by slightly over half. I had done this once a few years previously and it had worked out very well. The necessary paperwork was done and I assumed, because of my income, all would be rosy. Wrong. I was about to discover how up to my neck I really was.

The loans officer did a quick scan of my credit history. Her response to my loan application was a decided "not on your life." She asked me if I was aware I had an R8 rating on one of my credit cards. I queried if that was good, knowing full well what the answer would be. She informed me with a grave tone that this meant repossession. I smiled and quietly responded that I was keenly aware of that fact, the memory of that disastrous lunch still painfully sharp. She mentioned the Credit Counselling Service of Metropolitan Toronto and strongly suggested I pay them a visit. She told me they would organize my debt and work out a palatable agreement with my creditors. "They're tough," she warned. "No tougher than Attila the Hun from the collection agency," I thought to myself. Because my debt was reasonably small and I was only dealing with three creditors, it never occurred to me I could take advantage of such a service. (The average debt load of people at Credit Counselling of Toronto in 1994 was $17,000. The average number of creditors trying to collect from these people was seven[4].) Credit Counselling of Toronto is one of 25 such agencies in Ontario. Many credit counselling organizations are nonprofit and have a charitable licence. They may charge a nominal fee of $25 to $125.

Through credit counselling I learned many things, but the first lesson was the importance of a good two-way relationship with your counsellor or advisor. After sitting down with my first counsellor and going over the grisly details, I was astonished when this gentleman suggested I consider marrying a wealthy man as a solution to my problem. I immediately retorted that a wedding would take 20 minutes. What, would he suggest, I do next? He looked at me blankly. It was evident he had missed my point. I excused myself and asked to see another counsellor. With my new counsellor, I devised a workable payment structure based on a realistic budget (shudder) that I religiously adhered to. The service contacted CIBC and the Bank of Montreal, the two holders of my cards, and my personal favourite, Mr. Attila of the collection agency, to inform them of our intentions. Once credit counselling came on the scene, all harassment from the collection agency and the nasty "pay or die" letters from the bank ceased. The total balance was around $5,000. It didn't take long to pay off.

It is noteworthy that financial institutions monetarily support these nonprofit organizations in an effort to help reclaim some of their bad debt. Banks and major department stores will waive the interest you owe and you become responsible for only the principal part of the debt. Unfortunately, this type of service is only available in Ontario and Newfoundland. The other provinces offer a scaled down version through the government, generally the Ministry of Consumer Relations. Here, however, you have to have a minimum of two judgments against you before they will talk to you and they do not have the resources to offer financial counselling. For people caught in the trap of overextended credit, credit counselling organizations can be very helpful. I am a living example of how it can work.

Getting in deep financial trouble can feel very isolating. I was shocked to learn how not alone I was. The highrolling '80s saw pervasive rampant spending. There seemed to be a theme at all levels of society of misusing credit. Not only little ol' me, but companies of all sizes, as well as our esteemed government were doing it. Canada and the United States have created enormous deficits by simply spending more than they received. The shortfall was financed by borrowing. As a result, the Canadian national debt is so large that interest payments amount for more than one-third of all annual expenditures made by the federal government. Debt is the total amount of money owed, the deficit is the annual difference between what the government spends and what it brings in, in terms of revenue. So, the deficit is added to the government's net debt each year. Hence the vicious cycle. (I strongly identify!) For until the national debt is reduced, it is impossible to reduce the deficit. But until the deficit is eliminated it is impossible to reduce the debt.

It is very clear to me now that one's credit rating is a privilege, not a right. Once the dust settled and we had effectively implemented damage control, I made a sobering discovery. I had unknowingly destroyed my credit rating. Here I was in full swing specializing in financial planning for women. I had cast off the old ways with a vengeance and transformed myself into a financially literate person. There was a certain irony in the fact that I was teaching people the necessity of proper planning and I couldn't get credit. It had been five years since my last bout of trouble. My nose had been clean the whole time. But when I applied again for a card, I was turned down.

Ellen Roseman, Associate Managing Editor of *The Globe and Mail's Report on Business* advises people in her seminars who have a tendency to abuse credit cards to perform "plastic surgery." I had followed her advice. When my credit cards were finally paid off (a feat more easily accomplished when I stopped using them), it was my honest intention not to use them again. Ever. This was proving to be more difficult than I had imagined. Have you ever tried ordering flowers or writing a cheque without one? Taking clients out for lunch became a problem. It was hard to impress the senior partners of a prestigious law firm when you try to pay for lunch discreetly with a pile of bills that would rival the CN Tower. The change in my attitude toward money was so pronounced and on such a fundamental level that it now seemed absurd not to have a credit card. I couldn't even get overdraft protection with the damage I had inadvertently done. So, I took the bull by the horns. I contacted the credit bureau to find out the exact status of my rating. I was fascinated by how the whole process worked. It was frightening to discover how much in the dark I had been about something that had such an impact on my life. I firmly believe information on how to make and break your credit rating should be on the high school curriculum. I often wonder, had I known how the system worked, might it have changed my cavalier attitude toward credit?

HOW CREDIT RATINGS AND THE CREDIT BUREAU WORK

The quickest way to establish a good credit rating is to borrow money from a financial institution and pay it back promptly. Your credit record begins once any kind of application for credit is approved. Maintaining a good rating is as simple as making payments on time and not taking on more debt than you can handle. However, times are tough out there. Although critically important to aspire to, this may be harder than it sounds.

The greatest misconception about credit bureaus is that they determine your credit rating. In fact, they are simply the clearing house for information that credit grantors may want access to in order to determine your credit worthiness. They are not interested in any personal data. The reason it is important to make timely monthly payments is that your records are updated every 30 days by information provided by your creditors on what balances remain and what payments have been made or missed. You are also assigned an R rating. R1 means you are glowingly perfect, all the way up (or down) to R9, which is very delinquent and essentially deadbeat status. This is when they call in our friend, the bill collector, and the debt becomes classified as a bad debt.

My R8 rating became an R7 as soon as I consolidated my debt with credit counselling. If I could have mustered a logical explanation for the R7 rating, the bank might have given me a bill consolidation loan. Unfortunately, financial stupidity doesn't qualify as a logical explanation. The first time I was one day late for a credit card payment and went over the allotted 30 days, my rating changed from R1 to R2. It was as simple as that. When I was off work with my injury and consistently owing two months' payments as well as being 60 days in arrears, I was silently downgraded to an R3 rating, and so it went. When the loans officer did my credit check, she saw a series of R3 ratings, most of them from several years back. At the time, while out of work, I had been ashamed and fearful that they might take away my only source of credit should I tell them I wasn't able to work and therefore make regular payments. In the eyes of the creditors, based on the little they know of your situation, an R3 rating tends to show that you are "light" in the financial discipline department. It's not likely they will extend you more credit. Once the payments are made, however, the ratings don't change. The file of late or missed payments becomes a permanent part of your record for six years. The good news, however, is that derogatory information, such as collections or judgments, has to be removed by law from your credit file after six years.

You don't actually receive an overall R rating. Each of your creditors or lenders has different credit requirements. Harry's Discount Furniture Emporium will have different credit standards than American Express. Your rating for each form of credit you have is matched with the lender's own specific requirements for granting credit. These R ratings are part of what is evaluated when an institution decides whether or not it is going to give you credit. Current income and ability to pay are, of course, major factors as well. There is a point system. Being the president of a corporation for 20 years and living at the same address in the exclusive Montreal neighbourhood of Westmount for 30 years will rate you pretty high. If, like myself, you have been mobile and

TABLE 2.1 MAKING THE CREDIT GRADE	
RATING	R#
Too new to rate: approved but not yet used	R0
Pays within 30 days; and all payments are up to date	R1
Pays in 30 days to 60 days, and is not more than 1 payment behind	R2
Pays in 60 days to 90 days, or is 2 payments behind	R3
Pays in 90 days to 120 days or 3 or more payments behind	R4
Account at least 120 days overdue, but not in collection	R5*
Making regular payments under consolidation order or similar arrangements	R7
In repossession	R8
Account is in collection or debtor can't be found	R9
* There is no R6 rating	

have missed a few credit card payments, you will likely be rejected and feel the humiliation that comes with a "Sorry, but we aren't going to let you have any" letter.

It is very important that you keep on top of what is in your file. Mistakes do, in fact, happen. Credit can be denied based on inaccurate or insufficient information. In 1991, the CBC program Market Place asked Canadians to visit their credit bureau and check the status of their file. A staggering 47 percent of the files had varying levels of inaccuracy and 13 percent had mistakes serious enough to lead to a possible decline for credit.[5] The credit bureaus are under provincial jurisdiction and have to ensure that their files are accurate. They guard carefully against unlawful use but at the same time have to make sure that the information is easily available to the customer. If you have a difference of opinion with the information found in your file, you have every right to dispute it. Equifax Canada, which is the largest credit bureau in Canada, handles approximately 800,000 customer requests for inspections each year.[6]

And mine was one of them. It seems the only thing standing in the way of my securing credit was an old R7 rating from the Bank of Montreal for my Mastercard. This debt had been paid off in full over five years ago. I figured it was time to give them a call. I had a lengthy discussion with a woman in their credit department who chuckled when I told her what I now did for a living. It seemed she also had a finely tuned sense of the absurd. She understood completely my dilemma and suggested I write a letter to the bank asking them to remove the bad rating. I did and they did.

I now had a completely clean credit rating for the first time in many years. I have come a long way in terms of saving and investments from that day, but little has given me as much satisfaction as that did. For the first time, I was beginning to feel like an adult. It really wasn't so bad. To this day I will use only two credit cards. The balances are paid off in full faithfully every month on the pain of death, no exceptions.

TYPES OF CREDIT

My next step was to create an emergency fund. I had been caught too many times in my life without one and was therefore forced to make dumb decisions such as cashing out a cash value life insurance policy when it was only three years old. It was going to take some time to accumulate enough for a suitable emergency fund. I started to consider the value of a personal line of credit to cover me until the industry standard "three months salary after tax" was attainable. But like so many people, I found the variety of loans, overdraft protection and personal lines of credit confusing. Each type of credit serves a particular purpose. I wanted to be sure I wasn't putting a square peg in a round hole. My bank manager was only too eager to help.

INSTALLMENT CREDIT (PERSONAL LOANS)

This type of credit is most often used to acquire those big-ticket necessities that life is so bleak without, like cars, boats and holidays. This is often the most appropriate type of loan for your RRSP contribution if you are short one year. My bill consolidation loan was this kind of loan. Its principal characteristic is a specific repayment schedule, that is, equal monthly amounts for a set time period such as 48 months. You can pay it off at any time with no penalty. You generally have a couple of options as to which type of interest rate you choose, variable or fixed. If it's a fixed rate, the payment amount is assured to be the same each month for the term of the loan. A variable rate is tied to the bank's prime lending rate. This means your monthly amount could fluctuate with the changes in the prime rate. This is ideal if you believe interest rates are heading downward in the future. (As if anyone really knows!) These types of loans are granted only for a one-year time frame and are subject to annual reviews so that the bank can evaluate the impact of interest rate fluctuations during the year.

Depending on what you are purchasing, your loan may be secured or unsecured. My bill consolidation loan, for example, was unsecured because I didn't have to offer up any collateral. This type is generally for things like a trip to Florida or Kate's orthodontist's bill.

My first car, however, was bought with a secured loan. This means that if I reneged on payments, they could come stealthily in the dead of night and whisk the car away. What you are actually purchasing becomes the collateral. This item is called a chattel. When I purchased my car, the bank had me sign a chattel mortgage. This is an intimidating term that simply meant that my car secured the loan. Chattel also means asset. For example, let's say you wanted to renovate the old homestead (jokingly referred to by those who have survived the experience as the second leading cause of divorce). You could secure a personal loan with the equity that has been built up in your home. The difference between what the property is worth and what is owed is your equity. In this case, a legal document called a collateral mortgage is required. This way you are not locked into a conventional mortgage and you have the freedom to pay it off anytime without penalty. You also don't have to renew an existing mortgage. Secured personal loans will generally receive lower interest rates than unsecured loans. Residential mortgage loans are actually a form of installment credit. They will be dealt with in detail in a later chapter.

OVERDRAFT PROTECTION

Many people confuse overdraft protection with a personal line of credit. They are completely different animals. Overdraft protection is for those of us who are mathematically challenged and bounce cheques. A godsend to many when you consider a bounced cheque these days can cost you anywhere from $15 and up. Not to mention the acute embarrassment associated with being the issuer of an NSF cheque. Overdraft protection will cover the shortfall up to a predetermined amount, the maximum usually being $5,000. This is strictly a short-term solution. The interest rate for this type of credit is generally higher than credit card rates. In other words, outrageously high! You don't have to make regular payments but the banks do want to see a positive balance in your account at least once a month. The service charges vary between institutions, but there is no charge if you don't use it. It's only when you forget to deposit your paycheque and your chequing account turns to rubber that the charges kick in. The charges can be significant so be careful that this is used for emergencies only. Overdraft protection is available on most types of chequing accounts.

After my credit was reestablished, getting overdraft protection was the next step I took. Though I had many financial faults, bouncing cheques was not one of them. Even so, this type of protection can give you a certain peace of mind in the event that the uncertain becomes certain. You apply for this as you would any form of credit.

PERSONAL LINE OF CREDIT (PLC)

I believe this to be a wonderful invention providing it is managed properly. It is not for the individual who can be enticed by easy access to ready cash. PLCs had traditionally been reserved for the wealthy but in the 1980s the banks began to market them aggressively. It's as though a permanent pot of money were stashed somewhere that you don't have to pay for if you don't use it. (Some institutions may charge a nominal annual fee in the $10 range.) In one Canadian bank's guide to credit, a personal line of credit is described as follows: "If you are likely to require a number of loans in the future for whatever reasons, your application for a personal line of credit may be the last time you ever have to apply again." What makes it so ideal is that if you are involved in a long-term project such as a house renovation, or even in a short-term cash crunch, you can borrow on a per need basis instead of borrowing the entire amount up front. This way, you can save a small fortune on interest costs. This type of credit is an excellent way to consolidate two or more bills to reduce your monthly payments. A PLC and installment credit are the two types of credit available for bill consolidation.

You apply for a PLC as you would any other type of loan. The difference is that once you use the money and pay it back, the money is available for use again. And again. And again. It works like a regular bank account that you can access anytime through bank machines or cheques. You pay interest only on the amount you have actually used. The interest rates are tied to the bank's prime rate, which means that they are on par with regular personal loans and therefore can be half of what you pay on your overdraft protection and credit cards. Let's say I have a $25,000 line of credit. I borrow $5,000. Two months later, I pay the $5,000 back. I get to use, at any time, the $25,000 or a portion thereof again. If used properly, the PLC is like a magic purse that never empties. If used improperly, the purse will snap shut on your fingers never to open again! Banks are understandably quite strict with this form of credit.

As with personal loans, you can have a secured or unsecured line of credit up to an established limit. Depending on the amount, it may be secured by real estate, stocks, bonds, cash value life insurance and GICs. If you secure it, you often get a break of a percentage point or two on your interest rate. There is no fixed period for repayment. Usually a minimum of three percent of the amount outstanding is required as a minimum monthly payment. If you have a secured line of credit, you can arrange for interest-only payments.

As with any form of credit, a PLC must be treated with respect. They are designed for above-average income earners who have demonstrated good credit sense and have a stable employment record. Banks watch PLCs pretty carefully, particularly in today's difficult economic climate. They are much harder to get than they were in the roaring '80s. Less than one-third of those who apply actually receive a personal line of credit.

There are several things the banks watch for:

1. As soon as you get a PLC, do you jack it right up to its limit, then pay only the minimum three percent per month from that point on for an extended period? Banks really hate that.

2. If you miss one payment, most banks will call you. Banks are justifiably nervous these days. There have been a frightening number of defaulted PLCs over the last few years as the recession has taken its toll.

3. Banks actually want you to use your PLC. If it has been dormant for an extended period of time, they have the power to yank it.

4. Your PLC is reviewed every year on the anniversary date. If the banks don't like how the credit line has been managed, or if there has been a change in your circumstances, such as losing your job or having a lower-paying one, don't be surprised if they close that purse.

5. Banks are now doing routine credit checks of their client list against the files Equifax keeps. This is to catch "bad trending." This routine applies to all forms of consumer credit, including credit cards. If you had the misfortune of getting poor ratings on more than one payment record, the bank will assess your ability to pay. You will be asked to renegotiate your debt repayment, or you may lose your credit line. Whether we like it or not, there are new realities in the '90s. The '80s cakewalk is over.

CREDIT CARDS

Credit cards are the most popular, most convenient, most abused and least understood form of credit. According to the Ministry of Corporate Affairs and Industry Canada, there are an estimated 58 million credit cards in circulation in Canada, which works out to 2.6 cards for everyone over 18 in this country. Of these, 27.5 million are Visa or Mastercard, 25.5 million are department store issue and 3.2 million are gas cards. In 1994, the accumulated outstanding balance on Mastercard and Visa was a staggering 15.4 billion dollars, an increase from 11.2 billion two years before with the total volume of sales being 55.1 billion dollars. The average size of transaction was $72.40.[7] The Ministry says only 54 percent pay off their Visa and Mastercard balances each month. Sixty percent pay off their retail cards in full monthly.

This is a very big business. I used to contribute significantly by not paying off my balances in full every month. Banks received enough interest from me to build my own gold-plated automated teller in my front hall. Today, exactly on the due date, I walk up to the bank machine and pay the bill. This way, I earn interest on my money right up to the last minute and avoid paying any interest costs. I have saved hundreds of dollars each year by managing my cards properly.

I also discovered through my own painful experience and that of many of my clients that you *never* put anything on a credit card that you don't have the money for in the bank or expect to have by the end of the month. I thought credit cards were a natural extension of my paycheque. This thinking was, I discovered, the quickest route to financial disaster. First of all, there is a difference between a charge card and a credit card. Credit cards are revolving credit and require minimum monthly payments. They're like expensive lines of credit extended to you through a bank or trust company. Visa and Mastercard are examples of credit cards. Charge cards, on the other hand, require that the balance be paid in full each month. American Express, gas and retail cards are examples of charge cards.

Credit and charge cards are for convenience. Period. Full stop. They are a way to get free money for 21 days. They are, however, the most expensive way to finance purchases if you don't pay off the balance each month. If you find that you are consistently carrying balances from month to month, explore a less expensive form of credit, like a personal bank loan or line of credit. I didn't bother because I assumed the interest rate was no big deal. I didn't do the math until it was too late. The average interest rate on charge cards is in the stratosphere of 28 percent. Credit card rates vary, but average around 17 percent. Personal lines of credit are somewhere between 8 and 10 percent. Which would you rather pay?

It's worth knowing how interest is calculated. If the balance is paid in full by the end of the grace period, there is no interest charge. However, with credit cards, if you go past the grace period, interest is calculated from the date of purchase, not the statement due date. Certain charge cards will only charge interest from the date the statement is sent out. This can make a noticeable difference. But not to those of us who pay balances in full each month. This should be as automatic as filing your taxes and paying your rent or mortgage. The way interest is calculated varies from institution to institution and can be confusing. Banks, trust companies and credit unions offer a 21-day grace period on their credit cards. This means you have three weeks from the statement date (the date when the monthly statement is issued) to pay your balance before you start paying interest. Retail stores and gas companies offer anywhere from 25 to 30 days. American Express gives you a 30-day grace period. This being said, however, American Express also demands full payment upon receipt of the statement. You can pay up to 30 percent per year on unpaid balances. If the balance remains unpaid, they send the charge card police after you and cancel your privileges. They need to be strict because there is no spending limit on this card. It is only for the financially mature. I shudder at the thought of having had this kind of card when I was younger. At the same time, however, I would have avoided the humiliating experience of being exposed as a financial reprobate in front of my clients. Let's assume you do not pay your credit card bill off entirely the first month and the second bill comes in which states it must be paid by November 15th. Interest is still accumulating from the month the bill is issued until the bill is paid and that interest will show up on the third month's bill even though the balance has been paid off in its entirety. At the very least, make it your business to know exactly how interest is calculated with your choice of card.

The other sobering point I learned about credit card interest is how it relates to the power of compounding. Our parents told us the value of letting money sit and letting compound interest do the work for you. The rule of 72 states that if you find an investment that will net you a 10 percent rate of return, your money will double every seven years. Compound interest can be your best friend, but watch it! It will turn on you very quickly when it comes to credit cards. The power of compound interest can work in reverse. To graphically illustrate the point: Before most financial institutions decided to waive credit card interest, I paid over $700 in interest on an outstanding $1,100 Visa bill while at credit counselling. This is because it took me a period of time to pay it off and the interest continued to compound. At 28.8 percent, the interest rate on department store credit cards will double its money in $2\frac{1}{2}$ years.

When choosing which type of card you should have, interest rate will be the least of your concerns if you pay in full each due date. If you don't, consider the one with the lowest rate. There are a few new low-interest cards that offer limited services. I do, however, adamantly maintain that this is the worst way of financing your purchases. Most cards have annual fees for the privilege of using them, but there are a few that offer a no-fee set-up. These fees are generally to cover administration and transaction costs and can range from $8 to $130 for a Gold American Express card. At the time of writing, Bank of Montreal, National Bank of Canada and National Trust offer a no-fee basic Mastercard.

There are premium or status cards like the gold cards that offer an abundance of features, but you pay dearly for them. Some of these features may be worth the expense, however. There is a particular feature offered on the American Express Gold card that significantly enhanced my quality of life. Or, I should say, my accountant's. It's work to be financially organized. I have always maintained that if you can get someone else to do it for you better and more easily than you can do it yourself, then go for it. I detest going through receipts at tax time trying to figure out how much I spent where and how often with whomever. The Gold American Express card offers a once-a-year summary that beautifully organizes your annual spending into different categories like education, health care, gas, airline travel, professional services and so on. It even details the charges for your account. It will also break down the information further and provide a month-by-month analysis of your spending. This service alone justifies the annual $130 in my particular circumstances. I use my credit card for everything and this summary provides an accurate snapshot of the kind of year I've had and of my spending patterns. My accountant was jubilant when I moved to this system. It sure beats the shoe boxes stuffed with tiny folded pieces of paper.

If you travel out of the country, some gold cards provide travel health insurance. It is mandatory that you read the fine print on these benefit plans. On some cards travel insurance is available that will pay a death benefit in the event of an accident. There is also trip cancellation and interruption coverage if someone becomes sick or injured or there is an emergency back home.

If you purchase merchandise, most gold cards offer a 90-day warranty for loss or breakage over and above the regular warranty. I love the commercial one company uses to sell this benefit: A little boy emulates his father as he cheerfully feeds his oatmeal to Daddy's brand new VCR. The credit card company ensures its replacement.

It is interesting to note with whom the credit card companies have been getting into bed lately. Some keen, young assistant V.P. of marketing must have got her creative juices flowing one morning after her fourth cup of high-test coffee and second chocolate donut and decided that the banks needed to expand their horizons. Little did she realize the monster she had created Many of the status cards offer rewards in the form of points based on what you spend monthly that you can cash in for merchandise or discounts on certain events or purchases. The first association was with the airlines that allowed the customer to earn air mileage points with credit card purchases. Hence the CIBC Aerocard (Air Canada) and the Canadian Plus card (Royal Trust and Canadian). American Express will allow you to choose between airline miles or merchandise. The car companies must have felt slighted, so now you can have a GM Visa or a Ford Visa. Your points go toward up to five to seven percent on the purchase of a new car. If that wasn't enough, you are now able to save for a new home with a Bank of Montreal Mastercard that will help you save toward a mortgage up to $3,500. (Certain restrictions apply.) What next?

I envisioned a card with a "Moriarty's Funeral Home" logo on the corner that is designed to ensure you are laid to rest in that finely crafted mahogany coffin you so richly deserve.

There is another little-known, unadvertised option that banks offer which is ideal for someone digging out from under a financial mess or who has no credit history. Some banks will allow you to secure your credit card request with a deposit equal to your credit limit. A typical example would be a $500 RRSP for a $500 credit limit, which is then left in the hands of the bank. GICs and term deposits are other examples of security. Though very big in the U.S. (over 700,000 Americans hold a secured card), they are more of a customer service than a promotable item in Canada. Your bank manager is the best person to talk to about this type of credit card. It works like a regular card subject to the same interest charges and potential abuses. If you miss too many payments, wave good-bye to your deposit. However, if you are on the road to financial recovery, this is a wonderful way to earn a better credit history. You can negotiate with your bank manager the length of time before the black mark on your credit history is washed away. If it is a bankruptcy, that could take years; but some credit messes could take as little as 18 months to get out from under.

Choosing a credit card has become much like choosing running shoes these days. This choice of card may be fine, but be sure you understand exactly how the different cards work and how much they cost. They have become very popular and the banks are finding that customers are already redeeming the car bonuses in reasonably large numbers. If it doesn't cost you any more than a regular card or entice you to make *unnecessary* car, home or travel purchases, my question to you would be "Why not?" It is always a good idea to get no-fee cards when you can, though they are becoming rarer. If you can justify them by your business, lifestyle or income, the premium cards can be an asset. If you want to know whether you should consider this type of card, here is a good guideline: If you are a heavy but responsible spender (say $10,000 a year) or you are a frequent traveller, such a card would likely be worth it for you. Don't fall into the trap of seeing prestige and status as reasons for carrying one of these cards. If *you* know you are important, everyone else will figure it out eventually. Because merchants often

TABLE 2.2 FINANCIAL INSTITUTION CREDIT CARDS*

Card Issuer	Fees ($ annual)	Interest Rates (% annual)	Grace Period (days)	Interest Calculated from Date of Purchase
Master Card				
Bank of Montreal				
Standard	–	18.90	21	X
Prime +	18	12.75	0	X
Air Miles Reward	35	18.90	21	X
Canada Trust	8[1]	18.00	21	X
CS CO-OP	–	18.90	21	X
National Bank	–	18.90	21	X
National Trust				
Basic	–	16.75	21	X
Low Interest Option	30	9.90	21	X
Niagara Credit Union	–	18.25	21	X
VISA				
Bank of Nova Scotia				
Standard	8	18.50	21	X
Value Visa	29	12.90	21	X
CIBC				
Standard	12	18.50	21	X
Ford Visa	20	18.50	21	X
Confédération des caisses populaires et d'économie				
Desjardins du Québec	12	17.50	21	X
Laurentian Bank	10	17.50	21	X
Montreal Trust	12[1]	17.50	21	X
Royal Bank				
Standard	12[1]	17.50	21	X
Option	25	13.50	21	X
Toronto-Dominion Bank				
Standard	12[1]	17.75	21	X
GM Card	–	18.75	21	X
Vancouver City Savings	12	18.50	21	X

* As of June, 1995. Since credit card terms and conditions may change, you should contact card issuers directly for the latest information.

[1] Under certain conditions, fee may be reduced or waived entirely.

Source: Office of Consumer Affairs, Industry Canada.

TABLE 2.3 OTHER CREDIT CARDS*

Card Issuer	Fees ($ annual)	Interest Rates (% annual)	Grace Period (days)	Interest Calculated from	
				Date of Purchase	Date of Statement
Canadian Tire	–	28.8	30		X
Eaton's	–	28.8	30		X
Home Card	–	28.8	30		X
Hudson's Bay	–	28.8	25-30		X
Petro-Canada	–	24.0	30	X	
Sears	–	28.8	25-30		X
Simpsons	–	28.8	25-30		X
Zellers	–	28.8	25–30		X

* As of June, 1995. Since credit card terms and conditions may change, you should contact card issuers directly for the latest information.

Source: Office of Consumer Affairs, Industry Canada.

complain about the cost of honouring American Express, not everyone accepts it. It is wise to carry another card for those circumstances. Also note that because I use credit cards for business, I can write off credit card fees on my income tax. This applies to all fee-based credit cards. Be sure you do the same if you qualify.

TABLE 2.4 CHARGE CARDS*

Card Issuer	Fees ($ annual)	Late Penalty Rates/Delin- quency Rate (% annual)	Grace Period (days)	Late Penalty Calculated from	
				Date of Purchase	Date of Statement
American Expresss	55	30	30		X
Diners Club/enRoute	65	30	30-60		X
Imperial Oil (Esso)	–	24	30	X	
Irving Oil	–	24	25		X

* As of June, 1995. Since credit card terms and conditions may change, you should contact card issuers directly for the latest information.

Source: Office of Consumer Affairs, Industry Canada.

WOMEN AND CREDIT

Up until the mid '70s, a woman was often turned down for credit simply because she was a woman. This practice was based on stereotypes and myths about women's ability to manage money and understand the complicated world of finance. It was also done because they earned so little of their own money. It was commonplace for women to have to have a male cosigner. Nowadays, it is illegal to discriminate on the basis of gender, marital status, race, religion or age. There have been general improvements in financial institutions, especially in their awareness levels, but women feel they are still fighting for fair and equitable treatment. Barbara Blum, President of Adams National Bank in Washington, D.C. (formerly the Women's National Bank), says that while blatant sexual discrimination against women has stopped, more subtle bias still occurs: "It has gone underground and this will not change until there are more women bankers at all levels of banking. It is still dominated by white males."[8]

The following is a story that acutely illustrates that bias. I recently went to my bank, armed with a comprehensive business plan, to ask for a business operating line of credit to fund expansion. I assumed it wasn't going to be easy because, like most women, I had no hard assets except for the one between my ears. Because my ideas were good and my business plan was solid, the bank approved my request in no time. I was greatly heartened. A couple of days later I was in my account manager's office to clean up the paperwork. While my banker, Kathrine, and I were going over the goods, the credit lending manager who actually approved our request walked by. Kathrine called him over so he could put a face to a name. The exchange went like this. "Thank you, Chester, for your vote of confidence. I appreciate your far-sightedness in approving a line of credit for such a non-traditional business." He then said: "No problem, that's quite a little hobby you've got going for yourself!" The room fell completely quiet as Kathrine and I digested what he had just said. Hobby?!! There were five people whose income depended on this so-called hobby. This was one of the few times in my life I have been rendered speechless. Chester left and Kathrine began a litany of apologies on his behalf. You've heard it before, "the white, middle-aged man who doesn't know better" argument. I don't buy this excuse for bad behaviour anymore. What this incident proved to me was discrimination wasn't the problem. What does exist, and does so in spades, is gender bias. My request for credit was approved — no discrimination — but the comment referring to my business as a "hobby" clearly showed a powerful gender bias. You can rest assured if it were a man with the same business, he would *never* have heard a demeaning comment like that one.

The ironic twist to this story is that Women and Money Inc. was hired to provide gender-awareness training for this bank, and our first branch to train was, you guessed it, Chester's. He was going to be in the training. A couple of weeks later, when I had suitably recovered from the shock of Chester's comment, I decided to go talk to him about it. He was the most pleasant person. I got quickly to the point. I repeated the conversation verbatim and watched the look of horror spread across his face. "I actually said *hobby*?!" he asked incredulously. Kathrine was there to verify it. I nodded my head. As he had daughters of his own, Chester was appalled and suitably regretful. Bless his heart, he even gave me permission to repeat this story while he was in the room in front of his own peers so we could illustrate the difference between gender discrimination and the much more insidious gender bias. Since then, Chester and I have grown to respect each other immensely. He even sends me cartoons from the paper that are relevant to gender difference.

Maybe Chester fell into that category of truly not knowing better. In fact, I wouldn't be surprised if there were a large percentage of men who are exactly like Chester and only need to be told what the boundaries are. People are confused as to what the rules are today. Perhaps, if they are addressed with tact and a touch of humour, many of the biases will disappear gradually if the offending person knows they are out of bounds. If they aren't told, how can their behaviour change? Chester's eyes are so wide open now, I can guarantee you his daughters will benefit greatly from his new insight. I salute the Chesters of the world. They are the real heroes in my opinion.

I have read the literature from all the chartered banks in Canada, and they all make it very clear that they do not discriminate on the basis of gender. They state, in writing, *that they treat everyone the same*. Can you see the failed logic here? They believe that lumping all people together to evaluate their credit worthiness is fair. Unfortunately, it's not. Their basis for credit is based on "who earns the most wins," meaning the more income and assets, the better the chance of getting credit. Women earn on average two-thirds of what men earn. Most of their disposable income goes toward living expenses, not asset accumulation. The majority of women work in the service sector, which is traditionally lower paying. Those women who aren't in the pink collar ghetto will often hit their heads on the glass ceiling in corporations and law firms. Women who open their own businesses (they are doing so at a rate three times that of men in Canada) find themselves at a disadvantage in getting credit because of the nature of most women's businesses. One out of every four small-to-medium sized companies opening in this country is opened by a woman and mostly in the service area. This often means there is no collateral since the business revolves around the woman and a service she provides. Credit, therefore, becomes extremely difficult to get. The Business Development Bank of Canada says women tend, when starting a business, to use their own resources such as savings, RRSPs and cash value insurance because of the difficulty in getting credit. Banks tend to offer credit to people who fit a certain financial profile. Most often it is men who fit this profile since men have had and continue to have the financial and career advantage. In the spring of 1995, the Canadian Federation of Independent Business released a comprehensive study which showed that on average, the difference in refusal rates for women and men is around 20 percent. Therefore, they concluded it is 20 percent more likely that a female business owner will have her request for financing refused than will her male counterpart. CFIB also reported that account managers charge women business owners higher rates of interest than they do men with similar profiles in the service and retail sectors. Furthermore, the amount of collateral required for a personal line of credit is higher for women than for men. The reaction of banks to this study was swift and severe. Previous studies done by CFIB have indicated there is little or no difference in the banks' treatment of women. The words of Catherine Swift, president of CFIB, became immortalized in Canada's national press: "Equality in financing has finally been achieved but only because men and women are being treated equally badly by the banks."

So why the different results now? Swift explains that the time frame of this study was the recession. Many women-owned businesses are on the margins of acceptability because of the nature and type of their operation. In tough times, banks tighten their lending policies, and women-owned businesses, because of their positioning, may have become caught in the stranglehold.

There is a growing awareness, not only among the lending institutions but the government as well, that women are finding it tough to get credit, but there is much more that must be done to translate this awareness into action.

In 1994 the current federal government created a standing committee on small business lending. After listening to senior-level bankers and related individuals, the committee tabled a working paper on what could be done to increase the access of small business to credit in this country. Even though women-owned businesses employ more people in North America than the Fortune 500 companies do worldwide, not a single banker addressed the issue of the special problems, perceived or otherwise, that women business owners encounter in obtaining credit. What was even more amazing to me is that no one on the committee even asked about this major problem. When I heard about this through my contacts within the industry, I was furious. I contacted the chair of the committee, David Berger, and lobbed a very direct and heated complaint. He seemed suitably aghast at the oversight and allowed us to submit a very detailed questionnaire that was then sent out to all the banks on government letterhead. Because banks do not keep gender-specific statistics, they were unable to answer three-quarters of the simple questions asked, like "What percentage of women are turned down for loans?" This exercise brought home our point. No one, including the banks, really knows for sure if it is harder for women to get credit than it is for men. There are no hard data being kept by the banks. We have to rely on anecdotal evidence, which can undermine the credibility of the complaints by women about banks that are rampant. I argued that if the banks kept gender-specific information, everyone would know, once and for all, if the perception of discrimination by banks against women is accurate. It seems Mr. Berger listened. The report was amended to include a recommendation that banks collect gender-specific data. This information could then be used to see if the problems really exist as women say they do or if, as the banks maintain, they don't. This was a small victory, but it could have a strong impact on the old "no there isn't, yes there is" debate.

Generally speaking, the progress banks have made toward understanding the small business market, including women entrepreneurs, has been noteworthy. Some are clearly better than others, but most banks have initiated internal gender awareness training for staff. One bank, Royal Bank of Canada, has taken this a step further: it is implementing this training nationally to sensitize its business account managers to the needs of women entrepreneurs. TD Bank and Royal Bank have seminars that specifically target women entrepreneurs. TD Bank took the initiative to create a position called National Director–Women in Business in order to address this market specifically. CIBC has a similar position and has community seminars as well but CIBC tends to use an inclusive method of marketing as opposed to addressing women specifically. Most banks sponsor women-oriented events and centres such as Mount Saint Vincent University's Centre For Women in Business and the Canadian Women Entrepreneur of the Year awards. All banks have in place programs to encourage advancement of women within the hierarchy. The most notable in this respect is the Bank of Montreal which, in 1994, won the Catalyst award from New York's highly regarded Catalyst Foundation for its tremendous efforts in advancing women.

Though executive suites have a very sparse population of women, middle management ranks are beginning to swell. In retail banking, the number of women and men managers is pretty equal. It is when you get into commercial or business banking that the number of women starts to significantly decrease; the average number of women business centre managers is around 20 percent.

It may be difficult to believe, but most banks are really beginning to listen. They readily acknowledge that their credit lending policies during the recession really hurt small business and are taking steps to redress the problem. Having the government continually hammering away at their head is always good incentive. I truly believe that we are going to see a radical and positive difference in the attitude and policies of our chartered banks over the next few years. The women I've met and worked with in this industry make me certain that change is imminent. The old-boy network better keep looking over its shoulder.

In terms of women needing their own credit rating, it's essential they have their own because, as the experts warn, 90 percent will be on their own and looking after their own affairs, frequently through divorce or death of a partner. Women live longer than men so they will most assuredly be looking after their money at some point. Also more and more women are staying single. The message here is why wait until catastrophe hits? Be proactive instead of reactive.

Women who become divorced or widowed often find themselves in a terrible bind when they realize they can't get credit. I have seen too many women destroyed emotionally and financially because they left the financial matters to their spouse. One client of mine suddenly became a widow at 49. She had worked in the home raising the family for over 20 years and was totally dependent on her spouse for *everything*. When he was killed in an accident, this woman didn't know how much money they had, had never opened a bank account and didn't even have a driver's licence. Her husband had set up charge accounts for her at a taxi company, drugstore and the local grocer. Though she paid these bills out of her housekeeping allowance, her money management skills never progressed beyond that point. She was denied credit because everything had been in her husband's name. She went by Mrs. John Doe, not even Mrs. Jane Doe. As a credit entity, she didn't exist. It was only after repeatedly imploring the bank to give her a credit card because of the gravity of her situation that they finally relented. But they did so only because there was money coming in from the sale of the house. It was her first credit card. She was given a $500 limit. It was under these circumstances that she was forced to learn about financial planning.

You may think this is an extreme case, and it is. But it is not unique. Women are often motivated into taking financial control through such terrible circumstances. There are a few precautions you can take to ensure this doesn't happen to you.

1. Make it your business to know what is going on with the family finances. At the very least, know where everything is. With the woman I wrote about above, I had to go through boxes filled with cancelled cheques to see if there were any payments being made to an insurance company. It was the only way to tell if there was an insurance policy, since we couldn't

find one in the husband's office or at home. I did find a couple of entries in his records, but upon calling the insurance companies I discovered the policies had lapsed a few months earlier. It was well over two years before we determined all of the husband's debts and assets and the process was an inordinate amount of work.

2. *Always* have your own account. Too many joint accounts have been emptied by whoever gets there first in a nasty divorce, and the remaining partner is left with no cash resources. If your partner dies, often all the assets, including credit cards in your partner's name, are frozen until the will is probated. (The exception is life insurance proceeds that have a named beneficiary. The money bypasses probate.) It is not inappropriate to have your own money stashed away somewhere in case a crisis occurs.

3. Get your own credit rating. Open up your own line of credit and have your own credit card *in your own name*. Become an individual, an identifiable person in the eyes of the financial institutions. At your request, the credit bureaus will open a file in your name and will list the accounts that you use in your partner's name and the accounts in your partner's name for which you are contractually liable for payment. But you must contact all your creditors directly and tell them to report the credit history of both you and your partner.

4. Even though the *Family Law Act of Ontario* and other similar provincial legislation dictates that everything is split 50-50 upon divorce, that doesn't include what you brought into the marriage. Be sure to list everything that was yours and his before the nuptials.

Before I leave the subject of credit, there is a story I want to share with you. This story will show you how vulnerable women can be in the area of credit.

My mother hails from an era when women married their financial plans. Mom worked in the home and was dependent on my father for her money. When we were young, she did work on occasion selling Beauty Counsellor cosmetics and Sarah Coventry jewelry through home parties. But this was only when Dad could baby-sit. These occasions were always squeezed in around her primary job which was raising us kids and maintaining the household. Like any woman who chose to work at home, my mother received no pay, benefits, security or pension. Dad represented all those things for her. This was the accepted norm for that generation. Dad was busy climbing the corporate ladder to success, hypertension and ulcers. He also had the responsibility of providing financially for a wife and three children. He left the running of the home and the child care completely to my mother as his father had done, and his grandfather, and so on in perpetuity. My mother wouldn't have had it any other way, even if there were other options.

I consider my mother to be the eighth wonder of the world. She managed the household finances and could turn a loony into a ten-dollar bill. My dad, on the other hand, was remarkably adept at turning a ten-dollar bill into a loony. He always said that anything we had was a direct result of my mother's financial acumen. My father has always been a wonderfully generous man and loves to spend money. That is, after all, what it was invented for. Mom, on the other hand, was much more frugal in order to balance her partner. It is evident who my role model was in the early years. If it were a choice between Mom's "bring a lunch and save a little over time" or Dad's "put that stereo on credit and worry about paying it when the bill comes in," Dad's way won hands down.

Like myself, my father always managed to make a very good living, but never kept any of the money. In 1976, while living on the East Coast, my father received an excellent job offer with a significant salary increase that he couldn't turn down. Around the same time my parents bought a new home and completely decorated it with new furniture. My mother co-signed the loan for a part of the down payment. The house was in my father's name only, which was not unusual at that time. It never occurred to my mother that it should be any other way. This turned out to be a blessing. Dad's salary had increased but the debt load was increasing disproportionately. Credit cards were my father's nemesis. It seems I came by my affliction honestly. The worst happened. The '70s recession was especially pronounced in the Maritimes. Shortly after we moved into our new house, my father was laid off from his new job.

Lay-offs were happening at a fearful rate and the financial institutions were experiencing critically high loan default rates. The

bank turned on my mother with a vengeance that can only be de
scribed as brutal. It was simple. She co-signed, she was now liable
for the debt. She received threatening phone calls at all hours. She
was terrified. It was a horrible experience for someone who took
debt very seriously and managed what money she did have brilliantly. Like most women of her generation, my mother was raised
to "listen to your husband because he will take care of you." Her
wedding vows included "love, honor and obey." She let Dad
manage the money even though he was terrible at it.

To keep the bank at bay, my mother worked double shifts at a
department store cosmetic counter to try to keep up with the payments. She was paid minimum wage. When I think back to this
time, I remember her always rushing and being chronically exhausted. I don't think I ever saw her taking time to read a book or
sit still for more than a moment. There was still the laundry to do,
meals to plan and prepare, the house to clean and so on. I pitched
in as much as any teenager would. But I was going to school and
worked part-time at the mall so I was not around a lot. When my
mother took on those double shifts, her responsibilities at home
didn't change. That's when I remember her beginning to age.

It wasn't long before my parents realized they couldn't keep
up the payments on everything. Dad had found a job that paid
commission, but with the recession, there was no income to
speak of coming in. My mother carried the debt for a few months,
until the end of the school year, but my father was finally forced
to file for personal bankruptcy. My family then moved to begin a
new life in Ontario. Even after bankruptcy had been filed and
my family had moved to Ontario, the bank harassed my mother
long distance. The harassment did finally end when my mother
lost her legendary Thomas temper with an unsuspecting representative from the bank who had just taken over my parents'
case. They never called back.

The ramifications of this experience were tremendous. Children
are resilient, but I did not escape unscathed. One afternoon, my
boyfriend and I were walking home from high school. As we
rounded the corner, we saw strange men loading my bedroom
furniture into a truck. Everything had been repossessed. I stood
there in complete shock, the tears streaming helplessly down my
face. I was shaking in disbelief. My parents had told us this was
going to happen, but actually seeing it was too painful to bear.

Chris put his arm around my shoulders, wheeled me around and started walking quickly in the opposite direction. At that moment I felt a physical sensation that can only be described as "shutting down." My cavalier "here today, gone tomorrow" attitude toward money solidified.

But our possessions were just things. The real losses were far more dramatic. We not only lost our home and possessions, my father had also destroyed his credit rating and my mother lost her innocence. My father had to deal with the devastating feeling of letting his family down. He had been taught it was a man's responsibility to bring home the bacon. My mother lived through the death of the dreams and ideals she had held since childhood. Her whole thought process had to be realigned. Everything she had been taught about life had to be unlearned and relearned. It was a terribly painful time for her. This was how my mother buried her knight in shining armour syndrome.

My mother began to rebuild her life, as did my father, on a much more realistic emotional and financial foundation. She had received a college diploma in business administration many years previously and snagged her first full-time job at the tender age of 40. Though she had many years of earnings and pension to make up, she remained undaunted. She started to build her own financial base, much the same way I would have. Her first step was to get a credit card in her own name. She then started her own savings account and got her own life insurance. She has since paid cash for every car she has owned or trip she has taken. My mother stopped depending on others and took control of her own financial affairs. In her own words, "I stopped being a passive little twit and started to develop some backbone. One has to be their own person and not be afraid of what that might entail." Today she is a coordinator for a company that provides homecare services to the terminally ill and the elderly. Like most women in this industry, she is paid well below her worth. However, she has a quiet dignity and confidence that come from surviving a trip to hell and back.

BAD DEBT AND GOOD DEBT

We have seen where the extreme mismanagement of money and debt can lead you. The point I can't emphasize enough is how easy it is to get caught in the downward spiral of debt. Most interest rates that you pay on consumer debt like credit cards, overdraft protection and those "Don't Pay A Cent" events far and away exceed what interest you would earn on most investments. That's why you should pay off your nondeductible debt before investing your money. Or at least make sure your debt is manageable before you start. A good way to do that is to consolidate your debts with an appropriate loan from your bank that has significantly lower interest rates than credit cards and other forms of credit. What would you rather pay in interest, 17 or 18 percent on a Visa balance or eight to ten percent on a bill consolidation loan? What you save in interest payments alone could be enough to start a savings program. All you need is $50 a month in a preauthorized chequing program to start most types of investments.

But the reality for many of us is that if we wait until we pay off our debts before we start to save, we will be buying our first mutual fund out of the death benefit of our life insurance policy! Use common sense when determining your ratio of debt versus savings. Much will depend on your lifestyle and weekly paycheque. Every financial advisor on the planet will tell you to avoid consumer debt at all costs. It's solid advice. However, I would like you to do an informal survey of people you know and tabulate all who are completely free of consumer debt. Out of a hundred, there may be three. This is a very "I want and deserve it now" society with little encouragement for waiting until you have the cash to do "it," whatever "it" might be. I think back to my grandmother's and mother's generations. Life was radically different. What did these people do without credit cards, lines of credit, overdraft protection and "Don't Pay A Cent" events?

They saved their money until they had enough to pay cash for it. My mother recalls the story of her grandfather pinning a huge wad of cash to his flannel shirt pocket when he went into town to buy a new tractor. A little hint: Save for your purchase until you have enough to buy it outright. Then buy it with your credit card and pay the card off in full on the due date. That way you earn interest for an extra 21 to 30 days and you don't have to pay any credit card interest providing your full payment is made by the due date.

Yet, after this lengthy diatribe against debt and all its evils, there is, in fact, good debt. That's the type of debt that results from investing in yourself or an investment of some sort. Some examples of debt that are worthwhile are Canada Student loans or business loans because they advance your station in life.

There are RRSP loans that should be used if you find yourself short and can't make your contribution. The interest on these isn't tax deductible but you are further ahead having a loan (which should be paid off in 12 months) and an RRSP than no loan and no RRSP. We will consider this in more detail in a later chapter.

Another reasonable form of debt is your mortgage. Very few people, in my circle of friends anyway, can afford to pay cash for their home so this form of debt is quite acceptable, though again, the interest is not tax deductible.

There is also investment debt which, if used carefully, can be advantageous. Let's say I borrow $10,000 to buy a mutual fund. The interest on this loan is tax deductible. Our government likes it when we invest in ourselves so they give us a bit of a break. This type of investment debt is also called leveraging. One must be very cautious in using it. Leveraging was responsible for wiping out many people in the '80s. People borrowed and used other people's money to invest in everything from investment real estate to the stock market. When everything crashed, these people not only lost their own money, but were still responsible for the money they had borrowed.

Make sure the investment you choose will earn higher interest than the interest you are paying on the loan. It doesn't make sense to be earning five percent on a GIC when you are paying eight percent on the loan to buy it, even with the deductible interest.

Something to keep in mind about investment debt is that if owing money keeps you awake at night, forget it. Save this method of investing until after you have built your financial base and have successfully accumulated your first million. We are most interested in securing your financial foundation. Leveraging is not foundation material.

Your debts are now paid off and you have gained a working knowledge of credit that ensures you will stay out of trouble, inadvertent or otherwise. When I reached that point, I felt it was a major accomplishment under my belt. I was now eager to do something sexier. I wanted to embark on a whole new experience: amassing unimaginable wealth. Or at least open a savings account.

BUILDING YOUR FINANCIAL BASE: TACKLING SOME FUNDAMENTALS

"Money is one of those rare things where quantity is quality."

Anonymous

With the worst behind me, I found myself actually looking forward to learning more about the mysterious world of money. That, and good-naturedly sparring with Elaine. In our next session, she dropped the bombshell. "I have to give you money?" I feigned incredulousness. I was ready to commit to financial security but I had hoped I wouldn't have to give up money to do it. Elaine looked at me with ill-disguised exasperation. That horrid pyramid stared up at me from the desk, permanently imprinting itself on my brain. My chest heaved with a resigned sigh.

"Joanne," she began, "tell me what happens when you re-ceive your paycheque each month."

"I pay my butler, Steed, Lance, the chauffeur, and last but not least, I send Costner, Selleck and Gibson their retainer fee to be on call when I need them." I wasn't going down easy.

Ignoring my sarcasm, she pressed on. "What's the first thing you do when you get paid?"

"I, uh, pay my bills, I guess. It's much more relaxing now that I have banished Attila to greener pastures. Let's see. I pay my rent, utilities, food, credit card bills, that kind of stuff first. I might buy a suit or dress if I see one I like."

"So whatever is left over, you save?" she asked. Elaine's expression was dead serious.

I snickered. "Yeah, Elaine. That's how I got to buy the 40-room mansion I live in. Ah...no. Whatever is left over I spend, woman!"

"Aren't you tired of doing everything backwards?" The problem with working with your advisor is that he or she takes certain liberties with you. "Joanne, have you heard of the famous story, *The Richest Man in Babylon?* In 1926, a gentleman named George S. Clason wrote this story that helped millions of people get on the right financial track. The plot is simple. Paraphrased, Clason said the first bill you should pay every month, before your rent or mortgage payment, kid's orthodontist bill, or Gibson's retainer, is the bill to yourself. And I don't mean pay yourself with that new camera or Group of Seven painting that your life is worthless without. I mean savings—treat your savings as a bill. These savings can be for a wonderful business opportunity that comes up or maybe a cottage. It's entirely up to you how you use the money. You work hard for your money, you deserve to have it when you want it. First, though, we must protect you against yourself and the demands of day-to-day living."

"Pay myself first?" I repeated softly. I could do this. Since I had a long history of self-indulgence, the idea of paying myself first fit right in. "I'll become the Richest Woman in Scarborough!"

"Before we decide where your millions are going to go, you need to understand a few basic investing principles." She went on to explain a number of things that became the premise on which my own financial base and that of my clients were subsequently built. I share them with you here as a simple, easy-to-understand primer on the basics you need to help with your financial planning and investment decisions. It's always good to know why you are doing something. Develop the habit of a three-year-old and always ask *why.*

INFLATION

I have seen more women who had anywhere from $5,000 to $60,000 sitting in a bank account earning three percent interest and who believed they were taking care of business. One client had sold her house three years ago and had $120,000 sitting in a chequing account earning three percent. I saw to it that it did not remain there long. This is not investing, this is resting. And it is not enough. Investing does not mean dumping money into a low-interest-bearing account. I was perplexed to discover that there is work to do in order to have my money work in the best way for me. An emergency fund, although essential, is not nearly enough. There are hundreds of financial products out there designed to do very specific jobs. They are also taxed differently. There are Registered Retirement Savings Plans for retirement. There are stock-market-based mutual funds best suited for long-term goals that may include retirement. There are money market mutual funds or general purpose savings accounts for short-term goals like an emergency fund or the mandatory week away at a cottage. There is life and disability insurance and investment real estate (not for the weak of heart, these days). One paltry, little savings account will do nothing for you in the long term. In fact, it can be a guaranteed recipe to lose money.

We have been accustomed for so long to think in terms of "interest rate" but that thinking will get us nowhere fast. During the '80s I was delighted to be earning 15 percent interest on a Canada Savings Bond. I took one out for forced savings (read spending) purposes. Around the same time the newspapers and television were filled with talk of "runaway inflation." It had no impact on me whatsoever. I thought inflation was some techno-economic term eggheads used to describe a phenomenon that only affected corporations and big business.

Wrong. I thought I was in line telling Elaine I wanted 15 percent for my investments. After all, that's what I got during the '80s. She quietly suggested that this was not so. She said 15 percent may have been the interest rate but it was not the "real" rate of return. "Real, smeal," I retorted. "I had a little piece of paper from the bank in one of my shoe boxes that said I was earning 15 percent."

It seems that didn't matter much. I discovered that the rate of return the banks say you are earning on your money is not the final story. You must subtract the rate of inflation and taxes to get your "real" rate of return. Elaine informed me that I had been getting closer to two or three percent. All of a sudden I found myself curious about these concepts of inflation and taxes.

Uninformed conventional wisdom suggests that it's great to have high interest rates so we can earn more interest on our money. But when we have high interest rates, high inflation generally lurks close behind. This is not good news. Inflation is another way of saying cost of living. When you clutch your heart from shock when the real estate agent tells you the price of that one-bedroom, 900-square-foot house located just next to runway two; when the same amount of money that filled your grocery cart last year buys you this year a head of wilted romaine and one-day-old bread, you know inflation is running amok.

The consumer price index is used to measure inflation. Imagine a shopping basket of consumer goods and services. Each year the cost of these items is compared with previous years. The result gives us a sense of how inflated or deflated our economy has become. In 1971, the consumer price index was set at $100. That means $100 of cash bought $100 of goods and services. If you fast forward 20-odd years to now, the same stuff would cost you around $250. Another example: A dollar in 1974 is worth 14 cents today. How about this one: Allowing for five percent inflation, a 30-year-old earning

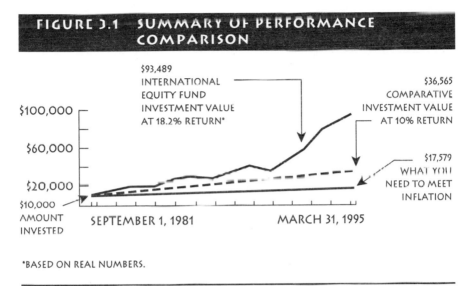

FIGURE 3.1   SUMMARY OF PERFORMANCE COMPARISON

$93,489
INTERNATIONAL
EQUITY FUND
INVESTMENT VALUE
AT 18.2% RETURN*

$36,565
COMPARATIVE
INVESTMENT VALUE
AT 10% RETURN

$100,000

$60,000

$20,000

$10,000

AMOUNT
INVESTED

$17,579
WHAT YOU
NEED TO MEET
INFLATION

SEPTEMBER 1, 1981

MARCH 31, 1995

*BASED ON REAL NUMBERS.

Source: Trimark Mutual Funds 1995. Reproduced with permission.

$40,000 a year will, at 55, make $135,454. He will need it. This is inflation.

Imagine someone like my grandfather who retired at 65 on a fixed pension. He died when he was 79. He had 14 years to struggle through on the same amount of money each month. His Canada Pension was indexed to keep up with inflation but CPP represents on average 39 percent of your total retirement picture. For women, the picture can be very grim. The latest Statistics Canada figures show women live on average to age 81. That's, on average, six years longer than men. These are *retirement* years when you are not working but they must still be planned and paid for. If you don't factor in the impact of inflation in your financial planning, your golden retirement will be tarnished.

The average rate of inflation in Canada has been about five percent per year over the last 20 years. That means it costs, on average, five percent more each year for essentials like food, shelter and clothing. The key word here, however, is average. The '80s saw what economists call double-digit inflation when inflation hit 12 percent or more. That's when interest rates jumped up. High interest rates encourage people (including foreign investors and people like me) to invest in our economy. It was then I purchased a Canada Savings Bond at 15 percent. Inflation was also running at 12 percent. After I took into consideration the increase in my cost of living, what I was left with was a sobering three percent as a "real" rate of return.

When you see interest rates as low as they are now, that *usually* means inflation is under control. Even though my guaranteed investments are only earning around four to six percent, I'm still in the same position I was in in the '80s. Inflation today is around two percent. Therefore my "real" rate of return is the same.

The bottom line is to be sure to factor in inflation in any long-term planning. Given women's life span, the risk of living longer than your money is high. People in general are living longer so inflation is a serious concern for everyone. Inflation does fluctuate so a good rule is to target twice the average rate of five to six percent over the long term. You should look for a *minimum* growth in your net worth of 10 to 12 percent each year to keep you swimming. Five or six percent growth will keep you treading water, period. Many advisors will tell you to make sure your investments keep pace with the rate of inflation. That's at the very least! Financial planning is not about staying flat or static.

As if worrying about inflation wasn't enough. In this country, we have another serious matter to think about before making investment decisions. And that's everybody's favourite thorn: taxes. After I internalized the barrage of bad news about inflation, I had to then face the effects of taxation on this "real" rate of return. Though guaranteed investments play an important role in your portfolio, because of taxes and inflation, you should never

"Make sure your money lasts at least as long as you do."

have only these types of investments. The key to any successful portfolio is diversification. A little bit of many is better than a few of a little. As usual, nothing was as easy as it seemed. The idea that you could put your money away in a little, old bank account and forget it was blasted to smithereens. "Ignorance truly is bliss," I groaned. "However, Elaine, the good news about inflation is that you can live in a more expensive neighbourhood without moving out of your home!"

Elaine ignored my optimistic observation and levelled me with one of those looks that said, "Alas, you have so much to learn!" The craving for M&Ms had never been stronger.

"What can people do about inflation and taxes?" I cried. "Nothing," came the abrupt answer.

I was to learn that you can, however, make investment choices that will work *with* inflation and taxes. Elaine showed me a graph (Figure 3.2) that illustrated how well guaranteed investments did as compared to the stock market over a 43-year period. Inflation was also shown on the graph. I was flabbergasted. Even though the stock market resembled a roller coaster more than the interest-bearing investments did, over the long term, the market outperformed both inflation and T-bills.

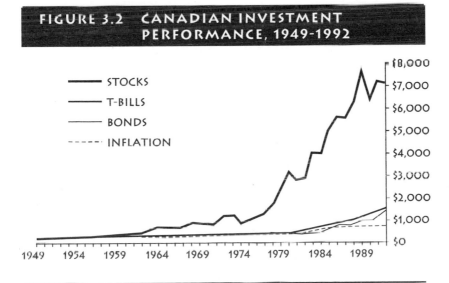

FIGURE 3.2   CANADIAN INVESTMENT PERFORMANCE, 1949-1992

Source: Reprinted with permission from McDermid St. Lawrence Chisholm Ltd.

A case in point: During the 43 years between 1950 and 1993, the Toronto Stock Exchange's 300 Index gained an average of 10 percent a year, U.S. stocks came in around 13 percent and GIC's annual growth was eight percent for the same time period. To graphically illustrate this: a $1,000 investment maintained over this time period would have given you $19,880 with Canada Savings Bonds, $27,367 with five-year GICs, $60,240 with TSE 300 stocks and $184,443 in U.S. stocks through Standard and Poor's 500 Index.

So what's the answer? The answer is to be sure a portion of your portfolio goes into investments that have a history of out-running inflation. The allocation of what goes where is based on many different factors such as age and goals, so be sure to talk to an advisor about it.

The light bulb went on. "I guess it's a good idea to have your money working for you, not against you," I said. "But the stock market! It gives me and many other women I know the willies. Don't forget it wasn't that long ago I thought the stock market was a place for the disgustingly rich or to sell cattle!"

"Wrong on both counts," Elaine countered. "Mutual funds allow the not-so-disgustingly rich, in fact, the downright poor and financially challenged, to take advantage of the good, the bad and the ugly of the stock market. There is, however, an important step to be taken before one runs off half-cocked, blinded by the allure of equity funds." As I had been finding out, anything worth having must be worth waiting for.

THE REAL SECRET TO GETTING RICH

Elaine leaned forward with a delightful air of conspiracy. "I can make you rich." She had my attention. I was awash with images of tall, dark and wonderfully mysterious men lolling about my palatial estate. This was the bonanza. This was what I had been waiting for throughout this painfully slow process of deciphering the financial planning maze. Finally something with sizzle.

She said, "Pay yourself first. Ten percent. That's the secret."

I was incredulous. "That's it?!" I demanded.

"That's it," she quietly affirmed. "Take 10 percent after tax from every paycheque. That should be the minimum you're squir-relling away. You've heard it before. It's called 'getting rich slowly.'" Then the reality hit me. Ten percent seemed like a lot to take away from the so-called necessities of life. No, I was sure this was too much. I started to balk.

"Hold on, before you write this notion off completely," she interjected. "We both know how well your stellar financial skills have served you in life, so hear me out." The sarcasm was hard to miss. "Let's say your company came to you and said, 'Sorry, Joanne, we have to lay you off.' However, the suits also

"Pay Yourself First"

say they are prepared to offer you an option. That is, if you take a 10 percent drop in pay, you can keep your job. What's more, they will invest that 10 percent for you so that when you retire, they will give you a million dollars cash. What would you do?"

"Duh, I'd quit," I shot back. "Of course I'd take the 10 percent drop in pay."

"Every so often, your good sense surprises me. OK, Joanne, I want you to fire yourself right now and hire yourself back at 10 percent less."

I'd been had. The strange thing about this 10 percent rule was that I didn't even notice it. The money came out first thing each month and it didn't make a perceptible difference in my lifestyle. I really hated it when Elaine was right. Initially, I put my 10 percent into a special account I'll describe in detail a little later. I needed to establish a financial cushion first before getting into higher-risk investments. The 10 percent would eventually evolve into "take advantage of whatever comes along" money. Thanks to this 10 percent, I was able to take almost a year off to write this book.

If you don't think you can afford it, look for the "black hole" in your financial plan. We all have one. Where does a disproportionate amount of your lifestyle maintenance money go? Mine was easy. Eating out and frittering. I was a world-class fritterer. If you gave me $50 in the morning and asked me before bedtime where the money went, I would be hard pressed to tell you. It can be as simple as cutting out your daily coffee and donut or chicken wings and beer on Friday nights.

This rule should be adhered to whether you earn $17,000 or $170,000 a year. It's all relative. Oh yes, ideally this should be over and above your annual RRSP contribution. Your RRSP provides a tax deduction that lowers the amount you have to pay in taxes or, even better, gets you money back. The money you save or get back should be used toward next year's contribution. Remember, the 10 percent rule is something to work up to. If you can afford only five percent, that's five percent more than you had last year. Every little bit counts. If it's a choice between the two, and you are in a higher tax bracket, go for the RRSP. If it is an emergency fund you are trying to build with your 10 percent, which must also include your RRSP contribution because of budget constraints, put half of your 10 percent in savings and the other half in your RRSP.

Women in particular need to be sure to implement this strategy. The divorce rate and the fact that they are the primary caregivers make women more financially vulnerable. The catch-22 is that women earn on average less, but often need the financial safety nets more. Most of these suggestions, like emergency funds, mutual funds, or any type of investment, can be started with as little as $50 a month. It doesn't sound like much, but it's a respectable beginning. One day I asked Elaine, "How does this 10 percent racket work?" "Next lesson," she offered. "There is only so much even your brain can assimilate." As I took my leave, I shot her a withering glance. She sat back in her chair, grinning broadly.

THE LAZY PERSON'S PATH TO WEALTH: COMPOUND INTEREST

I was settled in for another rousing session of Financial Planning 101. Elaine and I did a quick summary of my financial accomplishments, quick being the operative word here. There was still some distance to travel. Debt gone? Check. Credit reestablished? Check. Emergency fund/PLC/overdraft protection in place? Check. Ten percent savings set up? Check.

"Inquiring minds want to know, Elaine. How can a measly 10 percent make you rich?"

"Rich is a subjective term," Elaine replied. "There are as many definitions of rich as there are people who have them. But to answer your question, it all comes down to compound interest, which needs time to work." It's the rule of 72. In its simplest form, it means that if you find an investment that will net you a 10 percent rate of return, your money will double every seven years, at six percent, it will double in 12 years and so on. All you need to do is divide 72 by the interest rate to find out when your money will double. It's another way of saying interest accumulating on top of interest.

The following is a classic story of the power of compound interest. Krystal and Vanessa, twin sisters, were having dinner one night. Over exceedingly decadent cheesecake, they discussed their impending retirement. Vanessa had been known for her free-spirited ways in her youth, but she got it together at age 30. She started a monthly savings plan that she adhered to religiously right up to age 65. Vanessa began: "Thank God I got on track so many years ago. I'm looking forward to a leisurely yet lavish retirement with no financial headaches. I worked so hard for my money and often couldn't make my RRSP contribution without having to borrow for it. One year I even postponed buying a much-needed winter coat to make my contribution. In fact, there were lots of years like that." She stabbed her cheesecake with a frustrated air. As she looked over her shoulder, she leaned forward toward Krystal. She pushed a piece of paper across the table and said in a conspiratorial whisper, "Can you believe I've saved this much?! I suppose it's the least I should expect after 35 years of saving." Krystal glanced at the statement and smiled benignly.

Vanessa went on. "Honey, you are going to be so sorry you didn't look after your retirement all these years. How does it look for you?" Krystal hadn't saved for 35 years. She had been able to save for only 10 years. Krystal started saving when she was 20. When she reached 30, she had to stop as she started her family and became a stay-at-home mom. Since she didn't work in the paid labour force, she couldn't make her own RRSP contributions and she didn't qualify for the Canada Pension Plan. She also didn't have access to a private pension plan. Her husband had died the year before leaving absolutely nothing behind but funeral expenses. Vanessa believed she had every reason to be concerned about her sister's future. Krystal could easily become one of the 60 percent of women her age living at the poverty line or lower. What separated Krystal from many women in her situation was the nest egg she had tucked away. She had 10 years worth of savings that she had left untouched for 35 years.

"I'm ahead of you, Vanessa," Krystal said. "In fact, about 10 years ahead. I knew I wasn't going to send my body out into the paid work force, so I decided to send my money out instead. You started at 30 and stopped at 65. I started at 20 and stopped at 30, but didn't touch the money." Krystal turned the statement over and wrote down a number. She slid it across the table to her sister and in a quiet voice said, "I'd swallow that cheesecake before you look at this." Vanessa looked down. As her eyes widened in disbelief, she started to laugh—a big, hearty belly laugh that comes from immeasurable relief. And shock. Krystal had much more money than her sister. In fact, she had almost double what her sister had. After 35 years of consistently investing $2,500 annually and earning a 10 percent return, Vanessa had a net worth of $745,317. Krystal, on the other hand, could only invest her $2,500, which got 10 percent as well, for 10 years. But she got a 10-year jump on Vanessa and ended up with $1,231,671!

That is the power of compound interest.

Once I understood the principle of compound interest, my desire to save was greatly enhanced. After all, easy money appeals to everyone's sense of greed. Like Krystal, I began to figure out that there are really two ways you can make money. The more traditional way is to send your body out to work, but you can also send your money out to work. Sending your money out to work can really help ease the pressure. You work hard for your money. Let it take some of the burden. It is never too late to start. Especially with women's lifespan, they could start at 65 and still have 15 to 20 years to enjoy the remarkable benefits of compounding.

EMERGENCY FUNDS

"OK, Elaine! I trust we are finally at the part now where we get to talk about something more exciting. I'm debt-free and I'm ready to let you rob me of 10 percent of my hard-earned money," I exclaimed, greedily rubbing my hands together. "I want to talk about something that will give me a really high rate of return each year though completely liquid so that I can get at it if I need to."

Elaine simply smiled at me. She said, "Tone down your mani-acal enthusiasm, Joanne, I have some bad news." That's when my lofty expectations collided with reality. She showed me the dreaded priority pyramid again. "Emergency fund?!" I groaned. "How positively dull." The only thing I knew about emergency funds was the mad money my mother used to make sure I had when I went out with my friends. I see now that I never did realize the appropriateness of my mother's gesture.

I had established my own personal line of credit, but I had not yet created a true emergency fund. The next step I was required to take was to create a safety net for myself. I had spent so much of my life walking a financial tightrope without pro-tection that at first the idea seemed silly and foreign. I did, how-ever, intuitively understand the need for it. There had been many times over the years when a little nest egg would have saved me immeasurable heartache and difficulty. But any time I had saved up an appreciable amount of money, I'd blow it on some-thing necessary like a trip or a gift for someone. I saved money to spend it. The idea of saving money to have "just in case" seemed downright weird. It did, however, make sense that if I was going to create a healthy financial situation for myself, an emer-gency fund was needed to protect it, and not just for the obvious disasters and pitfalls.

Let's say I had an extensive RRSP portfolio but nothing else. If something happened, this would be my only source of rev-enue. I would end up damaging the very thing that the investment was supposed to do in the first place: provide for retirement and tax sheltering. RRSPs are the world's worst emergency fund. I do not advise using them before retirement under any avoidable cir-cumstance. One reason is that Revenue Canada will hold back 30 percent of the value of your withdrawal on amounts of $15,000 and over. That means you only get 70 cents for every dollar. (It's 10 percent for under $5,000 and 15 percent for $5,001 to $14,999; it's higher in Quebec.) And that's just the beginning. Once you file your tax return, there may be more held back depending on what you owe Revenue Canada. Another important reason is that it is hard enough to save for retirement without having to access your major source of income at retirement. People are outliving their capital these days because of increasing lifespans. Don't sabotage your retirement plans.

If all your money is in equity mutual funds or the stock market, you can rest assured that your catastrophe will coincide with the day the stock market nose-dives. You are then at the mercy of the market. Having an emergency fund protects the integrity of each of your investments and allows them to do whatever they are designed to do. And I repeat, "investments" does not mean a savings account.

Ideally, you should take three months' salary net (after taxes) and put it aside into something earmarked for emergencies only. (Emergencies don't include buying a framed, mint condition, original Woodstock album that your life is meaningless without.) Through the miracle of preauthorized chequing and the 10 percent rule, I started an emergency fund in a savings account with surprising ease. A predetermined amount comes out of my chequing account each month and is deposited into a special account that I nicknamed "On Pain of Death Only."

I found a savings vehicle that was perfect for an emergency fund. Because I can succumb to the allure of a camera store in an instant, I needed something that I couldn't easily get at when my spontaneous urges flared up. After all, as I discovered, money didn't grow on sprees. (Sorry, couldn't resist…). But the fund had to be accessible in case I lost my job or had to move unexpectedly. (I have experienced both with no cushion. Not fun.) Life insurance companies have a type of savings account often called an investment account. You can set it up through preauthorized chequing but what makes it particularly appealling is that you can't access it through a bank machine or write cheques on it. So far it sounds like a regular savings account. But you also can't step into a branch office, fill out a piece of paper and walk out 10 minutes later with cash in hand to buy that collector's album or camera. It usually takes seven to 10 working days to get your money. This was perfect for me. It was impossible to be impulsive with this type of account. Most events that constitute emergencies usually allow a 30-day payment period anyway. The interest rate is comparable to, if not marginally higher than, standard bank savings accounts. Because it is with an insurance company, you can name a beneficiary, which means the money will not get locked up in your estate should you have the misfortune of dying before you spend it. The money goes directly to your beneficiary, no strings attached. It is also creditor-proof.

This approach may not suit everyone. For those of you who aren't bothered by debilitating impulse spending, a regular savings account or money market fund that is more accessible is fine. Check with the financial institution you are dealing with to see if they have a similar product that would be ideal for your emergency fund given your spending habits.

There are many different opinions as to how much money should be in an emergency fund. I believe that the amount of your emergency fund should be based on your lifestyle and occupation. If you are in a volatile profession and could be laid off or if you have a home and/or children dependent on your income, three to six months' net salary is mandatory. That is a lot of money, but believe me, it won't seem like much when you have lost your job and the rent or mortgage is due. For the self-employed and commissioned sales people, a three months' salary nest egg is recommended. This will help you ride out the cyclical nature of business and sales.

As a single professional, I found three to six months high for my lifestyle. The problem with emergency funds is that they have to be reasonably accessible, which means a lower interest rate. There is a fundamental rule in the world of investing: the easier it is to get at, generally the lower it pays you. I couldn't see tying up that much cash in something that was paying low interest relative to other options that were available. For people earning high incomes, the three to six months rule could mean having $20,000 or $30,000 in a low-interest-bearing savings account. An Italian woman in one of our focus groups attended 11 weddings in one year. She could have used a large emergency fund. Otherwise, this isn't necessarily the best option for those who have secure jobs and can't foresee having an emergency that would require that kind of cash outlay. An option for people in this category might be to put a portion of their emergency money into one or more of the many types of mutual funds. Over the long term, these will give you better bang for your buck. It is important, however, to be sure that you always have on hand adequate resources to maintain your day-to-day lifestyle.

I chose the mutual fund route. To help alleviate the anxiety of being caught short, I established a personal line of credit to make up the difference. I don't have to pay for it if I don't use it. That way I freed up a good chunk of my money that I invested more wisely. Caution! Remember from our earlier discussion of PLCs that they are for the credit-sensible only. Use only if you are certain of a reasonable source of continuing income. The worst thing that could happen to someone is to have to go into debt for an indefinite period because of an emergency.

When I started talking to women and advising them on money matters, I was quick to learn that very few had emergency funds. Having an adequate emergency fund can buy you time for making important decisions that could affect the rest of your life. The worst time to learn about financial planning or to make financial decisions is when you are under tremendous stress. It can also buy you the freedom to leave a failed marriage or relationship. Too many women are forced to stay in unhappy or unhealthy situations because of financial dependence or ignorance.

With so many women working at the low end of the income continuum, starting an emergency fund can be tough. Often women are forced to spend their earnings on lavish luxuries such as food, shelter and clothing. There is little, if anything, left over for emergency funds. My mother went through much of her life depending on Dad as her emergency fund. At the same time, she managed to squirrel away a little bit here and a little bit there for stuff that the family might need. Mom certainly didn't spend this money on manicures and afternoon teas. In fact, it is safe to say it was never spent on herself. I call this the "teapot syndrome." Women throughout the ages have had emergency funds stashed in their "teapots" to bail out husbands or pay for the kids' summer camp. The focus groups we conducted included an overwhelming majority of women whose mothers saved little bits of money where they could but only spent it on others. Many contemporary women have carried on that trait. The reality of today's world suggests that it is time to break the pattern.

There is no easy answer. Credit can be harder to get for women at the lower end of the earning scale and for those lacking collateral, but that is not to say one shouldn't try. Do try to work up to the 10 percent rule. Be resigned to the fact that it is going to take time to build up. Just getting started, however, gave me a huge psychological boost. The key to building a proper financial plan is to be systematic with your approach. With your 10 percent each month, once your cushion is firmly in place, keep going. That's when you can start to branch out into other investments like mutual funds. Once I had an adequate fund for my purposes (which was almost immediately because I chose the PLC route until I had three months' salary tucked away), I started to invest in a long-term, growth-oriented equity mutual fund. I could do so comfortably because I could now afford the risk. If the mutual fund lost money, my lifestyle would still be protected by the emergency fund. Remember, when Noah and his wife built the ark, it wasn't raining.

THE HILARIOUS WORLD OF BUDGETS

I reconciled myself to the fact that there was much to do, not the least of which was to get all this stuff organized. In her naiveté, Elaine suggested a budget. After my howling laughter subsided, she acknowledged she got the point. Fewer than 10 percent of Canadians do any sort of financial planning, let alone entertain the nasty "B" word. I am about to utter what is considered veritable heresy in financial planning circles. Budgets don't work. I know budgets don't work from my own experience and that of thousands I have dealt with on a professional level. The idea of budgets is very sane and very credible. There is one minor detail, however. People don't stick to them. Human nature runs contrary to the very idea of what budgets are about. Budgets are based on needs and wants. The needs (food and shelter) should get priority and attention. We then save or budget for wants (compact disc player) afterward. I don't think this is what really happens for most of us. Remember, we live in a "Get it now! Don't pay a cent until 2099!" world. Immediate gratification has become the basis for much of our existence.

Watch how quickly a want becomes a need and throws the delicate balancing act of your budget out the window! I have heard people emphatically state that they *need* that compact disc player so they can mellow out after a stressful day at the office. Who am I to judge? My approach has always been to justify absolutely anything I wanted. I was brilliant at it. I could justify with the deftness of a senior diplomat the purchase of a $800 suit over a perfectly adequate $400 one in an instant. I'd worry about how to pay later. I love what David Chilton, Canada's very own Wealthy Barber, says about budgets. According to him, very few people can budget effectively. And those who can, he says, aren't fun people.

The difficulty with budgets comes from the fact that they require us to retrain our money behaviour. This is especially true for the many women who lack financial training or the belief that they need to manage their own money. When I designed a financial plan for someone, I told them after their first visit to come back with a budget in hand. Knowing full well how people detest budgets, I described it as an "approximate forecast of the outcome of your spending." I used a very simple one-page form so it shouldn't have been too daunting a task. Fewer than 20 percent came back with one completed. People fight budgeting. To many, a budget means life is over as they know it. They will be banished to Kraft Dinner at home with "America's Funniest Home Videos."

In theory, a budget is supposed to be used to allow you to live the way you want to. One of my favourite stories is of a woman who had close to $7,000 on both of her credit cards. When asked how long she had been carrying this debt, she replied since her divorce. That wasn't particularly helpful so I pressed on. "When might that have been?" I queried, expecting a year at the most. "Six years ago," she calmly replied. After I picked myself up off the floor and dusted myself off, I asked her if she was aware of the monumental interest she had been paying over the years. She said she was but had come to accept it as a matter of course. It hadn't bothered her in the least. This woman had gotten caught in the "rob Mary to pay Sally" routine. She would get a cash advance on her Visa to pay off Mastercard, then switch it around the following month. After impressing upon her the importance of paying off this debt and establishing a healthier form of budgeting, I noticed the familiar "eyes glazing over." I knew I had lost this soul. She wasn't ready to break out of this insidious trap yet and I was right. The idea of budgeting scared her off. I never saw her again.

Abuse of credit cards is the most common way that people sabotage their budgets. There is a well-known story of a woman who took her credit cards and put them in a deep plastic container filled with water. She then put them in the freezer in an effort to stop her impulse buying that regularly threw her budget off. I had a client who, after hearing this story, thought she would give it a try. She came to realize early on, however, how inane this really was. The minute the first impulse hit, she simply put the container in the microwave for 30 seconds and was off, armed and ready for the next onslaught. Thirty seconds isn't a long time to talk yourself out of your urges. Today, she is happily on the road to financial recovery after discovering scissors worked infinitely better than ice.

But the real kicker came in the form of one of the most accomplished women I had ever met. Lisette had a Bachelor of Commerce degree, an MBA and a PhD in Organizational Management Theory. She had worked as a financial analyst with a major computer company for 10 years analyzing corporate financial trends and developing strategies with immense budgets. Her decisions could affect the company's bottom line in the millions of dollars. When I met her, she had moved on to become a professor at a prestigious university. Lisette had an extraordinary background in finance. Yet this woman could barely manage to pay her rent. In her own words, "I came alive at the poverty line! The idea of having my own money intimidated me to such a degree that I found a way around it; I married an alcoholic so he could spend it for me." Needless to say, this was not an effective money-management technique. Lisette eventually found her way through the maze but had to experience tremendous pain before she was able to get her money act together. She often said she didn't feel that she "deserved" to have money so didn't pay it much attention even though she worked like a Trojan and was an extremely skilled woman. How women think about themselves can have a huge impact on their success with budgets, financial planning and investing.

The vast majority of women I have dealt with, however, do have a pretty good idea of what they can afford to invest. There are a few notable exceptions that I send packing to credit counselling. There are also people who could afford to save more but who are not prepared to make any changes to their lifestyle. An important point to note here is that financial planning should not be painful. It may pinch a bit here and there, but it should never require a radical shift from your present situation, unless, of course, you are in dire financial straits with a strangling debt load. In such circumstances, some drastic measure like credit counselling or, in the ultimate worst case, declaring bankruptcy, may be necessary. If you take on more than you can handle at first, the chances are high that you will end up dusting the whole notion within six months. Frustration and overzealousness are the two leading causes of premature deaths of financial plans.

While in private practice, I often suggested starting at half or three-quarters of what the client thought she could afford to save for the first three to six months. It's the "try it on for fit and comfort" method. There is always something people "forget" to include in their budgets. This method often flushes it out. In almost every case, however, people increase their savings and investing to the original, and often higher, amount.

So, if budgets (in the traditional sense of the word) don't work for most people, what can you do? First of all, let me say straight out that budgets are designed to give you at best a sense of your situation. It is impossible to calculate right down to the penny the comings and goings of your money. If you try, you'll fail. Corporations have a hard enough time at this, and let's not even mention our esteemed governments. It is, however, important to know how much is coming in and going out consistently each month. Things like rent or mortgage, savings, insurance, anything that remains reasonably constant, are easy to account for. Balance these expenditures with your regular income.

This is especially important for commissioned sales people or people who receive bonuses. Base your budget on what you know absolutely is going to come in each month. Commissions and bonuses should be considered gravy. Also try to look at a full year or even a five-year period to get as accurate as possible a handle on your boom and bust cycles and plan accordingly. When you attempt your budget, if you don't have taxes deducted at source, be sure to remember the inevitable tax bill. Setting up and budgeting for a monthly tax account is mandatory in these circumstances. Remember, if you are self-employed or a commissioned sales person, you can only write off 50 percent of your business meals and entertainment expenses, instead of 80 percent as in previous years. This reduction applies to the goods and services tax credit for business meals and expenses. The self employed also need to consider budgeting for their own extended healthcare, life and disability insurance, and retirement since pension plans aren't available. Your maximum RRSP contribution amortized over the year should also be a monthly expense.

I found a way to "budget" that worked for incorrigible finan-cial habits like mine—preauthorized chequing and a company payroll deduction plan. These helped me more than anything else to establish an effective working budget. My 10 percent sav-ings, life and disability insurance, RRSP, car payments, *everything* came out of my account on a predetermined day. The money was out and gone before I could get my hands on it. I was rich for approximately 20 minutes on payday, then preauthorized chequing would wreak hell and havoc on my chequing account. The good news was that I was free to spend guiltlessly what-ever was left over. OK, some months the spending capacity was-n't so good, but I sure slept well at night. I want to stress again, it doesn't matter how much you earn or think you can afford. If you do nothing else but save 10 percent net of your income, the chances are very high you will be financially secure. When (and if) you do your budget, right at the top of the list of expenses should be *10 percent savings.*

Budgets can be as simple as the scribblings on the back of a napkin (I have seen hundreds of these) or as detailed as a cash flow analysis (I have seen two of these). There is a plethora of budget forms available. Find out what works for you. Financial ad-visors can be very helpful in this area. Remember, budgets are de-signed to give you the big picture. Don't get hung up on the word. They can actually help to make your money world feel safe again. One last budget tip: A good exercise is to write down a wish list. Some people call this goal setting if it's anchored in the real world. Such a list set down on paper does seem to make your financial goal more tangible so possibly more achievable.

THE GENDER TAX

"Gender-based selling, where none is called for, keeps bouncing back on Main Street, notwithstanding what laws there are or what liberationist attitudes are nominally displayed. Nothing can surpass sharper shopping, questioning and acting to expose and avoid bias in the marketplace. If more women, knowing their rights and equities, individually reject the notion that to have taste means you can be taken, or that insecurities are fair game for a targeted market campaign (recall the Virginia Slims ad "You've come a long way, baby"), then the practice of change becomes widely emulated. Girls begin to learn these wiser ways from their mothers. Mothers can press for more education in the schools as part of existing courses to teach their daughters about this discrimination in the marketplace and how to end it. Billions of dollars of wasteful promotion, poor quality merchandise, unnecessary surgery, drugs, and car/home repairs would be squeezed out of the economy. Greater health, safety, efficiency and peace of mind would be achieved."

Ralph Nader, Washington, D.C., January 1993

WHERE DO WE FIND ALL THIS MONEY?

It isn't easy to find the money to do all the things we are told to do to become financially independent. For many women, it becomes essential to cut out waste. We are all familiar with the drill about bringing our lunch, washing our own cars, ironing our own clothes, cleaning our own homes, quitting smoking/drinking/ dancing the night hours away and so

on. These ideas have merit since it is hard to overspend in a convent. However, very few women can realistically give up time-saving services. Women frequently depend on outside help because of their already heavy workloads. As illustrated earlier in the Statistics Canada Study, women clearly have two full-time jobs.

Cutting out the "unnecessities of life" can be an admirable place to start. But for those who don't have much wiggle room in their budgets, the choices are few. Or are they? I have a new passion: becoming conscious of money spent unnecessarily as a result of the manipulation of and discrimination against female consumers that is rampant everywhere — the gender tax. Since I developed my newfound awareness, I have saved myself, and possibly other women, hundreds of dollars each year.

I refuse to pay more for drycleaning, haircuts and clothing than men do. Very few women, or men, are even aware that women pay more for a vast array of products and services for no other reason than that they are female. Not only do I refuse to pay more, I will boycott the establishment and tell everyone I know about their discriminatory practices. I turn into their worst nightmare. The following situations, which happened within a two-week period, show how I stumbled across and started to become aware of this pervasive problem.

I was sitting in the waiting room of a well-known beauty salon in downtown Toronto. Next to me sat a young man in his mid 20s who was also waiting for his stylist. We made light, easy chatter about the cost of everything these days, especially haircuts by these so-called "senior stylists." There were two of these senior types at this particular salon. He was seeing one and I was seeing the other. We were summoned simultaneously by the words, "the hairstylist will see you now." It had the "commoner visiting the queen" flavour about it. We were seated side by side to have our hair washed. We were then led to the stylists' chairs that, you guessed it, were also next to each other. As I sat down, I jokingly inquired if he was following me. We got on with the business of having our tresses coiffed. Finishing at the same time, we both headed to the change rooms. (Yes, they were, in fact, next to each other.)

The receptionist had prepared our bills in advance and they were sitting on the counter as we emerged from the change rooms. As I was reaching for my credit card, I caught the balance of his bill out of the corner of my eye. I did a quick double take. "Wait just a minute here!" I thought angrily to myself. I looked at his hair. It was short and brown. Mine was short and red. Our haircuts had taken the same length of time. Yet his bill was $20 less than mine. As he put his credit card down to pay his bill, I gently put my hand out to stop him. He looked at me, confused.

"How much does André charge for a cut?" I asked innocently. André was his stylist. The receptionist replied, "$55." "Oh, so he's the same as Karen (my stylist)," I observed, as I picked up the man's bill and quietly passed him mine. The gentleman started to catch on. When he saw what I had been charged, he shook his head slowly in disbelief. "Explain something to me," I continued. "Why is his bill $20 less than mine?" Without missing a beat, she said, "Well, his is men's pricing."

Neither of us said a word as we watched the dawning realization on her face.

"Wait a minute," she exclaimed as she grabbed both bills. "There is something wrong here." She got up, disappeared for a few moments and came back with the owner of the salon. It was a woman. We explained what had happened. I told her under no circumstances was I prepared to pay this bill unless they lowered the price by $20.

The reaction of the salon owner was unexpected. She apologized graciously and said that this kind of discrimination went against everything she believed in. She said the only reason the pricing structure was this way was because it had *always* been this way. Until that very moment she had never thought about it in terms of unfairness and discrimination. There was no reason to because no one had ever questioned it! She didn't try to insult our intelligence with the often used rebuttal that women's hair takes more time or that women are fussier. When an appointment is booked, whether it be for male or female, the same amount of time is allotted. She turned and said to the receptionist, "Take the price board down. We are changing the pricing. Starting tomorrow, men pay $10 more and women pay $10 less. Everyone is charged the same. Except these two," she said, pointing at the two of us. "Their cuts are on the house." With that, she turned and walked purposefully back to her office.

The three of us stood there somewhat stunned. The receptionist and the young man stuck out their hands in enthusiastic congratulations. I was blinking in disbelief. "Wow," I thought. "How much of this goes on that is completely out of our awareness? And how many would react with the intelligence and swiftness of this enlightened business owner?" Two weeks later, I found out.

This was my week to take in the drycleaning. I was on a first-name basis with the couple who owned the cleaners as we'd been going there for a couple of years. As I stood at the counter separating "his" from "hers," the owner told me they had increased their prices slightly. I couldn't tell you what I paid for drycleaning. It needed to be done, so it just got done, no questions asked. My pile had a white cotton dress shirt and a pair of dress pants. "His" pile had five or six white dress shirts and a couple of suits. I joked with the owner, "How many more millions are you going to take from me now? I have already funded two of your children's university educations and both your and Anna's retirement with the money I spend here!" He grinned as he went through the his and hers piles, writing the new prices down on the receipt. I snatched it up and, in customary fashion, stuffed it in my jacket pocket without looking at it, then bid him adieu.

Later that day, I was walking outside and, it being a typically brisk Canadian winter day, I had my hands in my pockets. While waiting for a light that was taking an interminably long time to turn green, I discovered the receipt from earlier that morning. For no other reason than boredom, I decided to look at it. It was pretty standard. All the stuff I had brought in was itemized on the bill with the new prices. However, something jumped off the paper at me. Maybe it was because of my experience at the hair salon that I even noticed this: Women's blouse — $4.75. Men's dress shirt — $1.20. "Oh, no!" I groaned in despair. "Not again."

I immediately turned and walked to our neighbourhood drycleaners. As I walked in, Gus greeted me with his usual warm smile and snapped a smart military salute. (Don't ask me why, he always did this with his customers.) "Wasn't it for tomorrow," he began before I interrupted him.

"Gus, my man," I started. "Tomorrow is fine, but I have some questions about your new prices." I showed him the receipt. "Why is my cotton shirt $3.55 more than his cotton shirt?" I asked.

The genial smile quickly disappeared and he became very defensive. "Women's clothes always require more care and the fabrics are more sensitive," he blustered.

"But Gus," I insisted, "they are both cotton shirts. How does one demand more care than the other?" He hit me with the "it's always been this way" explanation. Cleaning women's clothes always cost more. He was long on anger but short on a reasonable explanation.

"Cost more how?" I persisted. He couldn't answer me. He suggested that I try other cleaners if I was unhappy with his service. "Gus, it's not your service. I'm simply asking about the inconsistency of the pricing. If you can give me a logical explanation, I'll be happy. I'm not an unreasonable person!" At that he went to the back of the store and came back a few minutes later with the crumpled-up clothes I had brought in earlier. He asked me to take my business elsewhere. He then walked away.

It took a while, but I did eventually find a cleaner who didn't charge according to gender. I was astounded at how hard I had to look.

Research proves it. According to a number of sources, including Ralph Nader's Center for Study of Responsive Law, women in North America pay anywhere from 30 to 50 percent more for goods and services like haircuts, alterations, cars, cosmetics, contracting services and drycleaning. Robert Kerton, an economist at the University of Waterloo, notes that price discrimination exists in the marketplace "any time you can get more from one group than another, whether it's based on their wealth, or their degree of information, or their urgency. The question becomes, "when you raise the price, does the person pay it or leave? It depends on the priority the person places on the item, how important it is to them."[9] "We've been conditioned to the fact that that's the way the market has always operated (with men paying less for a haircut)," says one retail industry analyst. "Until you have people asking the difficult questions, you won't see any change."[10]

The purported reasons for gender-based pricing are wide and varied. One of the worst culprits, the hairdressing industry, claims that women are fussier, take longer and use more hair products. It's an odd claim considering women are not *asked* if they want these products used on their hair and a large contingent have very simple cuts that take no more than 10 or 15 minutes. As for being fussier, this definition is typically and conveniently the stylist's, not the client's. Men can be as fussy as some women. Women can be as "unfussy" as some men. Men can take 15 minutes *or longer* for a cut, have it done by the very same hair stylist, may even use the same hair products and still pay up to 50 percent less. This industry has continued to perpetuate a standard that is nothing short of ancient and has also continued to allege that *all* women take longer and therefore must be charged more. Using these sweeping generalizations that may have once been true will sustain healthier bottom lines but at women's expense. Women should no longer be subsidizing the cost of men's haircuts. Of course no one objects to a healthy company profit, but the line must be drawn when one group experiences blatant discrimination in order to subsidize the cost to another group that isn't foolish enough to pay the higher prices. *The issue is not the cost of the haircut; it's why the same cut can cost twice as much for women as it does for men.* Men also have the advantage of a low-cost option: barbers, most of whom won't cut women's hair.

Consider this: if black men were charged more for haircuts, there would be revolt in this country. But because it's women, a blind eye is turned. It is time this industry charged according to the time the service takes and eliminated the gender category entirely. If what *they* say is true, a time-based price structure will have no impact on their profits. Women who take longer to have their hair done will continue to pay more, but so will men. Men and women (like me) who zip in and out in 20 minutes will pay the same. Though seemingly simple and fair, the problem with this approach is this: men won't pay the higher prices. The industry knows this, so gender-based pricing continues.

The drycleaning industry also supports gender-based pricing. Basic women's blouses usually cost much more than men's shirts to be cleaned and pressed. We are often told that women's blouses are too small to fit the presses (ironically known as bucks) that are designed to accommodate only men's size clothing. Therefore, women's garments must be hand-pressed. It is most curious that an expandable press hasn't been designed to accommodate a mere 52 percent of the population, and it is even more odd when you consider that women are 45 percent of middle management in corporate Canada. That's a lot of drycleaning. Nobody is saying that women shouldn't pay extra for special drycleaning needs — delicate fabrics, ruffles and pleats, buttons and bows — but why should our plain, tailored garments cost more than men's? Many women are beginning to refuse to pay more just because the drycleaning industry hasn't seen fit to accommodate women's clothing in their press technology. When we talked to various drycleaners during the course of our research, many were just as baffled as we were. In fact, several commented that if an expandable press were ever developed, they would be the first in line to purchase one.

There is a plethora of evidence, mostly anecdotal, that proves gender-based pricing runs rampant in Canada. Though scientific and statistical evidence is lacking in Canada (compared to the U.S.), it's my opinion that anecdotal evidence can, in fact, be even stronger. Anyone can manipulate statistics to support their view. But real stories from real people carry much more weight. Canada is far behind U.S. accomplishments in this area, but thankfully at least the Canadian media has jumped on the bandwagon and has done much to elevate general awareness of this issue. The following is but a tiny sample of the thousands of stories I have collected over the last year.

- The issue of gender-based pricing was brought home by a CBC television program I did that sent a man and a woman into a Vancouver drycleaners with the identical cotton shirt. Both were wearing a hidden microphone. The man was told it would cost $5.00 to have his shirt cleaned. Three minutes later the woman was sent in with the same shirt. She was told it would cost her $6.50 to have it cleaned.

- City TV in Toronto did a story on the gender tax in hair salons. What struck me about this one was the complete lack of awareness exhibited by the person interviewed. The manager of one very high-priced Yorkville establishment was asked how much it cost to cut men's hair. He replied, "$60." When asked about women's hair, without an ounce of hesitation he answered, "$120." When asked why it was twice as much, the manager shrugged his shoulders dismissively, smiled smugly at the reporter and said in an unmistakably sarcastic tone, "Be damned if I know."

- As if this smug attitude wasn't offensive enough, in the same neighbourhood of Yorkville I noticed these posters in elevators and on the street featuring a pouty, scantily dressed young woman with enough cleavage exposed to make Hugh Hefner blush. Her hair was wet (the erotic looking wet, not the drowned rat look most of us have getting out of the shower) and she had a towel wrapped around her neck. I couldn't make out what this poster was advertising until I looked closer and saw a small tag line at the bottom proclaiming, "We charge according to time, not gender." There, in black and white, was a sample price list from a hair salon with a column of pricing for men and a column of pricing for women, as well as the owner's list of prices. It read: Men's cut, shampoo and blow dry: $20.00. Women's cut, shampoo and blow dry $35.00. The owner's prices were twenty dollars higher in both categories. I blinked, trying to understand what was being said. The poster claimed they didn't charge according to gender but the price list showed glaring gender-based pricing. I walked into the salon and asked for a price list in case I was missing something—it had the identical tag line and prices. I was very confused, as was the guy at the reception desk when I asked him about it. In a suspicious and defensive tone he told me that he would not talk to me and that I would have to talk to the owner, who, to my surprise, wasn't in at the moment. I was also informed that the sexy woman in the poster was the owner's wife. I just rolled my eyes and left. Rarely have I run into an establishment that believed to this degree that the population at large had I.Q.s marginally higher than those of shoelaces. How I wanted to reproduce that pricelist in this book for you to see! But, it seems my publisher has this silly little fear of lawsuits.

- BCTV did a piece on gender-based pricing using one of our representatives in Vancouver. During the piece our representative announced there was a petition available and gave out her home phone number on the air. Within three hours, she had been flooded with over 150 phone calls from people wanting copies of the petition. She called me in a total panic, claiming jokingly that her husband was threatening to leave her if the damned phone didn't stop ringing!

- Shaughnessy Cohen, Member of Parliament for Windsor/St. Clair in Ontario, Vice-Chair of the Federal Liberal Women's Caucus and, by trade, a criminal lawyer with 15 years' experience, shared a great story with me. She took on a drycleaner's a few years back when she discovered she was paying "women's pricing" to have her "court shirts" cleaned. What made this so ironic was that court shirts only came in men's sizes. Her male counterparts were charged 80 cents to have their court shirts cleaned and she was being charged $2.50. Even after she explained this to the cleaners, they still refused to lower the price. She rectified the situation by giving her shirts to a male colleague who took them in with his shirts. She has since found a cleaners that doesn't subscribe to gender-based pricing.

- I have an aunt who is bountifully blessed. There is lots of her to hug. After reading *Balancing Act* she was equipped with a new awareness that she drew upon when picking up her size 18 blouse at the cleaners. It was plain, boasting no frills or shoulder pads, yet she was charged "women's pricing." She was incensed. "I'm larger than half the men I know." It was clear her garments would easily fit on that silly buck. She refused to pay women's pricing; they finally relented and charged her the more reasonable men's pricing. As you can see, whether the garment fits the press is often not the point. It's a women's garment, therefore let's charge more! Aunt Margaret's point to the cleaner: it's the detail and what the shirt is made of that should determine the price, not who wears it.

I recently went back to a hairdresser I used to go to years ago who had just opened a new shop nearby. As we were catching up, I let him know that I was the culprit behind the grief the hairdressing industry was getting of late. Fascinated, he started, with some trepidation, down the usual road of "women take longer, they're fussier" and so on. As he was talking, he broke into a big grin and said, "That is such bull! I've embarrassed myself with the drivel that just came out of my mouth. The real reason women pay more is because men won't." He was almost talking to himself, saying that men had gone to barbers until the 60s, when beauty salons went unisex. In order to capture the men's market, unisex salons kept the price of men's cuts as close to barber levels as possible. No one has bothered to equalize the prices since. I could have jumped out of my chair to hug him. Since the recent controversy had been raging, he had been toying with the idea of eliminating gender-based pricing. All of a sudden he felt greatly motivated. Since he owned the salon, he set the standard. He and I and a third hairdresser who worked there figured out a price schedule that was fair and equitable not only to the client, but to the hairdresser as well. One stylist's clientele was three-quarters male and she was charging them $15 less than she was her female customers. She split the difference between both genders: men paid $7.50 more, women $7.50 less. My stylist was very senior and had an established clientele primarily of women. He bumped men up to the women's level of pricing, easily justifying the move by pointing out that most of them take as much time as women. We then put together copy for a sign to put in the front window of the store announcing the fairer system and the elimination of gender-based pricing. Besides knowing in his heart that it was the right thing to do, this business person saw dollar signs. Very smart man.

Marketing 101 teaches there are two main elements in determining the cost of goods and services. One is the cost of bringing the product to market and the second is what the market will bear. It's the second part of this equation we are working against. No one objects to paying more if it costs more or the service takes longer. But if it's an arbitrary price set because that's what the market will bear, then it's up to the market to change that situation. Women have been paying these higher prices for years, complaining to each other, but not doing anything. This is not surprising when you consider women's socialization: be nice, don't rock the boat and accommodate others at all costs. It's time to claim our voices and collective strength (since women control 85 percent of the consumer dollars spent in North America) and place our concerns on the laps of those people subscribing to gender-based pricing. If you don't think you can make a difference, remember Rogers Cable and the negative billing fiasco. (This was when Rogers automatically billed you for the new cable stations. If you didn't want them, you had to contact them to cancel.) The people's voice was so strong, Rogers was forced to back down and submit to the will of the consumers. The same thing happened with Intel and the flawed pentium chip they released. In their arrogance, Intel actually told people they didn't have to worry about the problem since it only affected one in a jillion. They refused to recall and replace the product. The people said, "Oh yeah?" and proceeded to lash out at Intel with such vehemence that they were forced to back down. There are great lessons here.

WHAT WE HAVE DONE SO FAR

In July 1994, with the help of my staff at Women and Money Inc., I started a gender tax awareness campaign that has been fully supported by the Canadian media. By August, I had conducted over two dozen print, radio and television interviews. The media's interest in this issue is tremendous and they have done it a great service. I thank them wholeheartedly for their support. I speak to audiences all over Canada on the problem of gender-based pricing. At every financial planning keynote speech or seminar I give, I devote a section of time to educating the audience on the gender tax. In one year, I have spoken directly to over a hundred thousand women, not including those I have reached through the media. And people wonder why this issue doesn't seem to go away! These people will carry the message elsewhere until it snowballs into an all-out movement. Here are some examples of the impact your message can have:

- When I spoke in Victoria, B.C., writer/researcher Marianne Scott brought the Assistant Deputy Minister from the Ministry of Women's Equality to one of my seminars. The two women were captivated by the issue and the ADM asked Marianne Scott to submit a proposal to study the problem of gender-based pricing in British Columbia. The proposal was accepted and the Ministry hired Scott to research the issue.

- I spoke recently in Vancouver. There was a representative in the audience from the Women's Committee of the Airline Division of CUPE. She asked that we send her a gender tax package complete with one of our petitions. That petition was then sent out to CUPE locals, potentially reaching their membership of 8,000, 80 percent of whom are women. The committee also covered gender-based pricing in an article in their newsletter.

- *Homemaker's* magazine interviewed me for a piece on the gender tax. They included our address so people could send for a copy of the petition. We were flooded with so many requests we had to work serious overtime to answer them all.

- In June 1995, I spoke on the gender tax at the annual meeting of the executive of the Canadian Federation of Business and Professional Women's Clubs in Toronto. This organization lobbies the government on a variety of issues that affect women's lives. They became so fired up over the issue that they drafted an emergency resolution to include gender-based pricing on their agenda that also covered taxation of child support payments and the protection of the confidentiality of medical and counselling records of rape victims. I was astonished at who got to hear the message. At their meeting, there were representatives from:
  - Department of Industry,
  - Department of Citizenship and Culture — the Honourable Sergio Marchi accompanied by the very vocal and effective rabble-rouser M.P. from Halifax, Mary Clancey,
  - Department of Justice — Though the Minister, Alan Rock, was not in attendance, the women were assured by the representatives that he was very aware of gender-based pricing and his Ministry was working on finding a solution.

- Department of Human Resources and Development,
- Department of Health and Welfare,
- Status of Women — the Honourable Sheila Finestone attending.

- Both the Department of Justice and Status of Women indicated they are interested in doing some investigation in this area. Most of the ministries that BPW met with were very interested in their point of view and offered encouragement in continuing the lobby for change. We should *never* depend on the government to do anything, but getting the issue known at these levels cannot possibly hurt. One never knows where it can snowball.

- I received a phone call from one of "Nader's Raiders," as the employees of Ralph Nader's Center of Responsive Law in Washington, D.C. are sometimes called. His name was Aaron Freemen, a brilliant young man who was Mr. Nader's associate editor and who had worked on the U.S. book on the gender tax *Why Women Pay More* by Frances Cerra Whittlesley. It turned out that Aaron is a transplanted Canadian who feels as strongly about this issue as I do. He had heard about the work we were doing and wanted to know if he could help. I could not believe our good fortune.

  At a downtown Toronto bakery Aaron and I outlined a 12-month plan to expose establishments that continue to subscribe to gender-based pricing, and to reward those that don't. We plan to cover all the major cities in Canada with a report on hair salons, and a few weeks later one on drycleaners. After our return to Toronto we intend to do a follow-up survey in order to keep public attention focused on the issue. The survey will name the most egregious offenders by region and reward those companies that have dropped gender-based pricing. It will also highlight what the major chains are doing. The reports will then be released to the media. Clearly, we have no intention of waiting for anyone, including the government, to "research" or "look into" the problem. Shame the retailers into action, I say. It's time people learn how pervasive the gender tax really is.

  Once I started to dig around, I was flabbergasted at how little anyone in Canada actually knew about this problem. My sense was confirmed by the findings of the B.C. Ministry of Women's Equality that had commissioned the study referred to above to investigate gender-based pricing. The study confirmed what I already knew: no one knew much. There are no provincial or federal laws prohibiting gender-based pricing. According to the study, there are no identified cases of gender-based pricing that have reached the court system. Every province in Canada has a Women's Directorate though none has a policy in this area. Most, however, are only too familiar with the gender tax, and expressed relief that someone was looking into the problem. Now if only they *could* start investigating.... The Consumers' Association of Canada in Ottawa has not done any research into gender-based pricing, nor has it any files on the issue. The B.C. report reviewed the Canadian and provincial human rights legislation as well as case descriptions in the *Canadian Human Rights Reporter.* No complaints about gender-based pricing have ever been published or reached an advanced administrative level. Mariann Burka, Director of the British Columbia Council of Human Rights, and Rosemary Brown, Commissioner of the Ontario Human Rights Commission, both agree that their organizations are the places to bring individual gender based pricing complaints. Ms. Burka stated in the study, "On the face of it, gender-based pricing falls within our jurisdiction as alleged discrimination under services customarily available to the public." Most other provincial human rights statutes contain provisions similar to that of section 3 of the B.C. Human Rights Act, which states the following:

3. No person shall
   a) deny a person or class of persons any accommodation, service or facility customarily available to the public, or
   b) discriminate against a person or class of persons with respect to any accommodation, service or facility customarily available to the public, because of race, colour, ancestry, place of origin, religion, marital status, physical or mental disability or sex of that person or class of persons....

According to Shaughnessy Cohen and a few other federal government types I've been associating with over the last year, there *may* also be something that can be done about this practice through Canada's Competition Act. Cohen says, "Under the Constitution of Canada, we divide legal powers between federal and provincial governments and we try to keep those powers distinct. The regulation of commerce is a provincial matter, just as property rights are. Where the federal government *can* legislate is in defining what can be called a crime. The federal government would use criminal law power as it does with guns and drugs and the like to investigate the abuses of the free enterprise system, particularly competition." She goes on to explain, "As a society, we value competition because it helps our economy run properly so we look askance at individuals or corporations who unfairly conspire to defeat the marketplace by banding together to keep prices up, just as we look askance at anyone trying to monopolize a particular area. In practice, these things are really difficult to prove and prosecute. Under the Competition Act, gender-based pricing is price fixing and conspiracy to charge women more for goods and services would have to be proved. Unfortunately, it looks like it falls into a gray area." With a twinge of sarcastic humour, Cohen adds, "Pantyhose, on the other hand...!"

Therein lies our dilemma. I sincerely doubt that large groups of hairdressers and drycleaners skulk about under cover of night, wearing dark clothes and glasses, to gather in clandestine meetings at nondescript coffee shops, diabolically conspiring to keep women poorer by charging them more for their services. It is probably safe to say there are no overt, calculated price-fixing schemes in place. Most of it simply comes down to "It's always been that way." The bottom line is that this practice has continued long after the reasons for it have ceased to exist. I hope that we can find a loophole in the current legal system to make something work, but government legislation is not the "be all and end all." Market pressure is our best ammunition.

Compared to our neighbours to the south, we are babes in the northern woods with regard to the progress we've made in gender-based pricing. We could investigate this thing into the next millennium. But public awareness is reaching a critical mass, so it's time for some real money and time to be spent on making it disappear. We could capitalize on much of what has been done al-

ready in the U.S., but there is a clear reluctance on the part of legislators and consumer associations to move too quickly. As I said
earlier, plunking the issue of gender-based pricing squarely on the
laps of the legislators is only a tiny part of the solution. My ultimate frustration is in trying to *organize* efforts. Since I am only
one person with limited financial resources to dedicate to this
issue, it has been my goal to get the message out there as broadly
as possible so that someone, several someones or something will
fund a study (like the B.C. study) or help create public service an-
nouncements like the ones the Ontario government did on wife
assault and gay-bashing. Why hasn't the Consumers' Association
of Canada or some other policy-making body issued a stern warning like the Attorney General's office did in Boston where gender-
based pricing was found to be rampant in the drycleaning
industry? Where the hell is everybody??!?

EXISTING UNITED STATES LAW

It is important to understand the gains the U.S. has made in this
area. In California, the Unruh Civil Rights Act prohibits a business establishment from discriminating against a person because
of gender, race, colour, religion, ancestry, national origin or disability. It states that all persons are entitled to full and equal ac-
commodations, advantages, facilities, privileges and services in
all business establishments. However, complaints from women
suggested gender-based pricing was still pervasive.

In 1994 the Assembly Committee on Consumer Protection
held an interim hearing on Gender Discrimination in the Pricing
and Availability of Products and Services. Data collected in conjunction with the hearing documented that adult women effectively pay a gender tax of $1,351 annually, or about $15 billion for
all women in California. This created some forward-moving incentive to address the issue of pricing *specifically*.

Several consumer groups, as well as the California chapter of
the National Organization of Women, the largest and most powerful feminist group in the U.S., the California Nurses' Association
and California politicians have finally done something about gender-based pricing. A bill has been introduced to render gender
based pricing illegal and discriminatory in the state of California.

THE CALIFORNIA BILL

The *Gender Tax Repeal Act* (1994), the first of its kind, was introduced by Democrat California Assembly Member Jackie Speier to prohibit price discrimination on the basis of the gender of the purchaser. Insurance rating practices and health services plans are excluded from this bill as the gender differences in these price structures are based on sound actuarial principles. The bill provides limited remedies for violations of the *Gender Tax Repeal Act* which may be sought through the filing of a civil suit where actual damages and attorney fees may be awarded. Speier says, "All this bill does is say if you provide the same service, then you charge the same price.... Why are women forced to be assertive to get what should be available as an equitable position? Some colleagues say it's a marketplace issue and we should take our business elsewhere. But why should I be so inconvenienced?... It's a fundamental inequity that exists in the pricing of services and products for women as opposed to men when the products are the same likeness and kind."

Senator Charles Calderon, also of California, introduced a bill to coincide with Speier's that would increase the fine from $250 to $1,000 plus reasonable attorney fees for any establishment caught subscribing to gender-based pricing. This statute also directs the Department of Consumer Affairs to send notices to licensed barbers and cosmetologists informing them of what constitutes illegal pricing practices.

Earlier in 1994, Assemblywoman Speier introduced the predecessor to the *Gender Tax Repeal Act*, called the Equal Pricing Act, which was vetoed by California Governor Pete Wilson on the grounds that it was too vague and general. The governor's objections to this act have been removed through the incorporation of his suggestions in the new bill which now 1) only applies to services, not products; 2) specifically allows for differences in prices which are based on the differences in the services provided; and 3) amends the Civil Code instead of the Business and Professions Code. Thus, as of May 3, 1995, the amended *Gender Tax Repeal Act* has passed its third reading in the California Legislature. Though it has passed its third reading, the bill is not without opposition. Democrats favour the bill and offered anecdotal evidence to back up Speier's points. Republicans object to the measure as a needless intrusion on the marketplace. A well-documented argument in the U.S. press between Republican Assemblyman Bernie Richter and Democrat John Burton went as follows: Richter: "The most democratic system I know is the marketplace. You can vote with your dollar. You can vote with your feet." Burton: "You cannot vote with your feet or your pocketbook if you can't find a place to vote. The issue is economic rights for women."

One exchange in the raucous, often humorous debate that captured some attention was when Republican Assemblyman Stan Statham asked Assembly Speaker Willie Brown (Democrat), "How much do you pay for a haircut?" The Speaker, who is balding and has grey-flecked black hair on the sides, replied, "Whenever I am in a position to get a haircut, it is a celebration. Clearly I pay more than it's worth."

Opponents of the bill argue it is unnecessary because discriminatory practices are already prohibited under the Unruh Civil Rights Act. However, there is only one published court case in which the Unruh Act was used to disallow gender price discrimination and it was one that dealt with "Ladies Nights" at bars and "Ladies Days" at car washes. In other words, the ruling speaks to pricing discrimination against men.

Elizabeth Toledo of the California National Organization for Women says, "The basic premise of equal access is that you don't have to shop around town searching for equal rights. It goes against every law we have." Elise Thurau, a senior consultant at Speier's Sacramento office, says, "A dollar in the hands of a woman should purchase the same as a dollar in the hands of a man."

The California *Tri-Valley Herald* commented on June 1, 1994 that "The arguments against the bill would be funny if they weren't so pathetic. Opponents say it costs more to dryclean women's clothes, for example, because they come in widely varying shapes and sizes (and men's clothes don't?) and their buttons are on the opposite side from those of men.... Speier's law is a law that's only about 200 years late."

Brian Doherty, editor of *Regulation* magazine, published by the Cato Institute, a Washington D.C. think tank, argues that if there is no legitimate reason for charging women more, merchants who do so "are only hurting themselves and will perish in a free market." He believes this new bill "sounds like moral breast beating on the part of lawmakers." However, the *Wall Street Journal* comments, "Consumer markets don't always punish irrational behaviour. Some retailers can get away with charging more based on convenience rather than price. And many consumers don't have time for comparison shopping." When you consider that most women have two full-time jobs, it is self-evident that time-consuming comparison shopping is a luxury few of them can afford.

The well-worn argument used by drycleaners, haircutters and department store tailors is that it costs more to provide services to women. But when such arguments have been challenged by regulators or in lawsuits, they usually haven't prevailed. In a June 30, 1989 settlement with the Washington, D.C. Office of Human Rights, the Metropolitan Drycleaners Association wrote that it is "inappropriate" for its members to "charge separate or different prices for the laundering or finishing of shirts and blouses based in any way on size, placement of buttons, whether it is a man's or woman's shirt or whether it is brought in for service by a man or a woman." George Pon, manager of the San Francisco Barber College, disputes the idea that it's more difficult to cut women's hair. "If you know how to cut women's hair, it's a piece of cake." Cynthia Bozonier, manager of Supercuts in Santa Barbara, believes it's ridiculous for women to pay more than men. "If you're getting a haircut, the skill and quality of the hair stylist is the same," she said. "Hair is hair." Hair salons that insist that women take longer are being made to look foolish by the growing number of salons who do not charge according to gender.

In the *San Francisco Chronicle* on September 20, 1994, Michelle Fadelli wrote: "The Department of Consumer Affairs suggests that women exercise their consumer rights, hold business accountable for unfair business practices and, presumably, stop shopping where gender bias is practised. The department seems to believe that properly educated consumers and the free market will eliminate discriminatory pricing. They also state that if unfair pricing practices should occur, they could be easily handled in small claims court. A $3 drycleaning bill does not belong in small claims court, or any court for that matter. Where a single standard can be specifically outlined in the law to ban discriminatory pricing practices, it is time to enact such a standard."

A SMALL SAMPLE OF U.S. CASES AND SURVEYS

On September 3, 1994, staff writer Tony Bizjak reported in the Sacramento *Bee* an incident that had happened to fellow writer Michelle Fadelli and that beautifully illustrates gender-based pricing. "As she watched Sacramento department store tailors chalk and tag her new business suits last year, it dawned on Michelle Fadelli that she was getting socked with $142 worth of social injustice. That was the price ticked off, button by button and hem by hem, for alterations on four suits. But just a couple of weeks before, Fadelli had been in the same store with her husband as he bought suits. His bill for alterations: $0." Fadelli called the manager and complained. The manager grudgingly said the charges would be waived *"this time."*

ALTERATIONS

- A June, 1994 survey of three major department stores, Nordstrom's, Macy's and Weinstock's, found that all three hem men's pants and slacks for free but charge women $10 to $14 for the same alterations. At Nordstrom's, the alterations on men's suits are free, unless there is a jacket vent. Women will pay anywhere from $10 to $50 to have alterations on any suit. In Canada, some retail stores like The Bay and Eaton's have changed their alterations policy. These services are offered for free if the customer pays full price for the item. There is, however, a large but thankfully declining segment of the market that still charges women extra for alterations.

- In a suit filed in northern California, two business executives, Lorie Anderson and Muriel Kaylin, sued Saks Fifth Avenue for the additional costs Saks charged for alterations on women's clothing. Saks settled and changed its policies.

USED CARS

- Women were quoted higher prices in two out of five visits to used auto lots in the New York City area. Investigators visited 50 auto dealerships where 21 (42 percent) quoted higher final prices to female "buyers" with prices that averaged nearly $400 higher than those quoted to the male "buyers."

NEW CARS

- A study cited by Ralph Nader's Center for Study of Responsive

Law showed that women paid anywhere from $150 to $800 more for a new car than men did.

- As reported in the *Harvard Law Review*, another study was done by Chicago's Northwestern University in conjunction with the American Bar Association that showed that white women were quoted a retail price for new cars that was 40 percent higher than the price quoted to white men. African-American women were offered three times the markup as compared to white men. All buyers in the study were college educated, professionally dressed, followed the same script and used the same bargaining techniques and body language. The women were quoted a higher price when bargaining began.[11]

HAIRCUTS

- The New York Department of Consumer Affairs did a study in 1992 whose results showed that women paid 25 percent more for a haircut than did men. In a survey of 80 haircutting establishments, two out of three charged women more than they did men.[12]

- According to a study done by the California Assembly Office of Research, 40 percent of salons surveyed in five major cities charged between $2.50 and $25 more for women's services than for similar men's services.

- George Washington University law professor John Banzhaf and his students brought action against hair salons engaging in discriminatory haircut pricing. All the accused salons settled. Most now charge the same price for women's and men's cuts and if there is any difference in the cost, it is based on task, not gender.

DRYCLEANERS

- In 1989, these same law students at George Washington University visited 25 drycleaners in the Washington, D.C. area. Cleaners charged up to 200 percent more to launder a woman's shirt. They were told that cleaners use a press specifically designed for men's shirts and that no such press was available for women's shirts. As a result of the complaint, the cleaners and their professional organization agreed to stop charging women more for their shirts, even if the laundering took longer.

- In 1991, the Massachusetts Attorney General's Office sent out warning letters to businesses after a survey that showed pronounced inequities among drycleaners in the Boston area. Gender-based pricing is explicitly forbidden under chapter 93, section 102(a) of the Massachusetts General Laws, which states that "all persons within the commonwealth, regardless of sex, race, color, creed or national origin, shall have, except as is otherwise provided or permitted by law, the same rights enjoyed by *white male citizens*, to make and enforce contracts, to inherit, purchase, to lease, sell, hold and convey real and personal property, and shall be subject to like punishment, pains, penalties, taxes, licenses, and exactions of every kind, and to no other."

- In 1992, the New York Department of Consumer Affairs conducted a study that found women were charged 27.3 percent more than men for cleaning a plain, white cotton shirt.

- California's Assembly Office of Research found that 64 percent of laundries surveyed in that state charged more to clean a woman's white cotton shirt than a man's. Women can pay nearly 30 percent more than men for the identical service which includes laundering and pressing a basic white cotton shirt. An average of three suits and ten shirts cleaned per month results in an average increased cost of $77.52 or 17 percent over the course of a year. One establishment surveyed actually charged women double for the identical service offered to men.

WHAT TO WATCH FOR

Avoiding paying the gender tax whenever possible is a great way for women to start saving money. Boycott establishments that don't respond if you uncover inequitable pricing. The first step, however, is to speak with someone at the company. I would not have believed that people would take action had I not seen it with my own eyes, as I did at the hair salon that day. Start becoming aware of this kind of discrimination in your day-to-day activities; you could save yourself some money. Here are some things to watch out for:

1. Avoid places that provide free alterations for men but charge an arm and a leg for alterations for women.

2. Anything automotive, from purchasing a car to having it serviced, is traditionally a danger area for women. Women are often charged more for cars because of their supposed gullibility. A 1990 American Bar Association study found that women were charged, on average, a profit markup 40 percent higher than were men. A woman friend of mine told me it was going to cost $1,500 to have her car repaired. The next day her son and husband took it out for three more quotes, all of which came in under $505.

3. Watch out when purchasing big-ticket items. The Montreal-based magazine *Elle Quebec* sent a male and a female reporter out to haggle price on a variety of items, from computers to landscaping. In the end, the woman reporter's total was 92 percent higher. When renovating, commissioning repairs or shopping for pricey items like cars or appliances, get no less than 3 quotes. Let the sales people know you are shopping around. Be sure to do your research — what did your male friends pay for the same service? If you have time and are really curious about gender differences in the marketplace, send a male colleague in to see what price he is quoted. If you are treated condescendingly or rudely, take your business elsewhere, but not before the offender and his or her manager know why.

   Part of the problem is that women have not been socialized to bargain or negotiate price. Deborah M. Kolb, a professor at Harvard Law School, did a study called "Is It Her Voice or Her Place That Makes a Difference? A Consideration of Gender Issues in Negotiations."[13] She asks, "Both men and women are taking more active roles in the traditional domains of each other, giving rise to gender questions. Can differences in style and approach be traced to gender? And how do they impact on the process of negotiation?" There is a tendency to reduce gender to a set of sex-linked behaviours and traits that are considered essential qualities of the individual. Being aware of Kolb's findings can help you better understand the process of negotiating, thereby becoming a more astute negotiator.

   • For men, the substantive issues under dispute are the primary matters to be dealt with in negotiation. For women, the quality of the relationship is more important than the issues.

Women read the importance of relationships into negotiations and look for agreements that enhance relationships.

- Women see negotiation not as a separate and distinct activity but as a part of an ongoing relationship with a past and a future.
- Women often learn through dialogue — a sharing of concerns and ideas — rather than through challenge and debate.
- Because a woman's status in negotiations is not automatically assured, she often has to be tough and aggressive to establish her place.
- Stereotypes about the appropriate behaviour of women can impact on negotiations. Women are generally expected to be passive, compliant, non-aggressive, noncompetitive and accommodating and to attend to the social and emotional needs of those present. A great example of this was the quip overheard at a major chartered bank in Canada. A woman V.P. of a visiting company overheard a bank V.P. say to his cohorts in the boardroom: "Oh good. The women are here. That means the coffee has arrived."
- Despite doing the same thing or speaking the same words, men and women will often find that different meanings are attached to their behaviour. For example, aggressive women are thought of in a negative sense, i.e. as a "ball breaker," "man in a skirt" and so on whereas aggressive is an admired quality in men
- Certain "rituals" of negotiation, such as extreme opening demands, grandstanding and joke-telling, may put women at a disadvantage.

Suggesting that women learn to negotiate like men is not appropriate. To level the playing field in negotiations, we will have to think about ways to find equality in the face of difference. One of the steps Women and Money Inc. has taken is in the area of gender-awareness training. We go into corporations and teach gender differences in business styles, communication, negotiation and public speaking. Once the differences are recognized, we work to bridge the gender gap in the workplace so people can begin to celebrate the differences as opposed to becoming frightened or angered by them. This new awareness creates a cooperative environment that utilizes everyone's skills and styles. If you do not have access to this kind of program but want to train yourself to be a better negotiator, my recommended option is: practice, practice, practice. Give yourself permission to be uncomfortable and nervous the first few times you take on a car sales rep or hairdresser. Trust me, the more you do it, the better you get. I speak from personal experience. I was a wreck the first few times I attempted to negotiate or take someone to task for bad service. But once you begin to see improvement, you will be inspired to carry on and expand your horizons. Read the many books available on the subject of haggling as well as those on gender differences in communications, such as Deborah Tannen's *You Just Don't Understand*. This book will open your eyes to the different ways women and men use language and will go a long way to helping you win the communication (read negotiation) battle. I haven't paid "list price" for anything in over six years. Many merchants are willing to lower their prices within reason to keep you as a customer. I always start with a minimum 15 percent off just to ease the tax burden.

4. Be aware of clothing stores that sell unisex clothes for a lot less in the men's department than in the ladies' section. I buy whatever I can in small men's sizes because these items are invariably cheaper than women's. This includes men's socks, shirts, jackets, sweaters, running shoes and even men's cosmetics. Men's items tend to be cheaper because the retail industry believes women will bear the higher prices. One defence of this practice says that women demand choice and men don't. Some retailers have claimed that women pay more for clothes because of the enormous selection available to them — what we end up paying for in reality is the stuff that never gets sold.

I have a favourite story about a man I knew quite well who wanted me to help him update his closet. He was in his early 50s and had been married twice, the first time when he was a mere lad of 19, and had two grown children in their early 20s. He told me the story of his life as we went through his closet: "This was the suit I wore to my daughter's christening, this suit I wore to my wedding," and so on. When I queried him on his choice of suit, he informed me that it was the one he had worn to his first wedding, not his second! He was still wearing it. In fact, he was still wearing all of them. Then it hit me. Why do women's fashions change every season of every year when men, on the other hand, are lucky if they see a fashion change every 50 years or so? Their ties get wide, then they get narrow. Big deal. I hope that this man's example of wearing a suit for over 30 years was unique, but I know many men who wear the same suits for 10 to 15 years, my own father being one of them. Societal pressure on women to be "in fashion" is tremendous and, frankly, very, very expensive. How come men aren't targetted the same way? It's time to send a different message to women's clothiers.

In his bestselling work *The Woman's Dress For Success Book (1977)*, John Molloy lists some of the perennial complaints women have had with the fashion industry:

- Why, when a man buys a pair of slacks for $20 and a woman buys a pair for $80 in the same store, does the woman have to pay for tailoring while the man gets it free?
- Why are some people who sew men's garments paid more than people who sew women's garments?
- Why do women's blouses often cost twice as much as comparable men's shirts?
- Why do women's sweaters cost more than comparable men's sweaters?
- Why aren't there standard sizes in women's clothing?

5. Don't buy into the media's messages about having to be young, athletically thin without an ounce of fat on your tummy, perfectly made up and coiffed, toes and fingers perfectly manicured, all surface body hair regularly torn out by its roots with hot wax or other torture devices, delightfully fragrant and expensively clothed in the latest styles each year complete with three-inch heels for that extra "leggy" look before men will notice you. I used to be one of those women. Now, I work out at home, and I lost weight by good old diet and exercise. I shave my own legs, I wear high heels only on special occasions and I have come to like the hard-earned lines around my eyes. They are signs of maturity and wisdom. OK, and worry. The money I save from having realistic expectations of myself physically and emotionally funds a good portion of my annual RRSP contribution.

6. Watch out when buying cosmetics and personal hygiene products. Victoria-based writer and researcher Marianne Scott realized that women can pay up to 50 percent more for deodorant. After noticing that her local drugstore offered 11 different scents of Lady Speed Stick at 50 grams and 15 different Mennen Speed Sticks for men at 75 grams, both priced at $2.99, she felt compelled to call Colgate-Palmolive Canada in Toronto to ask why women were getting one-third less than men. "The representative said the wholesale costs of women's deodorant are somewhat higher because the fragrances used are more expensive. (I do wonder, though, how much more 'Country Fresh' for women costs than 'Fresh Surf' for men.) I asked about the unscented version. That product, said the spokeswoman, is 'price-equalized' with the scented versions. She then stated that Colgate-Palmolive reduces the size of the Lady Speed Stick — 'ergonomically designed' — because women use less deodorant (men's armpits are larger and have more hair). She added that men and women thus use up the deodorant at roughly the same rate, so we get equal treatment!" When Marianne and I talked about this incident, we did so between hoots of laughter and snorts of derision. The only way to describe this rationale is: insulting. Marianne also discovered that certain brands of women's shaving gel can be up to a dollar more expensive than men's shaving gel. Probably because of the hair disbursement patterns on our legs! Take a look at any line of men's skin care products, particularly the cleanser and moisturizer, and compare the price to the women's equivalent. Men's product lines are invariably cheaper, often by a substantial amount. I get the impression that marketers think men are a bunch of buffoons who only want the cheapest of everything and care nothing for selection or choice while women are considered to have such delicate senses and tastes that they need the most expensive of everything, including packaging and the inalienable right to choose between three hundred brands of women's shavers. Manufacturers and retailers have therefore concluded that it's only natural that we be willing to pay double for this privilege that *they* have decided *all* of us want . As Marianne Scott says, "Next time you need deodorant, buy the men's size — you'll get 50 percent more. If we all do it, Colgate-Palmolive and Johnson & Johnson will get

the message. Leave those 'equal' ergonomic sizes on the shelf. Show all those drug makers and drugstores that our little, delicate hands can somehow manage to hold those larger sizes."

Rosalind Russell, famous Hollywood actor and renowned beauty, said: "Taking joy in life is a woman's best cosmetic." The health, diet and beauty aids industry is fed billions of dollars by women who continue to subscribe to the pervasive social standard that women have to be thin and rich in order to be acceptable. Ralph Nader, North America's consumer guru, is quoted in "Why Women Pay More," by Frances Cerra Whittlesey, as saying: "Time and time again sellers will exploit women's vulnerabilities, anxieties and passive self-images as long as they can profitably get away with such practices."[14] I say it's time we begin to think more like men in this area. Women start to panic when they can't fit into the smallest sized clothes in their closets. Men, on the other hand, start to flip when they can't fit into their cars! Whittlesey says the problem can be partially solved through laws, but women have to stop spending on items that are impractical and overpriced in their effort to please men. "Women obsess about their appearance and fashion." Perhaps times are slowly beginning to change. On October 18, 1991, Louis Rukeyser reported on his PBS television show "Wall Street Week" that a *Women's Day* magazine survey of 50,000 American women asked whether they would rather be rich, beautiful, famous or younger. Fully 71 percent said they'd take the money and run!

I believe the practice of gender-based pricing persists because the attitudes behind it persist. Until society undergoes a paradigm shift in its thinking about women, we will be forced to rely on short-term solutions like buying as many men's products as we are comfortable with, including clothing, until we can get the retailers to wake up. It's a lousy and, quite frankly, offensive solution and in a fair and equitable world we shouldn't have to do it. So, Let's get angry. Grassroots and direct consumer intervention like boycotts and letter writing campaigns really work. Write to the managers of salons, drycleaners, retail stores, car dealerships. Write to your local MP. Let's stop being "patsys" and start shaking the rafters to let these people know we mean business.

We at Women and Money Inc. need help. Bodies, money, ideas, legal advice, all of it. This issue has finally caught the country by storm and we don't want to lose the momentum we have going. We would like to form a coalition of people representing communities across Canada to help organize, educate and fight this practice. We are looking for volunteers to help with our surveys in every major centre across Canada. Call Women and Money Inc. (number is in the resource directory at the back of the book) for more information. All ideas and suggestions will be warmly welcomed. Education and awareness work wonders at inspiring people to take care of their own corner of the universe. After all, isn't this how women won the vote at the turn of the century?

Today, there is a great deal of emphasis on pay and employment equity. How about market and consumer equity? As long as it exists, two-tiered gender-based pricing, also known as the gender tax, is going to stand in the way of women achieving true financial equality.

ADMITTING MORTALITY

LYNN'S STORY

Lynn and I have been friends for years. As good friends do, we have shared many a pizza and cheesecake, either celebrating or commiserating. The events of 1989 and 1990 tested Lynn's courage and emotional stamina almost to the breaking point. I lived very closely with Lynn through this heartbreaking period. The things that happened to Lynn in these two years underline the importance of understanding family law, wills, power of attorney, life insurance, tax and estate planning and other financial planning matters. The important lesson to be learned from her story, however, is how vulnerable women are who fail to take financial control of their own lives. Lynn is a walking example of a person who waits until catastrophe strikes before waking up to her own financial reality. It is for this reason that she has graciously allowed me to share her story here. We both believe there is much to be gained by relaying her experience.

From the outside, Lynn's marriage resembled a Norman Rockwell painting. It was traditional and reflective of an earlier time. Stan was a lawyer with his own thriving practice. Lynn worked in the home raising three rambunctious sons. Before Lynn married, she had been secretary to three company presidents.

But it was accepted by women and men alike that as soon as a woman married, she would quit her job in the paid work force and begin her career in the home. Lynn left her position as an executive secretary and remained out of the paid labour force for over 21 years. She entered into the marriage with no appreciable assets, believing, however, that her contribution to the home and family made her an equal partner.

In 1968, Lynn and Stan bought a big, beautiful, rambling house in one of Toronto's finest neighbourhoods. Their home was surrounded by almost two acres of impeccably manicured lawns and gardens. The house was in Stan's name. Lynn did not think twice about this. They had three children in rapid succession. Lynn's life was filled with her family responsibilities and volunteer work. The financial arrangement was that Stan paid Lynn a monthly housekeeping allowance of $400 (in 1968). This money was to cover all home- and child-related expenses as well as Lynn's own personal requirements. She had a charge account with a taxi company (Lynn never learned to drive), the drugstore and the local grocery store. These were the only bills she was responsible for. She had a spouse's credit card, but lost the privilege after getting into trouble with it. Lynn and Stan had a joint bank account and Stan had several accounts of his own.

When I asked Lynn if she had saved any of the allowance for her own purposes, like retirement or an emergency fund, she candidly replied, "It never occurred to me that I should save my own money. I came from an era when women married their retirement plans. Even if I had wanted to, I couldn't. There simply wasn't anything left over." Whenever Lynn approached Stan for an increase in her housekeeping allowance, there would invariably be an argument. Though Stan never begrudged giving Lynn her allowance, if she came to him for more money, she would have to justify her request and be reduced to a subordinate position in the partnership. There were times when Lynn approached Stan about returning to the paid work force, if only part time. They invariably fought as Stan consistently refused to "allow" her to return to work. Stan's explanation for his adamant refusal was the $1,200 tax exemption he would lose if she returned to work outside the home. In the 21 years of their marriage, Lynn had no idea of Stan's income or what he held in assets. Lynn did have a will and life insurance on herself. The monthly premiums for her policy came out of her housekeeping money. When she started experiencing financial difficulties, she insisted Stan take over the insurance premiums. He finally did but made no bones about his unhappiness at doing so.

Part of the problem was that Stan was trying to build his law practice. His overhead was high and when he felt financial pressure, he resisted doling out more money at home. Moreover, it was money he had no control over or knowledge of how it was being spent. Not being aware of the rising cost of children's clothes and food, he assumed Lynn had more than she needed. There was no question that in any marriage it takes two to tango. Lynn believed, however, that Stan had serious issues around control. He needed to be in control of all aspects of their life to an alarming degree. The marriage began to deteriorate seriously eight years after their walk down the aisle.

That was when Lynn first went to a lawyer to investigate her options for getting out of her unhappy marriage. But she had two experiences which shook her up enough that she shelved her plans to pursue a separation for another 13 years. The first lawyer she went to see told her outright that he wouldn't take her case because she was too afraid of her husband. This lawyer told her that because she had no confidence, her chances of getting remuneration were nil. (This was before family law reforms that ensure equal division of family property.) Lynn's fear, whether justified or not, was very real. Stan was, after all, a lawyer and would be very tough to beat at his own game. Lynn did manage to find a lawyer who would take her case without a retainer (upfront fee) and was prepared to take a percentage of the spoils. But Lynn knew she was in trouble by the third visit. She remembers the visit vividly. The lawyer had repeatedly asked her questions about Stan's net worth and income level. "He was drilling me again on Stan's income. I told him that I had no idea. I tried to make it clear to him that Stan never discussed his assets and holdings with me, though I asked many times. The lawyer was looking thoughtfully out the window when he said, 'I can understand that. In his position, I'd do the same thing.'"

That was Lynn's last visit to a lawyer for 13 years. The marriage continued in a backward slide until finally, in 1989, it reached an intolerable level for Lynn. Both Lynn and Stan were opposed to the idea of their children coming from a broken home. But enough was enough. As Lynn put it, "The home front was broken but now I wanted to fix it."

Lynn was still intimidated by the idea of taking on a lawyer. Nevertheless, without Stan's knowledge, she quietly began to seek advice. She wanted to be sure she and her children would be adequately protected before confronting Stan with her intention to end the marriage. The Family Law Act of Ontario had been in force since 1987, so there was some automatic protection for her in place. Lynn went to a woman lawyer who specialized in family law and was a very vocal spokesperson for women's issues. The first thing this lawyer did was demand a retainer of $3,000. Lynn was shocked and dismayed, not only because the lawyer refused to take her case without the retainer, but because Lynn had a grand total of $300 to her name after 21 years of marriage and child-rearing.

Lynn then realized she had to get a job somehow to raise the $3,000 necessary to pursue the separation. Because of her level of experience before marriage, she did finally manage to get a job as a legal secretary in one of Canada's largest and most prestigious law firms. But Lynn had difficulty adjusting to the new work culture. Technology was everywhere. She did her best to learn, but law firms are very fast-paced and everything is needed yesterday. It was not a patient environment. Also, after three months of inappropriate comments from her boss, Lynn lost her temper and snapped at him. She was fired two days later. Lynn was forced to sell her jewellery, borrow money from a generous friend and cash in a spousal RRSP to pay her legal fees. After all the years Lynn and Stan had been together, Lynn was flabbergasted to discover that there was only $2,500 in the spousal RRSP.

Once Stan realized that Lynn meant business, he agreed to a living arrangement that was palatable to everyone. He rented a duplex where he and Lynn stayed on alternate weeks. The week he was at the duplex, Lynn would stay at the family home and vice versa. The children stayed in the family home all the time. It was a dreadful way to live for Lynn and Stan. Their lives were very unsettled and all hell began to break loose. The negotiation of the separation agreement became acrimonious. The first thing Lynn's lawyer did was slap a matrimonial designation on the house since it was in Stan's name. This action removed any possibility of selling it out from under Lynn.

An extremely contentious issue was Lynn's demand that the house be in joint tenancy. She wanted to be sure that if something happened to Stan, the house would be hers and the children's. She had fought with Stan to change this over the course of their marriage. He had always refused on the grounds that "it simply wasn't necessary." But Lynn felt this was part of his control mania. He would never relinquish control of the house. At her lawyer's suggestion, Lynn had the house and contents appraised. The contents were valued at $100,000. The house was valued at two million dollars. Real estate had appreciated dramatically in 21 years. Herein lay much of the problem.

Finally, after a gruelling year and a half of vicious fighting back and forth, Stan agreed to the joint tenancy clause. This was a major move forward and the agreement was very close to being signed.

The agreement was back in Lynn's hands to sign when she noticed a clause that sent her into a rage. She would be required to pay tax on the child support payments she received from Stan but he would be able to use the payments as a tax deduction. She fired the agreement back to Stan's lawyer challenging it on the grounds that this was unfair and requested that her payments be increased to compensate her for the extra tax she had to pay. When Stan got word of Lynn's refusal to sign because of the tax clause, he became apoplectic. He refused to discuss the agreement further.

I offered what support I could to Lynn while she went through this agonizing period. My involvement in her life, however, was about to increase dramatically. It was months after the tax issue in the separation agreement exploded. Stan was no closer to budging than he had been before. I had just completed the licensing requirements to become a financial advisor and was due to start my new job in a week.

At this point, I had been away visiting the folks in Montreal for the weekend. It was late Sunday afternoon as I let myself into the house after a long, boring drive home. Out of the corner of my eye I caught the steady, insistent flashing of the red light on my answering machine as I struggled to take the key out of the front door. The display window on the machine flashed a staggering "22 messages." I had only been gone for three days. I started to get an uneasy feeling in the pit of my stomach as I rewound the tape. "Twenty-two messages!" I mused. "I'm sure Michelle Pfeiffer doesn't get this many calls in three days. Who the heck are these people?" I never got to find out. The first message simply said, "Joanne, Stan Greene was killed in a car accident this afternoon. Thought you might want to know." The message ended. With suitcase still in hand, I immediately turned and ran to my car.

Stan had been killed instantly when he lost control of his car and hit a light standard. Lynn's life turned from bad to nightmarish. The children were completely devastated at the loss of their father. Lynn found herself having to deal with the intense guilt that came as a result of the horrendous shots and slurs that had been uttered during the divorce proceedings. But that was only part of her anguish. Because the separation agreement had not been signed before Stan's death, the house had not been changed to joint tenant status. It was still in Stan's name and it was the only appreciable asset Stan had. Said another way, Lynn had lost control of an asset valued at two million dollars. It now belonged to "the estate." The estate was the sum total of Stan's assets and property and was being held in trust for the children until they reached a certain age.

Stan had had the sense to make a tape that outlined what to do in the event of his death. Unfortunately, because of the impending separation, much of what was on the tape had changed, but it did give us a place to start. I began the arduous task of looking for anything that resembled a financial document or insurance policy. Canada Pension Plan offered a small death benefit of about $2,000 to the surviving spouse and a very small monthly pension for each of the children until they graduated from school. We filled out the forms to get this started. It is not easy going through someone's personal papers knowing they have died. We had to go to Stan's office to deal with closing his business affairs. It turns out Stan's business had been in trouble. He had an abundance of outstanding debts.

It also turned out that there was still a $98,000 mortgage on the house that Lynn knew nothing about. Considering the house had been purchased for $112,000 over 21 years ago, it was obvious that Stan had been dipping into its equity. When we made that discovery, Lynn really began to realize the extent of her vulnerability and financial ignorance. She remarked to me one day, "If

Stan had defaulted on the mortgage payments, we would have lost the house. I'd never have known until it was too late." Lynn was beginning to understand the folly of leaving financial matters entirely up to one's partner.

The will was on file with the trust company so that part of the situation was simple. The will stipulated that Lynn and the trust company were co-executors although Stan had made sure that Lynn still did not have control over her financial affairs. Lynn was to receive the contents of the house free and clear. That was the extent of the assets that she could control with no conditions or stipulations from the trust company. Lynn received a house full of furniture as payment for 21 years of being a dedicated mother and wife. Lynn was distraught at the prospect of having to sell the family home. We tried to think of ways around it, but to no avail. We even considered converting the house to take on boarders but the trust company would never have gone for the idea. Anything Lynn wanted to do with the house had to be approved by them.

I told Lynn that if we could find a life insurance policy that named her as beneficiary, Stan's creditors couldn't touch the money and the trust company would have no control over it. It would be Lynn's exclusively. This was the only fighting chance she would have at living an independent life. We searched high and low. So did the trust company. There were no life insurance policies to be found anywhere. But Lynn was sure one existed because Stan had been a strong believer in insurance. In one last kick at the can, I began to go through cancelled cheques that Stan had kept, looking for one made payable to an insurance company. I found three stubs that had been written over a year ago to different companies. I called the insurance companies and the worst was confirmed: The policies had all lapsed within the last six months. Two were term life insurance policies and one was a property insurance policy. I also discovered that Stan had let the life insurance policy on Lynn lapse without her knowledge. We all but gave up hope.

It was late Thursday afternoon. Exhausted and bleary-eyed from wading through mountains of paper, I leaned back in what used to be Stan's chair in his study. "How can this be?" I tormented myself. "Can divorce make people so bitter that they lose all sense? I'm *never* getting married." I smiled to myself as I mentally paraphrased a famous piece of philosophy, "I think, therefore I'm single." I stared at the stack of mail piling up on Stan's desk. I decided to go through the pile to see if there was anything that needed immediate attention. As I ripped open an unobtrusive-looking envelope and scanned the contents of the letter, my heart started beating faster and faster. I yelled to Lynn to "get your fanny in here as quick as you can." Lynn burst into the study fearing I had had a seizure of some sort. I shoved the letter in her hand. It was a premium overdue notice from an insurance company. The policy would lapse if the overdue premium of $157 was not paid by the 28th of the month. The notice was discovered at 4:00 in the afternoon on the 27th. I said to Lynn, "This is the stuff movies are made of."

I called the insurance company to get the details of the policy. It turned out to be a substantial accidental death policy. Lynn and I were completely unsure as to what our next move should be. Should we pay the premium and not say anything? We decided to take the high road and call the senior management of the company. I spoke with the insurance company's representative and carefully explained the events leading up to the phone call. As expected, nothing could be done until the legal hacks had a go at it. We were told to "leave it with us." I reminded the woman bluntly that they had to respond immediately, if not sooner. The policy lapsed at 4 p.m. Friday, the very next day. She said she understood. That evening was one of the longest that Lynn and I had ever endured.

At exactly 9:01 the next morning, I called the insurance company. That was the first of a barrage of calls the company received on the hour, every hour. Every call was received with a "No answer yet. Legal hasn't dealt before with someone dying during a grace period so there is no clear policy." The blood of many generations of Irish-Italians started to boil. It was 2:00 in the afternoon and the insurance company payment office closed at 4:00. Lynn and I were getting very anxious. I called again and this time I uttered the words that would instill fear into the hearts of the coldest and biggest of conglomerates. I said simply, "I will go to the media." This met with the response, "I will be back to you in twenty minutes." Forty-five minutes passed. My patience snapped. I called Elaine. "Elaine," I barked, "these guys are trying to stall us until it's too late. Technically, they have to accept the money to reinstate the policy, don't they?" Even Elaine was unsure. It was a pretty unusual situation. Finally Lynn, Elaine and I came up with a last-ditch plan that we hoped would work.

Lynn and I scrambled to find $157 in cash. It had to be cash because we didn't want the insurance company saying a cheque didn't count because it had not been cleared by the bank by the lapse date. It was slightly past 3:00. We leaped into my car and drove furiously through Friday afternoon downtown Toronto traffic. We parked the car at exactly 3:35. There were 25 minutes left to settle everything. We took a moment to compose ourselves before walking up to the wicket. I passed the overdue notice through the wicket to the young man sitting behind the window. "I'd like to make a payment on this policy, please. The premium is overdue," Lynn said my voice sounded strong and confident. The voice she heard, however, must have come from someone else's body.

The young man was very pleasant and eager to please. I passed him the stack of crumpled bills and a handful of coins, turning slightly red in the process. Lynn and I couldn't look at each other. We kept our eyes on the clerk's hands as he counted the money. Then we heard the sound we wanted so desperately to hear: the thud of the stamp imprinting those wonderful words "Paid in Full" on the notice. Very calmly, I asked, "Is that everything you need? Is the policy still in force?"

"Oh yes, ma'am," he replied. "Everything is completely in order."

Only then did I venture a glance at Lynn. "Good," I replied, "I'd like to make a death claim." With that, I passed him a copy of Stan's death certificate.

He paled visibly. "Uh, excuse me?" he asked in a very confused state. "You're not serious?"

"Get your supervisor down here, please," I said. "We are very serious." It was 3:50, ten minutes before the business day ended. Lynn and I sat in the reception area, quietly waiting for the fireworks to go off. We were not disappointed.

The representative we had been dealing with over the last 24 hours miraculously appeared in the reception area no more than five minutes later. She was not smiling. "We would have extended the grace period because of the circumstances. It was unnecessary for you to come all the way down here," she began. "Unfortunately, we still don't know the status of the policy. Oh yes, by the way, Mrs. Greene, my condolences on your loss."

Both Lynn and I bristled at her manner. I stood up. "As of five minutes ago, your legal department has a whole new set of variables to work with. By our standards and that of your company clerk who readily accepted Mrs. Greene's money, this policy is technically in force." The woman tried to use a lot of legal manoeuvring to skate around the issue. Both Lynn and I were at our wits end. Lynn's life and that of her children were at issue here, not some legal precedent. Lynn graciously extended her hand to the woman and said brightly, "I'll have my legal department get in touch with your legal department." She turned and walked away toward the elevators. "Nice one!" I thought gleefully to myself. I turned to join her.

I would love to report that everything worked out in Lynn's favour, but it did not. Because the situation got into the hands of the lawyers, it took over three years and $45,000 in legal fees to settle out of court. In the meantime, Lynn was forced to sell the house in order to survive and pay the spiralling legal costs. The will stipulated that Lynn and the family were to live off the interest of the proceeds of the sale of the house. The principal belonged to the estate and was to be managed and controlled by the trust company. Because the principal had to grow, some of the interest had to be reinvested. It worked out that Lynn was to live off of 60 to 65 percent of the interest income. Lynn was very smart. When it became evident she had no option but to sell the house, Lynn refused to budge from her asking price of two million dollars. If she had to live off of 65 percent of the interest of whatever the house garnered, she was going to make sure that it would provide a decent living for as long as she was on this earth.

Interest on two million dollars sounds like major wealth, but in Lynn's case, it was not. Debts and taxes had to be paid. Even though Stan had died, Revenue Canada still required that a "terminal tax return" be filed for the income he had earned up to that fateful day in September. Even in death, they want their money. Actually, *especially* in death would be a better way to phrase it. The tax bill upon the death of a family member can come as a great shock to the survivors. Often people like Lynn are forced to sell assets just to pay debts and taxes.

Lynn was also concerned that declining interest rates could negatively affect her income. She had repeatedly told these "experts" that she intended to get the maximum she could to protect herself against inflation, taxes and dropping interest rates. I was impressed at how quickly Lynn was learning. Two million is what she asked for and two million is what she got. Sort of. What was actually left over for the trust company to invest was significantly less because of all the bills. The proceeds from the estate purchased a much smaller but perfectly lovely townhouse for the family to live in. However, a point to note here is that the estate owned the house, not Lynn. Anything she might want to do with it has to be agreed upon, in writing, by her sons.

It has been over three years since Stan's accident. Two of Lynn's children are in university and one has already graduated. Their life is only now evolving into a stable routine. Lynn recognizes how unbelievably lucky she is. Too many women share her dreadful experience and don't have a large house to fall back on. She has come a long way in understanding money matters. Lynn reads every book and attends seminars. I have set up savings programs for her children. Lynn and I continually preach to them the importance of financial literacy. There is no way that Lynn will allow them to follow in her footsteps. Oh yes, you may remember I was due to start my new career in financial services. I did start about three weeks later, when the maelstrom died down. Talk about getting your feet wet in a hurry. Lynn was my first client.

EVERYONE NEEDS A WILL

It was the first day of my new job. Elaine and I sat in my office trying to make sense of the tax and estate issues in Lynn's case. At one point, Elaine turned to me and said, "I suppose I don't have to ask if you have made a will. After all, you do remember telling me that paying your parking tickets was a big step forward?" I was quickly learning that honesty doesn't always pay.

Elaine continued, "Let's assume you were removed from the picture. Tell me exactly what situation your family would walk into. Would they know what to do? Do you think they would know what you would want them to do? And, pray tell, what do you think would happen to all your stuff?"

I pondered Elaine's questions. I imagined the disaster area that was my bedroom. After returning from Lynn's, I hadn't had much time to get organized before starting work. I thought about the journal I kept that I wouldn't want anyone to read but that happened to be sitting on my nightstand. Somehow, I didn't think this was the kind of thing Elaine was referring to. "What are you really asking me? Obviously, if I died, my family and friends would share the bonanza of my immense estate. That would be after a major blowout at a nondepressing, totally unfuneral-like place, say the SkyDome."

"You only wish," Elaine remarked. "My dear, if you die without a will, the government steps in and writes one for you. It's a way to guarantee that the folks you want to get stuff, won't, and those you don't want to get stuff, will! The chances of the government writing a will that is close to what you would write for yourself are slim to none. They call this dying 'intestate' or 'without a will.' You saw firsthand how complicated things can get even with a will."

She had a point there. After being so close to Lynn's trauma, I was only too willing to meet the next challenge in the priority pyramid. It was time to prepare for the day when I would meet my maker. I figured if I was being responsible and looking after my affairs while I was alive, why shouldn't I take responsibility for what would happen when I died? It made sense that I should clean up my own messes or ensure that there weren't any when I died. I made a call to a lawyer specializing in this field.

Having a will is a major, though not the only, part of tax and estate planning. Estate planning does not have to be complicated. Be prepared, however—it is time consuming. Remember also that estate planning is not for the dead but for the living: survivors such as your mate, business partner or children. Its purpose is to preserve what you have spent your life accumulating so it doesn't get chewed up by taxes and bad or uninformed decisions. It is part of the foundation of your financial plan. While I made my living as a financial advisor, I learned much about human nature. There is a very prevalent "head in the sand" attitude when it comes to admitting we are going to die. Oh sure, we all know it but we act like death really isn't possible. At least not today. And certainly not tomorrow. Consider the following true example of a couple who need a will. But do they have one? No-o-o!

These are two of my oldest and closest friends who both act as my power of attorney and executor. They have been married forever, have three small children (two are my god-daughters) under the age of five, a beautiful big house and lots of assets. Gretchen is a very successful account executive in the computer industry (I worked with her for many years) and, wait for it, Hans is a lawyer! Not only is Gretchen's husband a lawyer, so are her father and her sister. I hound these good people about getting a will almost every time I see them. Each time they enthusiastically agree I'm right. Every time we talk about it they promise to do something. They have been promising for five years now. I yell at the lawyer of the two: "For Heaven's sake, all you have to do is stumble out of your cushy little office and walk three feet! Everything you need is right at your fingertips." To which Hans invariably responds, "I'll have you know I have to take the elevator down three floors. It's not that easy."

I counter, "Name one good reason why you two bright people don't have a will." He says, "Uh..., we aren't going to die...?!?? OK, Joanne, I think maybe if I do the will thing, that's when *it* will happen! Show me one person that has signed a will who hasn't died!" Don't laugh. I've heard this many times. Whether consciously or unconsciously, some people are afraid to get a will or own life insurance. To do so acknowledges one's mortality.

Here is an indication of the depth of the problem. The Trust Companies Association of Canada did an extensive national survey and discovered that only half of Canadians have made wills. The survey revealed other disturbing news. Of those who had wills, only one in three had discussed what was in the will with the executor, the very person who was going to be administering their last wishes. A staggering 44 percent was completely unaware that their executor was financially responsible for any mistakes made while the will was being settled. Here are some other findings: 77 percent named an immediate family member as their executor while only six percent named a professional. Eighty-three percent of Canadians who had wills had had them drawn up by a professional (lawyer or trust company) and 13 percent had holograph wills (drawn up by themselves). Of those who didn't have a will, three-quarters thought they *might know* who would inherit their assets. One-quarter had no idea what would happen to their property, cash or personal belongings.[15]

Take a look at the following StatsCan statistics. There are over a million people widowed in Canada. Eighty-two percent are widows and 18 percent are widowers. The average age at which women lose their partners is 56 counting both death and divorce. Since women live on average to age 81, that's 25 years of being potentially on their own.[16] When you consider that one out of three widows lives below the poverty line (it is two out of three when they reach age 75), it is obvious that people are not paying attention to this important part of life.

Dying without a will can leave one's family dangerously exposed. There is enough grief and anguish to handle during this time without the necessity to deal with an added financial mess. The ability of the surviving family members to make appropriate decisions is often hindered by their emotional state. Outlining your final requests in a will not only makes the transition immeasurably easier, but it can reduce cost and minimize delays as well. If you die without a will, your assets are frozen so there is no cash to help wind up your affairs or for your family to live on until your estate is administered. My discussions with Hans and Gretchen on this topic were very lively. Our last chat started off with Hans's declaration, "You say we need a will, but do we really? We own life insurance and we have named each other as beneficiary so the policies bypass probate; we've also done that with our RRSPs and other investments. Our house is jointly owned and so are our bank accounts so we will automatically receive each other's share. We aren't as badly off as you think."

I launched into my speech. "You are forgetting something, Hans. What if you die together? This is called common disaster. If no one is sure who died first, the law in Ontario, for example, will presume that you predeceased each other. What this means is that, without a will, your stake in the house and RRSPs that are jointly owned passes to beneficiaries *other* than Gretchen's. And vice versa. Who chooses these beneficiaries? The law, Hans. Doesn't that make you feel warm and fuzzy? You lose control over who receives your estate."

I started to warm up. "When you go out for the evening, don't you always make sure I know where you are, whom to call if there is an emergency, where everything is to ensure the kids are properly looked after? You drive me crazy with your attention to detail and you're only going to a two-hour movie! Please explain to me why you don't have plans in place in case you don't come back from that movie. Does that mean you want *me* to raise your kids? Some of your family members might have something to say about that. You need to name a legal guardian or there will be hell to pay among your family. Even if you do name a guardian for your kids in the will, that doesn't necessarily mean that the court will honour your request. Though quite rare, if someone comes up with a good enough reason not to honour your choice, your request can be overturned. But it's still much better to name one in your will. If the guardian is named in your will, that fact can be very persuasive in the event there is a dispute.

"You have already decided your first-born is brilliant and is going to be a judge or surgeon. What if she excels and wants to go to an expensive specialty school but can't because she can't get to her money until she is eighteen? Or worse, what if she turns out to be a disaster with money and blows her entire share by sundown the day of her eighteenth birthday? Establishing a trust would take care of these issues. You could choose a trustee, who is often your executor, to manage how much and when." By now Hans is staring at his shoes and shifting uncomfortably in his chair.

"And what if you do die before Gretchen? I know you *assume* that Gretchen will get everything because that is what you want to happen. Forget that pipe dream. Depending on which province you live in, the government will divvy up your estate according to very strict guidelines. You and Gretchen live in Ontario. That means Gretchen receives the first $200,000 of your estate, one-third of the rest then goes again to her and two-thirds to the three children. If Gretchen had died before April 1, 1995, she'd receive $75,000, not $200,000 and the rest would be split proportionately. Since all three of your children are under eighteen, if you died now, their portion would be held in trust for them by the court until they reach the age of majority. You lose the flexibility to set up a trust to reflect your own personal situation. What if you wanted the kids to receive certain amounts of money staggered at different ages? You eliminate the ability to take into consideration any special needs of other family members."

I continued on. "I'm single, for Heaven's sake, and I have a will. If I didn't, my parents would get everything. If they died before me, then it would be my brother and sister and so on down the line. Now, I want my parents to be looked after well enough, but I also have twin seven-year-old nieces I'd like to see get a good start in life. My university alma mater is always looking for money because of the drastic cutbacks in the government's education funding. I'd like to leave a donation to breast cancer research. These are all near and dear to my heart. But, if I didn't have a will, I couldn't do these things. I would lose my ability to choose who benefits from my life's work.

"And Hans, there is something else I'll bet you haven't thought of. I know how much you *love* the taxes you have to pay. Your accountant receives big dollars to make sure you don't have to pay anything unnecessarily. If you take the time to draw up a proper will, you will save a bundle in taxes at the time of your death. But if you meet your maker without proper planning, your death will trigger a domino effect that will cost you plenty. Your cottage, common stocks and that headache you call investment real estate will automatically be taxed as though you had sold them. Welcome to the wonderful world of capital gains tax. You know that RRSP and pension plan you relish so much because you don't have to pay tax until you cash it in? Well, consider it cashed in. It will be taxed as income in the year you die. Assuming you have the good sense to wait until the kids are grown and the mortgage is paid off before you die, you will have accumulated significant RRSP holdings which will be rolled into your income. The result will be a lot of tax to pay." Hans was turning the most unusual shade of green.

"Actually, Hans," I said, not able to stand to see him cry, "even without a will, pensions and RRSPs can be rolled over to Gretchen's RRSP tax-free until she decides to use the money. In fact, anything you leave to Gretchen won't be taxed if she hasn't died before you. This is an automatic provision since the government considers a couple as one person. No tax need be paid until the last of you two die or cash the assets in. But remember, at best you can only hope to postpone paying the tax, you'll never eliminate it. The other consideration is that Canada Savings Bonds, cash and proceeds from life insurance have absolutely no income tax implications. Cash and non-growth-type assets are considered income on which the taxes are already paid. Apart from these assets you would pay tax on just about everything else.

"You and Gretchen are fiscally responsible. You wouldn't have acquired all that you have at such a young age without some savvy. The term 'estate' sounds like you must have a lot of assets when, in fact, if you leave 10 dollars when you die, that is still called an estate. And you know darn well there is no such thing as a free lunch. To administer your estate costs money. It will cost even more if there is no will. Your estate is *administered* if you die without a will. It is *probated* or *validated* if there is a will. In Ontario, administration and probate fees have gone up from $5 for every $1,000 value of the estate to a whopping $15. Probate fees vary from province to province with the average being in the $5 per $1,000 range with no maximum set. There are ways to lower the fees if you are proactive. Some of the things you and Gretchen are doing now. Have all your real estate holdings in 'joint tenancy with the right of survivorship' so they go directly to Gretchen, and vice versa, rather than becoming part of 'the estate.' For the same reason, your bank accounts should be jointly held.

"You have already made sure that Gretchen is the named beneficiary of your insurance policy, as you should be on hers. This is very good. If you named the estate, the creditors get paid first and your family gets what's left over. If a person is named directly as a beneficiary, the proceeds from the insurance bypass probate. That means a lot fewer $1,000s to pay the $15 on. The same principle applies to your RRSPs. You bought your RRSP through an insurance company so you can name anyone as your beneficiary and not have the proceeds form part of your estate, so again, fewer probate fees. Some financial institutions don't make provision for naming a beneficiary on your RRSP. It's always a good idea to deal with one that does.

"Now, Hans, do you know what you would like to have done with your body when you die? Do you want to be buried or cremated?"

Hans was feeling a little beat up at this point. He mumbled something about "...cremated, I guess."

"OK, who else besides you knows this?" I inquired.

"Uh, no one. Just me."

"Does that mean you want us to guess? Would it bother you if Gretchen goofed and made the wrong choice?" I was intent on hammering my point home.

Hans blanched. "OK, OK, tell Gretchen and put it in the will. I'm getting it. God, I hate feeling like a dufus. Go home, Joanne."

I don't think he was kidding. He was quick to see the theme developing here. "I guess the best reason to have a will is to protect yourself against what would happen if you died without one," he summarized. Bingo.

What a will really does is guarantee order and timeliness. A will distributes, according to your wishes, your compact disc player and your RRSP. That is why it is very important to put together a list of all your assets. This exercise will help you to figure out a fair distribution of those assets to your loved ones. Examples of the most common assets include your home, jewelry, household furniture, investments, life insurance, pension plans, RRSPs and any interest in a business. Don't forget your liabilities. All your debts must be paid immediately upon death. That's why it's important to insure your mortgage and any substantial loans you might have. A tax return has to be filed and income tax paid on the amount you earned in the year of your death. Canada has no specific death taxes. However, if you own real estate or have holdings in other countries, such as the UK, your estate will have to pay tax according to the laws of that country. Once all your creditors have been satisfied, whatever is left over will be distributed by your executor according to your instructions.

CHOOSING AN EXECUTOR

Being an executor can be a very big job. In Canada, the vast majority of people choose friends or family members as their executors. Intuitively, this makes sense. But remember, the role executors play is very time-consuming and, depending on the estate, complex. Be sure your executors are emotionally capable of handling the responsibility especially considering that they will be grieving while going through the process. Few people know that your executor can be held financially responsible for mistakes made relating to your will. Can they afford to pay? Your executor also has to be paid, usually a percentage of the value of the estate. This fee, called the Executor's Fee, is established by the court and varies from province to province.

Your executor should be knowledgeable in the area of tax and estate planning or have access to resources in this area. Trust companies that have tremendous expertise in estate planning are often used for large estates. It's not a bad idea to name a contingency executor in the event your first choice is unable to do it.

An executor is the mind, voice and hands of the deceased and takes direction and authority from the will. The job includes a variety of tasks. My lawyer insisted I have my mother as co-executor since he didn't want the responsibility of "looking in my top drawer and going through my unmentionables." Because my mother lives in a different city, I chose her plus another co-executor who lives in the same city as I do, thus making life much easier for everyone.

Here are some of the tasks executors must perform:

- Find the will and act on it. It is obviously important that your executor know where the will is.
- Make the phone calls to your lawyer, banker, broker, insurance agent and next of kin, not necessarily in that order.
- Arrange your funeral according to your wishes. (This is often done by family members. Make sure they know what special wishes you have. Don't take those wishes to the grave with you.)
- Arrange payment for the funeral, outstanding debts and taxes. (The money for these payments usually comes out of the estate.)
- Prepare a statement of assets and liabilities.
- Find someone qualified, like an accountant, to file your final tax return.
- Fill out forms for life insurance and Canada Pension Plan survivor benefits.
- Sell your property or any asset as you specified in the will.
- Distribute your estate to the heirs and see that any cash legacies, like donations to universities or charities, are carried out.
- Transfer assets or money to any trusts established under your will.

The situation will be made infinitely simpler if your executor knows who the key players are and how to reach them. Do as Stan did and make a tape to go with the will. Remember this is a very tough time for your survivors. Make it as easy on them as you can.

HOW DO I MAKE A WILL?

The experts agree that a will is not something to skimp on. Far too much is riding on it, and it may be complicated. Any mistakes may be very costly. Let the lawyers do it. They will charge you anywhere from $100 to $200 for a basic will. Holograph wills are wills written in your own handwriting, or typewritten for that matter. They are the do-it-yourself home version of what lawyers typically do. Though legally binding, they will be more trouble than they are worth if there is a mistake or misunderstanding. I doubt that most of us are qualified to write our own wills since there are variables we probably aren't even aware of that could dramatically affect the lives of our survivors. Lawyers go to school for many years to learn these things.

Review your will at least every three years. Remember that the minute you marry, your old will is rendered null and void. It's important that your will reflect any major changes in your life such as births, deaths, marriages, divorces and new business arrangements. You can have a marriage contract that will exempt you from any provincial laws concerning the distribution of assets. You do, however, have to leave your spouse *some* share of your estate. Have your own lawyer review your marriage contract *very carefully*. The Family Law Act of Ontario, one of the most comprehensive in the country, guarantees that the spouses share evenly in the assets acquired after the marriage, regardless of what the will stipulates. However, family law does vary among provinces.

One final note. Be sure to keep your will where it can easily be found. A copy stays with your lawyer but keep your copy where your family and executor can get to it without difficulty.

POWER OF ATTORNEY

I took up rollerblading. I would skate for hours, letting my mind wander, coming up with ideas that I could use to help my clients. I blew off a lot of steam while waiting for moments of inspiration to hit. One day, it wasn't inspiration that hit. It was me, meeting the highway in an intimate sort of way. A cyclist who had ridden by earlier had yelled to me that he had clocked me going 80 kms an hour. (I was skating flat out down a reasonably significant hill.) No more than two minutes later, my blade caught a pebble. I was in the customary posture, leaning forward over slightly bent knees. This contributed greatly to the velocity I experienced as I became airborne. The good news is that I was only in the air a matter of seconds. The bad news is that I dived and hit the pavement chest first, head second. Hard. Thankfully I'm not as stupid as I look. I wear protective gear: helmet, knee, elbow and wrist pads. These new-fangled wrist guards have a curved plastic piece that fits in the palm so that if you do wipe out, it is forgiving and allows you to slide instead of coming to an abrupt, dead stop.

Well, slide I did. Right across the paved highway. On my chest. With my hands stretched out in front of me. It was like high-speed body surfing—on pavement. I came to a stop when I hit the loose shoulder on the opposite side of the road. The only thing I could think of was that I should be dead or permanently damaged. My gray matter was rattling around in my skull from the impact of my not-so-graceful swan dive. My brain did function enough to realize I should stand up as quickly as possible to avoid contact with the steady stream of gravel trucks that used this piece of road. I leaped to my feet as gracefully as anyone could who had just been knocked silly and was wearing rollerblades. I did a quick mental check of all my body parts and discovered, much to my surprise, everything intact. Shaken, but intact. My t-shirt was the only thing that suffered. The decal on the front had been completely worn away.

When I relayed this harrowing experience to a friend, he comforted me by saying, "You came very close to becoming a nice, little turnip." Bad humour aside, I started to think about how close I had come to disaster. The accident wouldn't have been enough to kill me, that was certain. But without that protective gear, and at the speed I was travelling, I would have sustained serious head injuries and God knows what else. I would have been out of the loop for a very long time. The long-term consequences could have been horrendous. If I wasn't able to make decisions for myself because I was in a coma, what would happen to my house? my investments? Who would pay my bills so I wouldn't lose my possessions, my car for instance?

In reality, a power of attorney does the same thing as your executor does, except you're still alive...sort of. Let's assume I had been seriously hurt and couldn't make decisions. What would happen? The exact same thing that would happen if I died without a will. The government, otherwise known in Ontario as the

Office of the Public Trustee (Public Curator in Quebec), could step in and pick someone to act on my behalf. That person is now deciding when to sell my stocks and where to invest my RRSP. That's not the worst of it. If my mother or a friend wanted to get control back into the hands of friends or family, they would have to get medical affidavits which stated that I was incapacitated and then go to court to fight for control. In the meantime, no one can access my money except the Office of the Public Trustee. A note about this Office. An Ontario provincial auditor's report of December 1992 showed that, of 125 trust and estate files, 55 percent had been handled incorrectly. I have worked with women who were in dire straits because they couldn't quickly come up with the money to, for instance, pay for a nurse for a husband who had been judged incapable because of Alzheimer's disease. Many assume husbands and wives naturally step in and take over in the event of disaster. Actually, without a power of attorney, the scenario would look more like this:

If you tangled with a truck and lost, and you found yourself in the hospital unable to make any decisions for yourself, our friends the Public Guardian or Trustee could step in and automatically take control of everything. What makes this whole arrangement so unpalatable is that your financial and business affairs are frozen until the *court* determines who should be acting on your behalf. This means your partner can't get access to anything you own, not even *jointly* held bank accounts, until the court deems your power of attorney. Your loved ones have the daunting challenge of having to go through not only the legal bureaucracy, but the medical bureaucracy as well to get the evidence necessary to show that you are, in fact, really out of the game. Your family has to prove you really are incapacitated, and they also have to prove to the court that your power of attorney is really capable of looking after your finances. The court may ask the person to post a bond that has the same value as your assets. All this involves hiring a lawyer which, you can rest assured, will not put your family and friends in a good mood. Normally, a power of attorney would not apply if you became mentally incompetent; however, lawyers can cover that off by making sure your power of attorney is "enduring," which means the power continues past your incapacity. If you didn't do this, the court decides if you are incapable of managing your affairs and, frankly, that should be a private matter amongst family. Like your executor, your power of attorney acts for you, managing your assets, property, financial affairs and personal care until you can act for yourself again.

A power of attorney has other practical uses as well. Let's say you decided to "do Europe" for a year. You could designate a power of attorney to handle things for you but only for the time you were away.

As to whom you should choose, people tend to stay with family. This is fine in most cases but be aware of the fact that these people have the same rights over your financial affairs as you do. Make sure you trust the person, whether it be a partner, child or parent, to make the right financial decisions for you. Your power of attorney will be responsible for doing your banking, making investment choices, selling your house if necessary and so on. Ask yourself if they will understand the mechanics of making such decisions. When I was single, my mother, in partnership with my lawyer (who was also a personal friend), acted as my power of attorney. I have acted as power of attorney for many single friends. If you're single, brothers, sisters, lifelong and trusted friends, even parents, depending on their age, are all worthy of consideration.

Many people worry about giving someone *too* much power over their affairs. A simple way around this is to appoint two attorneys who must act jointly or leave your power of attorney with your lawyer along with written instructions on when to release it. Your stand-in can't act without the physical document. There is, however, a balance that is necessary here. Try not to make the document too restrictive as that will defeat the purpose of having a power of attorney in the first place. It is remarkably easy to revoke — simply tear it up. The more appropriate route, however, is to inform your attorney(s) in writing and retrieve all original copies.

These are some reasons why I now have a power of attorney. I want to have someone I know and trust to look after my financial affairs. That is precisely what a power of attorney does.

LIVING WILLS

Advances in medical technology have made it possible to sustain life, even in the face of life-threatening illness. In North

America, there are over 10,000 people in chronic vegetative states being kept alive by life-support systems. In almost all of these cases, the patients had no part in the decision that maintains them in this state.[17]

Power of attorney for personal care (also known as a living will, a health care or advance directive or a mandate in Quebec) is as important as those you designate to handle your property and financial affairs. Its primary function is to make health care decisions for you when you can't or to ensure your wishes regarding the very personal issue of how you die are carried out.

Let's go back to my rollerblading accident. Let's assume the injuries I almost sustained had been serious enough that I should have died but didn't because of technology. Let's also assume that the chances of my recovering were nil, but I was kept alive by the respirator which breathed for me. This situation would have been completely unacceptable to me. But where would my voice have been? How could I have made my wishes known? I couldn't. That is why I have a power of attorney for personal care or a living will. It takes the painful decision out of the hands of friends and family and informs the doctors that I don't want to be kept alive through artificial means.

For years, people have been attempting to have living wills legally recognized, putting forth the argument that quality of death is as important as quality of life. Living wills have been simply an *expression* of your wishes to your family and the medical community regarding the manner in which you die. Until recently, there was no way of really knowing if your final wishes regarding your death would ever be carried out. However, more and more doctors and lawyers are beginning to recognize their moral obligation to ensure quality of life *and* death and seem to be moving away from the "save life at all costs" philosophy.

My grandfather, who lived in Montreal, had a massive cerebral hemorrhage at the age of 79. He suffered so much brain damage that he had absolutely no hope of a decent life. Though Granddad didn't have a power of attorney or mandate, as it is known in Quebec, the doctor took the family aside and said, "If it were my father, I'd never want him to live like this." With the support of the hospital and staff, we quietly let him go. The point to be made here is that we were very lucky to have like-minded physician, but you cannot depend on this as a standard matter of course. The only way to ensure death with dignity is to write your wishes down.

Several provinces have decided to leap out of the dark ages, recognizing the urgent need for legislation in this area. Nova Scotia, Ontario, Quebec, British Columbia and Manitoba have made living wills legally binding or are in the process of doing so. You can take advantage of commercial kits, ranging in price from $10 to $40, available through provincial government offices like the Office of the Public Guardian and Trustee in Ontario, for example. Vancouver-based Self-Counsel Press publishes kits for all provinces. You can also buy 50-cent stationery store versions of a power of attorney for property and living wills but because the rules are complicated and vary from province to province, it is always wise to seek legal advice before signing anything. All of these options have flaws, however. They are either too simple or don't address setting up an alternate power of attorney if something happened to your first choice. In Ontario, the law stipulates that your power of attorney has to be paid. Commercial kits don't address the compensation issue. One need not have a vivid imagination to visualize the potential family squabbles that could ensue. Couples who have no adult children might rule out compensation for themselves, but not for a friend, for example.

Lawyers, who are feeling the effects of the recession like everyone else, are getting very marketing-oriented these days. Some are offering wills and power of attorney "kits" that you fill in for yourself. These are perfectly legal and can save time and money. I would strongly advise, however, that you only use these lawyer-provided "kits" if your situation is very straightforward. There are no choices in this kind of power of attorney other than name and address. This is why these should only be used in clear-cut, simple situations. However, these are much safer than the stationery store versions. Too much could go wrong with this latter type because there are too many choices you can make, which increases the possibility of error. You may save a few dollars up front, but end up paying thousands later in legal fees trying to regain control of your assets should something go wrong.

If you want to tailor-make your power of attorney to your own specifications, you have no option but to go to a lawyer. I believe it is always important to get your lawyer's advice on your power of attorney, both personal care and property, just as it is with your will. Both are very powerful documents. You can amend, add or adjust anything in your health care directive should you want to, though most come with standard boilerplate clauses that provide a good starting point. It's really important not to be too vague, like saying, for example, "please avoid using heroic measures or life-support systems," because this wouldn't be of much use to the doctor. What is heroic to one physician may be standard procedure to another. I have very definite feelings about the kind of treatment I want and don't want. The term *heroic measures* scares me silly and conjures up images that scaremeister David Cronenberg could do justice to. I want to leave this world as naturally as I came into it. Power of attorney for personal care and health care directives, and Quebec's mandate, are, in fact, more sophisticated versions of the living will. They are not restricted only to terminal conditions; they also allow you to name specific medical treatments you want applied in specific circumstances. Do you want a cardiac resuscitation or organ transplant, for example? A discussion with your partner and practitioner is always recommended so your living will can be tailor-made to fit your own health circumstances. Make sure you make copies for you doctor, lawyer and family. Look to pay around $150 for a power of attorney done by a lawyer, always the recommended option. You can save money by shopping around and comparing fees. Many provincial law societies operate lawyer referral services which give you the first half-hour of legal advice free.

LIFE INSURANCE

> *"I detest life insurance agents. They always argue that I shall one day die, which is not so."*
>
> Canadian humorist, Stephen Leacock

I was staring absent-mindedly out of Elaine's window, slumped in one of her stuffed chairs, which I propelled aimlessly back and forth with one hand against her desk. I was feeling very introspective. I was still living on a daily basis with Lynn's ongoing nightmare. Between her situation and Elaine's insistence that I consider preparing for my death, I found my thoughts eventu-

ally meandering over to life insurance. I had a will, living will
and power of attorney in place. Investigating whether I needed
life insurance seemed the obvious next step. "Elaine," I asked,
"should I get some life insurance?"

"What do you want it for?" she inquired.

"For sure I want money for funeral expenses. They will be
costly. I wonder what the SkyDome is going for these days?" I
joked. "Seriously though, Elaine, Lynn and I were shocked at
how expensive it is to die. It costs anywhere from $4,000 to
$10,000 to bury someone. Stan's funeral was close to $10,000. I
always figured, you know, a box, a hole in the ground, some
flowers and a minister. How much could that cost? The guy at
the funeral home said $10,000 was the average amount that
people pay, though there are less expensive options, like cre-
mation."

Elaine nodded in agreement. "People always forget things
like legal fees and medical bills for things that aren't covered
by a health plan. There are so many hidden or unexpected costs
that often the survivors are caught by surprise. OK, so funeral or
death-related expenses. What else?"

"Well," I pondered, "I don't have dependents, but I'd like to
provide the tuition for med school for my twin nieces."

"Medical school?" Elaine said, raising her eyebrows and
smiling.

"They are going to be Chiefs of Thoracic Surgery at Toronto's
Hospital for Sick Children. I know because they told me." I was
feigning complete seriousness.

"They actually said the word 'thoracic'?" Elaine rolled her
eyes.

"They're quite brilliant. Just the other day they chose, out
of two forks, the proper one for their salad without even being
told which one to use," I said, eyes wide in amazement.

"You're right," Elaine said. "They obviously show great aptitude for surgery. Or eating."

"You gotta think big, Elaine," I said, brushing off her shot.
"Imagine what it will cost to go to university 15 years from
now. Financial advisors will be asking parents 'Do you want
to buy a home or do you want to put your kids through school?'
Higher education is going to cost, on average, $20,000 a year.
Expensive stuff. I'd also like to leave something for my folks.

They're playing catch-up because of the bankruptcy, so I'd like to help their retirement."

"Funeral, twins, parents—all valid reasons. What else?" Elaine asked.

"I'm concerned about the tax problems of owning my own business. Let's assume that when I am 35 years old, the business is worth $50,000. Providing famine and pestilence don't hit, let's say it grows at 10 percent a year. If I have an early demise and die at 65, my business will be worth a whopping $872,450. Revenue Canada generously allows my business to earn $500,000 in profit before it taxes me. Considering it was worth $50,000 when I was 35, that leaves me with a gain of $322,450. Seventy-five percent of this will be taxable at my tax rate of approximately 50 percent. By my calculations, my tax bill will be a staggering $120,918.

"And it's not only business taxes I'm worried about. By the time I'm 40, I plan on owning a cottage on a lake approximately 60 miles north of nowhere. Since this place would be a second property after my principal residence, my estate could have to deal with another serious tax bill. Let's say, Elaine, I work really hard and manage to achieve my goal to buy this dream cottage for $100,000. If I'm lucky, this property will grow in value maybe seven percent a year. If I die when I reach 80, my little dream spot will be worth almost one and a half million dollars. My tax bill, just on the cottage alone, will be over half a million dollars!

"I don't want my family to have to sell my business or that country estate of mine when I die just to pay a tax bill. I want my insurance to pay my tax bill so my business and personal stuff can go directly to my family. It seems to me I have a choice of paying, say, three cents on every dollar in advance to pay my tax bill by using the tax-free death benefit from an insurance policy. Or, the other option is to pay a hundred cents on the dollar for my tax bill if I don't have insurance when I die. I know what makes more sense to me."

"You have been doing your homework," Elaine said, mocking surprise. "Your tax reason is a good one. And you don't have to be rich to be concerned about it. Almost everyone at all income levels, especially business owners, should think about the tax implications of death. It's funny, though—almost no one does. It's said that the only two things in life that are certain are death and taxes. These two go together more than people realize. The one thing you haven't considered, though, is that you might find some poor, unsuspecting fellow who marries you and manages to stay alive until after you die. If the cottage is in joint tenancy he will get it rolled over to him with no tax problems. That is, of course, unless he sells it; then he'll be hit. Revenue Canada will allow you to pass on your belongings and investments to your legally married or common-law spouse and defer the tax load to them. They're very generous that way. Remember, in this country, there is no such thing as tax-free, with the exception of the sale of your principal residence. There is simply tax postponement. If there is no spouse to pass this stuff on to, then yes, your estate is going to have a serious tax bill to contend with. Insurance can be the least expensive way to pay these bills. Good one, Joanne! And to think your high school algebra teacher said you couldn't add."

"I'll take that as a compliment whether it was meant as one or not. Let's see," I mused. "Another reason is my health. I'm in the pink at the moment, but as my rollerblading record will attest, that may not always be so. The cost of insurance goes up every birthday. I would certainly never let my good health and young age be the only reasons to buy insurance, but they do contribute another positive element to the equation."

Elaine only partially agreed. "Those are your personal choices. They definitely shouldn't be primary reasons to buy insurance. Naturally, once you are married and start a family, the reasons become self evident."

"Absolutely. I only need to find a date first," I deadpanned.

It is my considered opinion that, if you are single, insurance needn't be a priority in your financial plan unless you have personal, business or tax planning reasons to want it. I wouldn't be caught dead without it. (Pardon the pun.) There are, however, single people out there who wouldn't be caught dead with it. If you have enough assets to cover the winding down of your affairs and have no business concerns, you won't need it. Unless of course, like me, you want to leave a legacy behind. Either way is perfectly acceptable, as long as your survivors aren't saddled with the financial responsibility of cleaning up your messes. Debt should never last longer than the person who created it.

Do you need insurance? Absolutely no one can answer that question except you—with the help of a financial advisor. Having been in the insurance business and having spent a few years talking to people about their insurance needs, I know two things for sure. *One:* People are emotional about this topic. They either love it or hate it. *Two:* There are no hard and fast rules. There are as many different answers as to what you should do about life insurance as there are people who have opinions. People buy life insurance for many reasons, but its number one function is to provide financial protection in the event that you die prematurely. A person creates an estate, or adds to one, with an insurance policy. The decision as to what kind and how much to buy will not be an easy one. The world of life insurance is a baffling, controversial and often complicated one. I will try to steer you through the maze, but I cannot tell you what or how much to buy. Get enough facts to develop a working knowledge and then seek advice from a qualified financial advisor licensed to sell insurance.

It has been my experience that only part of the life insurance decision-making process is about math. There is also a very important human side. There are emotional considerations that come from a person's life experiences that must be taken into account when developing a life insurance portfolio. Moreover, this is a very sensitive subject: a person's mortality and their wish to provide financially for their family. At the same time, it is important to be on guard for those few who use an emotional sales pitch to sell this product. If you find yourself wanting to weep uncontrollably during your first visit from a new agent, get that agent out of your house as fast as you can.

Get the facts and apply them to your own personal requirements. Then, and only then, will you be equipped to make an informed decision about your life insurance needs. Your life insurance portfolio can be part of a very sophisticated and complex estate plan. Or it can be as simple as "pay my beneficiary something when I die."

There are only two types of life insurance—term and permanent (cash value). Anything else is a variation of these two. In fact, term and permanent insurance are essentially the same thing. They are just different ways of paying for a death benefit. Term refers to coverage for a specific time frame or term. Permanent is permanent coverage until you die.

TERM INSURANCE

Term insurance takes three seconds to explain. If you die while it is in force, it will pay your survivors a tax-free death benefit. That's pretty much it. It is the cheapest, simplest, purest form of insurance there is. That is not to say, however, that it is the easiest to buy. You can buy it in one, five, 10 and 20-year chunks, depending on the nature of the responsibility you want to insure. The cost of coverage increases at each renewal according to your age at the time of renewal. This type of insurance is used to cover obligations that will eventually disappear—things like mortgages, children (who eventually grow up and move out   with any luck), and major debts or business loans.

The *only* kind of term insurance you should buy is the renewable and convertible variety. This type of insurance allows you to convert to a permanent form of coverage should you decide you need it later in life. You also won't need to fess up to any health problems you may have encountered during the period you were covered by the term insurance.

The key with term insurance is to be sure that you find out how much it will cost to have yourself insured for at least 25 years. The cost may be unbelievably inexpensive today but it could be much higher in five, 10 or 20 years, depending on your age since you need to renew it after each term expires. It is interesting to note that the Canadian Life and Health Insurance Association of Canada says that fewer than one percent of term policies stay in force long enough to pay death benefits. Almost all term insurance gets dropped without paying out any death benefit. Be sure to ask if there is a cost to convert your term coverage to permanent insurance. The cost of term can vary dramatically from institution to institution. It pays to shop around and compare prices. Insurance brokers subscribe to a computer service that accesses over 60 insurance companies and compares over 300 types of policies. Let their computer do the walking.

PERMANENT INSURANCE

Get comfortable. This form of insurance needs some explanation because it does more than term insurance.

During the '70s and '80s, inflation reached alarming proportions, running at a double-digit level for almost an entire decade. Because of this inflationary pressure, interest rates on investments like Canada Savings Bonds skyrocketed to unheard-of heights of 18 percent. The rates of return on whole life or permanent policies were regulated and based on portfolio rates of three and four percent for the life of the contract. Bottom line: These policies were horrendously uncompetitive. The old way of doing things was no longer adequate. For insurance companies to survive, they had to begin to develop interest-sensitive products to compete effectively in this new world of extraordinarily high interest rates. It was around this time that insurance companies also began to unbundle their policies and to identify all the separate components of a policy. Examples are the non-smoking and gender-specific policies that were introduced in 1981. Universal life policies came soon after, which let the investor separate the investment part of the insurance contract from the insurance part of the contract.

Your insurance premium (the monthly or annual amount you pay) is based on your contributions, the interest the company makes on its investments, the cost of doing business and the mortality tables, which tell the insurance company how many people are going to die in a given year. There are events that impact the mortality rates. For example, AIDS has greatly affected the way insurance companies do business today. Anyone applying for a minimum of $100,000 worth of coverage must submit to an AIDS test. These tests are becoming more and more "customer" friendly. Many companies are using saliva tests that are administered by the agents themselves right at point of sale. These are much less intrusive than blood or urine tests and take much less time to determine the results. It is interesting to note that fewer than three percent of insurance applications are actually turned down for health reasons.

Your contributions, minus the company's expenses and mortality charges, are held in an account. The interest on the investments the company makes with your contributions and time help the account to grow. As long as the size of the account and the size of the death benefit that the cash value is supporting meet a predetermined benchmark (set by the government), the cash in the policy accumulates on a tax-sheltered basis. If the cash value exceeds this benchmark or you surrender the policy, tax then becomes payable. The purpose of the cash value in a permanent policy is so that it will pay for itself when the costs of insurance become prohibitive in later years. The older you get, the more expensive insurance is. The premiums charged in the earlier years are actually higher than the cost of the insurance. In the later years, however, the premiums are substantially lower than the actual cost of protection. The cash value begins to grow when the costs of the insurance are looked after, generally after three or four years. You can access this cash by borrowing it from the policy. This is the major difference between term and permanent insurance. With permanent insurance, you pay for the high costs of insuring in later life upfront, in the early years. With term insurance, you pay the escalating costs due to your increasing age as you go along.

This means permanent insurance premiums stay level, they don't increase each year. You will note, however, they are substantially higher than term insurance, most notably in the early years. The part of your premium that isn't used by the company to pay expenses and death benefits is socked back into your insurance plan in the form of dividends. These are not the same as stock dividends, which represent shares in a company's profits. Insurance dividends are a return of the unused part of your premium. These dividends can be used to automatically "buy" additional coverage to your existing plan, which makes sure your coverage keeps pace with inflation. Even though your premiums stay the same year after year, your coverage will actually increase by the dividend amount paid into the policy each year. You can choose this option or you can take the dividends in cash on an annual basis. This type of policy is called a participating or "par" policy. A policy that doesn't offer dividends is called a "non-par" policy. Most policies today are participating.

You can take advantage of what is called a "vanishing premium," which is available on whole life plans. Providing the cash value generates enough interest earnings, you can pay up your policy in seven to 10 years. Be very careful however. With declining interest rates many people are now finding themselves having to pay over a much longer period.

TYPES OF PERMANENT INSURANCE

WHOLE LIFE   As stated earlier, whole life is simply an insurance policy where the premiums remain level for your entire life. That's why the insurance company needs to collect more money up front than is actually needed. You have no say in how the cash value part of the policy is to be invested; that is the insurance company's responsibility.

UNIVERSAL LIFE   The rates of return on these policies are better than the traditional policies of the '70s. The same principle applies as with traditional whole life except that the policy expenses and charges as well as the investment part of the policy are disclosed. The cash value is invested in such things as GICs and mutual funds. The insurance and investment components are separate so you can manipulate each component independently. If you have extra cash one year, you can put it in a universal life policy to accumulate tax-sheltered up to a certain amount. In fact, you can put in enough money within a six-year time frame to cover your insurance costs for life.

You can also control the cost of the insurance by increasing or decreasing the death benefit. However, if you want to increase the coverage, expect to take a medical examination. The insurance costs do fluctuate as a result of changes in interest rates. The insurance company can also change the amount it charges for the actual insurance up to a certain maximum. If the costs of the insurance component rise and you don't add more cash to the policy, the amount of insurance coverage you have will be subsequently reduced. Be careful, there is a risk you could end up with less insurance than you really need.

TERM TO 100   Whole life coverage with no cash value. The simplest and least expensive permanent insurance plan. Those reaching the grand old age of 101 are out of luck. This, however, would be a chance I would be willing to take.

You can only buy permanent insurance from a licensed representative. Banks sell term insurance because it is very simple, but bank representatives are not qualified to offer advice in this area. Shop very carefully as prices do vary.

SHOULD YOU USE PERMANENT INSURANCE AS A SAVINGS PLAN?

> *"Those looking for tax shelters or deferral mechanisms may wish to explore the significant benefits that may be derived from an 'exempt' life insurance policy. While professional advice may be needed, it is to be noted that a substantial portion of the income from such investments accumulates free of tax, that such income can be utilized before death, and the proceeds are not subject to tax on death...such policies may be a powerful tool in the tax planning arsenal."*
>
> *"While many people think of life insurance as pure protection, and would not consider it to be an investment, let alone a tax shelter, the general choking-off of most shelters and the anti-avoidance rules ought to convince many investors to look more favorably upon life insurance.... The returns from virtually tax-free accumulation after the deduction of the insurance costs, compared to taxable accumulations, can be quite remarkable.... Those with capital to invest would be well advised not to overlook this important shelter (and eventual source of capital)."*
>
> The Coopers & Lybrand Tax Planning Checklist, CCH
> Canadian Ltd.
>
> *"Never buy whole life insurance as an investment...Whole life is a plan where your money goes into a 'hole,' never to be seen again. Whole life has literally cheated millions out of billions since its inception...Whole life is just a grossly overpriced term insurance policy with a mediocre investment attached."*
>
> Charles J. Givens, *Wealth Without Risk For Canadians*,
> Stoddart Publishing Co. Limited, 1991.

How's that for an answer to the question of whether or not you should use insurance as an investment? You couldn't get two more opposing views. I would not be exaggerating if I said I could fill a book with quotes like these, representing both sides of the "permanent insurance as a savings" debate. Opinions on permanent insurance as a savings tool run from glowingly positive to outright reckless.

One thing everyone agrees on is *never* buy life insurance as an investment unless you have a need for life insurance itself. If you are going to use permanent insurance as a savings vehicle, it is imperative that you have your debts paid off, emergency fund intact and your RRSP maximized. Remember, insurance is insurance no matter how you try to dress it up. Use it as protection first, and, if you choose to, forced savings second.

The kind of tax shelter referred to by Coopers & Lybrand is usually best suited for well-heeled investors who have their financial base intact. Cash value insurance plans are not short-term plans. Not even close. They are not like Treasury Bills or Canada Savings Bonds. Cash value insurance has the primary purpose of providing a death benefit for your survivors and keeping your insurance costs manageable in later years should you need coverage past age 70. (This is often when term plans expire.) The actual purpose of the cash reserve is to pay for what would otherwise be exorbitant costs later in life. This is why the cash value inside permanent policies enjoys tax-sheltered status. The government made sure in MacEachen's 1981 budget that no one could pour large amounts of cash into their policies and thereby avoid paying tax. That's when they set this benchmark that determined anything over this particular line is subject to tax. Cash value withdrawals are taxed as income. You are taxed on the difference between the cost of the insurance and the amount of cash you withdraw.

The rates of return on insurance policies vary depending on a company's expenses, how much it has had to pay in death claims and what the company has earned on its investment portfolio. There is no cash value usually until the third or fourth year and it is at this point you may begin to borrow from your policy, up to 90 percent of the cash value. Until the costs of providing the insurance for life are recovered, the cash value remains quite low for a number of years, at least eight to 10. You will pay interest on anything that you borrow, usually at prime. Remember that Stan had borrowed from his policy and when he died the outstanding loan had to be deducted from the death benefit. If you do borrow from your policy, be sure to pay it back or you may lose the valuable financial resources your family will need after your death. The cash value in these plans is accessible as soon as your policy is in a positive cash value position and can act as emergency funds as long as you pay the loan back. It can also bolster your retirement planning if you find you get to your golden years and don't need as much death benefit as you had anticipated. You can access the cash value in your policy to supplement your RRSP and other retirement savings.

One thing to be aware of: When an agent is showing you the projected cash value in a permanent plan, remember it is only a *projection*. Most insurance agents sell from computer-produced illustrations that will forecast the rate of return on a policy. This forecast is based on an *assumed* interest rate. This is the key. Be sure the interest rate the agent is using is realistic. It has been my experience that they generally are but be sure to ask for yourself. Projections used by insurance companies clearly state at the bottom of the page that the numbers are not guaranteed and they also generally reveal the interest rate used in the projection.

So, should you only buy term insurance and invest the difference? If you are sure you won't have a requirement for insurance in your later years and have a modicum of discipline, absolutely. It has been my experience, however, that many people will buy term and *spend* the difference. The old argument is that if you have enough discipline to make monthly contributions to a life insurance policy, you should be able to make monthly payments into something like a mutual fund. This should be true, it could be true, but it is not necessarily true. I have proven it in my own life and have witnessed, in my role as a financial advisor, hundreds of others who believe that if they can get at the money, *it will be spent!* The good news, however, is that such people can be rehabilitated with the help of a good financial advisor and their own willingness. They can even go on to write books on the subject.

Owning a home is a great idea because it forces you to save. If you are short one month, it is tough to sell the kitchen sink and then buy it back next month when things are better. Permanent insurance can work in a similar way. There is no incentive to take the cash out in the early years, quite simply because there isn't much. It's much tougher to get at than a Canada Savings Bond or a mutual fund. Plus, you pay interest on anything you borrow from your policy. Remember, the money is there to pay for your coverage later in life. If you borrow from it, you will impact how your policy will grow. The insurance company is banking on your keeping the money intact in the policy to offset later costs. If you take from it, you have to pay what the company would have earned on the policy had the cash value stayed put. This is to guarantee the insurance coverage remains stable. Buying term and investing the difference in a mutual fund, however, will invariably give you better results from an investment perspective. Buying term and investing in a GIC or Canada Savings Bond will give you about the same return as a universal life policy.

WHO NEEDS PERMANENT INSURANCE?

- First and foremost, those with estate tax concerns. If you want to keep your estate intact so it will be passed on to your survivors without having been annihilated by Revenue Canada, permanent insurance will provide the funds to pay your tax bill upon death.

- If you are a woman who works unpaid in the home raising a family while your partner works in the paid labour force, you need proper coverage to make up for pension inequities. This also applies to women who work part-time or in jobs that don't provide pension plans. There is a serious problem these days of people outliving their capital. Make sure you will be financially looked after should you live to 100.

- More and more people are having children later in life and in second and third marriages. If your insurance requirements will extend past a certain age, say 65 or 70, permanent insurance will be necessary.

- To protect your business, especially if it's a family business that you want to pass on to your next of kin. Your business could be hit with a tax bill so prohibitive that it could force liquidation of the company. Your family's source of revenue could, as a result, dry up. The good news is that there is a $500,000 business capital gains exemption that will ease the burden somewhat. But, if the business is a thriving one, the exemption may not be enough to protect your family's interests.

- If you have an RRSP, adequate emergency funds and no (read manageable) debt, you can use permanent insurance as a savings tool though there are much better investment options.

If you are young, have a limited budget and need a lot of coverage, you should only purchase term protection. Clients have come to me with two children, a mortgage, no RRSP or savings to speak of and owning $50,000 of permanent insurance. Their intention was to start a savings program at the same time as having their insurance needs addressed. This is nothing short of criminal. It not only doesn't provide anywhere near enough protection, but the savings element is so inconsequential for the first few years that it is virtually useless. If protection for your family is your main concern, get as much term as possible for your money. For $100.00 a month, depending on age and health, you can get $50,000 permanent insurance or $500,000 term. Term can always be converted to permanent later when you have more financial resources and, obviously, if you need it. Take the few dollars left over and sock them away into an RRSP.

Incidentally, permanent and term insurance can be blended together to give you the advantages of both. It doesn't necessarily have to be a clear-cut choice between them. If you choose a blended product, you will reduce the costs dramatically and it will still give you lifetime protection. People frequently need both. For example, you might have a need for permanent insurance to cover death, debt and tax expenses. You may also have a need for insurance to cover obligations that will eventually disappear, like mortgages, kids, business loans and debts. You can do two things here. You can have, in essence, two insurance plans: a small permanent policy for the permanent needs combined with a term rider for your shorter term needs. This way you will always have protection, no matter when you die, and you won't be paying the large expense of whole life insurance when you don't actually need it. The second choice is to buy a blended option, which combines the two types of insurance in one plan at a substantially lower cost than whole life on its own. There is enough cash value in the blended plan to keep it going until you die, but it resembles term because of its low cost. This type of plan may also have marginal cash value. Talk to your agent or insurance broker about your choices.

GROUP AND ASSOCIATION INSURANCE

Group insurance is the stuff your employer is kind enough to lend you while you work for the company. But it's kind of like living with your parents—chances are exceedingly high that you will have to move out eventually. In today's precarious economy, job security is a thing of the past. No matter what happens in your work life, a privately-owned plan will always be yours and completely transportable. Group insurance is a great way to augment your core insurance plan. I would suggest to you, however, that it isn't secure enough to be the only coverage you have. When you leave your job, it disappears. Even if you are lucky enough to get another job that offers group life insurance, it may not be enough. The amount of coverage varies from plan to plan. If you are unable to afford your own plan, your group coverage is at least something. The government has recently taxed life insurance group benefits on amounts up to $25,000, if your employer pays for this benefit. This could cost you $30-$50 a year. But remember, term is remarkably inexpensive. Depending on age and health, it could cost you as little as $15 a month.

Association insurance works much like group but it is provided by a professional organization or a university alumni. This type of coverage is a very inexpensive alternative but should be used only to supplement your privately-owned coverage. This form of coverage is subject to price increases and possible cancellation if the organization can't afford to offer it any longer.

INSURANCE RIDERS

Buying an insurance policy is like buying a car. You can add on features to tailor it to your own needs. It is important to know exactly what you are getting.

- *Waiver of Premium*—If you become *completely* disabled and unable to work at all, the insurance company will pay your premium for you. Now, we are talking down for the count, not a part-time problem. This is designed to help out only in the worst possible case scenario. You also have to be off work for a minimum of six months before this benefit kicks in. The insurance company will pay those six months of premiums retroactively, however. Under no circumstances is this to replace a disability insurance as they are two totally different animals.

Buy this only if you are really flush cash-wise. It's not an essential part of the equation.

- *Accidental Death Benefit*—This will double the benefit paid
  to your survivors if you are killed in an accident. This is a
  rarely-used option. You should buy insurance based on your
  need for it, not on the way you die.

- *Guaranteed Insurability Option*—This allows you to buy additional chunks of insurance every three years up to age 40 to
  45, regardless of your health. This is a good idea if you think
  you are going to need additional coverage later in life. It can be
  expensive, though. You are paying to guarantee coverage even
  if you become terminally ill. This does not come cheap.

WOMEN AND INSURANCE

Women have made important moves forward since the days when
a woman's life was thought not to have any monetary value. It is
still perplexing to me, however, that so few women own their
own life insurance or that, if they do, it's usually what Gram and
Grandad gave them when they were born. It would barely be
enough to bury them. Our research has also shown that as women
grow older or get married, their frequency of purchasing life insurance declines notably. Many women I speak with think they
own insurance when, in fact, they don't. The following story is a
good example.

I was talking to a client, Sherez, who worked in the home. She
was married and was raising three children, all under the age of
five. This conversation was the first of many like it.

"OK, Sherez, I'm starting to get a clear financial picture. Now
we are going to move on to wills and life insurance. How are
you in this department?" I asked.

"Absolutely fine. Both Miguel and I did our wills before our
first child was born. We have lots of life insurance as well," she
answered.

I pressed on. "How much insurance does Miguel have and
how much do you have?" Sherez became a little confused and
started to shift around in her chair. "I don't really know," she
said. "Miguel looked after that."

"Go back to the day you signed the application form when
you applied for coverage. Do you remember any amount being
discussed?"

"Oh, I didn't sign anything. Miguel met with the agent and did everything," she repeated.

"Sherez, that probably means you don't have coverage on yourself. You have to fill out a medical form, have medical tests if necessary and sign the actual application form. I think what Miguel did was get insurance on himself," I explained.

"Oh no," she emphatically replied, "I have insurance. If Miguel dies, I get whatever the policy is worth."

"Ah!" I said. "Now I understand what you are saying. Sherez, how much would Miguel get if you died?" I knew full well what the answer would be but I needed Sherez to understand the implications.

"Well, uh, nothing." She paused for a moment. "Good heavens, I guess I don't own any life insurance. Isn't that strange, I always thought I did." She had seen the difference between a husband owning a policy with his wife as beneficiary and the wife owning her own insurance.

"Sherez," I began, "take yourself out of the picture. What would your family situation look like if you weren't around? How would Miguel manage? Does he earn enough money to replace the work you do at home?"

"Oh, no," she said, shaking her head. "It would be an unmitigated disaster, quite frankly. Miguel doesn't know how to run a household. The children run for cover when he fills the dishwasher. Besides, he's building his business. He wouldn't have the time, let alone the know-how, to do what I do." She levelled a look at me. "It never occurred to me to put a price tag on what I do. Joanne, we had better talk about this some more."

I have had similar discussions with a disconcerting number of women who assume they have life insurance because they are the beneficiary of their partner's policy. These women range from work-at-home mothers to company presidents. A woman's life has value, economic and otherwise, whether she works at home or in the paid labour force. When life insurance agents or brokers do a life insurance analysis, it is standard practice to evaluate the cost of replacing what women do in the home. Many insurance companies use in the neighbourhood of $18,000 a year as the minimum average amount that it would cost to replace the services of someone who works at home. (I have seen replacement values as high as $50,000.) There is an old insurance industry adage: "There are two types of people who need insurance. Those who earn a living, and those who don't." There is more than an element of truth here, especially for homemakers who work in the unpaid labour force.

As was seen in an earlier Statistics Canada study, women working in the paid labour force are still solely responsible for child and homecare in the majority of Canadian households. It is essential to include the cost of replacing the unpaid work women do in the home in their life insurance analysis as the amount can be staggering.

If we look back over the years we see that many experts, then and now, have been advising their clients to buy insurance with the eventual intent of becoming "self insured." This means that you will have accumulated enough assets that you won't need insurance anymore. If this advice has been so sound, then please explain to me why so many women between 60 and 65 today live at or below the poverty line? It is safe to say that these women aren't living at this level because their partners were "self insured." More likely it is because there are very few assets and little life insurance. Today women are taking control of their own financial destinies, so the need for widows to depend solely on their partner's life insurance will diminish accordingly. Another point to consider: If you accumulate enough assets to be technically "self insured," the chances are good you will need life insurance to pay your tax bill.

INSURANCE ON CHILDREN

What about insurance on children? This is a tough one. Many consider the idea downright morbid. In the past, I didn't often suggest this option unless parents wanted to use the tax-sheltered savings feature to save for a child's education. Recently, however, there was a tragic incident that opened my mind to the other side of the argument.

Matthew, the five-year old child of close friends, was killed in a car accident on Christmas Eve. His parents were completely destroyed by their loss and had tremendous difficulty functioning from day to day. They went through counselling and were told that time was their only ally. Because they had a large mortgage and, like most of us, lived close to the bone, Scott was forced to go back to work sooner than he wanted to. Anne was a nurse, but because of the grave emotional responsibilities of her job, was unable to go back to work. She needed and wanted to stay at home with their two-year-old daughter. So they lost Anne's income. What prompted me to think about the benefit of insuring a child was a comment Scott made to me one day. He said that, had he been able to financially, he would have taken off a lot more time to allow himself to grieve properly. As it was, he could only afford to be away from work less than a month. Though many psychologists suggest going back to work can be good therapy, if one does it too soon, it can be detrimental to the natural grieving process. Scott's adjustment to having to go back to work so soon can only be described as torturous.

After this experience, I began to think that insuring your children may not be so reprehensible. Certainly, the death of a child is a long shot and not something one wants to contemplate. But the loss of a child is catastrophic enough without having to worry about money if you are unable to go back to work right away.

If you do buy an insurance policy on your child, it may be wise to take advantage of the guaranteed insurability option. I bought a policy for my twin nieces when they were born. Regardless of their health, they will be able to buy additional amounts of insurance at designated ages. Let's say they develop juvenile diabetes and become uninsurable. The policy I bought for them will ensure that they will always have coverage and be able to buy more when it's needed. I'll transfer the responsibility for the payments over to them when they are in a financial position to handle it.

One last word: Never consider insuring your children unless you, and your partner, are fully covered. Any application for insurance for children will ask directly how much the parents are covered for. Insuring your child should only be considered after you have taken care of building your financial base. There are other priorities.

GENERAL RULES

There are some general principles you should follow before making any insurance decisions.

- First and foremost, never buy life insurance before having a proper need analysis done. There are standard formulas for how much coverage you need, such as 10 to 12 times your salary, but these are too loose and general. The worst time to find out you don't have enough is when it's too late. You could also be paying for insurance that you don't need.

- Never buy life insurance based on what *you* think you need. I have done more life insurance analyses where the absolute minimum amount required was triple what the people thought they needed. People are always shocked at how much is really required. Canadians like life insurance but remain woefully underinsured as a group.

  A proper life insurance analysis doesn't mean the agent or broker determines the amount of coverage for you. The agent will ask you a series of questions about your financial requirements. You decide, with the guidance of your advisor, the costs you think will be incurred for funeral, medical, legal and other expenses. Things to be factored into the analysis include mortgages to be paid off or rent payment funds to be established, child care, debts, education costs, salary replacement to provide an ongoing income, retirement planning and inflation.

- If you are single, or just want enough to bury you, a comprehensive analysis isn't quite as important. But with family or business obligations, you must know exactly how much you will need. And always take into account the potentially devastating impact of inflation. Since life insurance is about a lifetime, be sure to consider carefully your death benefit's future buying power.

- Do not be influenced by what your neighbour or accountant has done. Every person's requirements will be different.

- You will often hear that life insurance makes a lousy investment. But please remember, investments make lousy life insurance.

- All insurance company products, not just life insurance, are creditor-proof in the event of bankruptcy. You can name a beneficiary on anything from a term deposit to a mutual fund so it will bypass probate and go directly to your beneficiary.

- Should you ever leave your place of employment and you are uninsurable, be sure to take advantage of the opportunity to convert your group plan into personally owned insurance.

Most group policies have a 30-day conversion clause that allows you to do this and you don't have to prove your insurability. It may be the only chance you get to own your own coverage.

- Insurance companies all adhere to the same mortality tables so the cost of the actual insurance is the same. Where costs begin to differ is in how well the company is run and its overhead. Costs will vary, so it pays to comparison shop.

- Never let another agent talk you out of your existing insurance plan and into a "new and improved" version until you are absolutely sure you have been medically approved by the new company. Be sure that it is in your best interest to change plans. (This generally refers to replacing one cash value policy with another.) Don't be fooled by agents telling you that the rate of return on their policy will be better than the one you currently have. Remember, the projections are based on an *assumed* interest rate.

  If you have had a cash value plan for a long time, say five or more years, and someone is suggesting you cancel it and buy term, be very, very careful. Sometimes replacing an improperly sold policy may be the correct decision, but work out the losses in cash value, the now higher cost to insure yourself because you are older, and whether you will need coverage for life before making your decision.

- The insurance industry monitors this practice of replacement closely to be sure the client isn't being misrepresented. If an agent or broker wants to replace a client's policy, that person must fill out an extensive form that spells out in detail why it is being replaced. Then you, as the client, must sign the form before it is sent off to the original agent who sold you your first policy. This procedure ensures that nothing underhanded occurs and that the first agent gets a chance to warn you if you are about to make a bad move. Be prepared, the first agent will obviously try to resell you. This isn't a bad thing and I would encourage you to always give the original person a chance. Review with this agent your reasons for buying their plan in the first place.

- There is a common belief that insurance agents and brokers only sell expensive permanent policies to make a whopping commission. The truth is, some do but many don't. If a policy lapses within a three-to-five year period, no matter what the reason, the agent pays back the bulk if not all of the commission that was earned, assuming they still work for the company. It certainly isn't in anyone's best interest to sell the wrong product. However, if your agent offers whole life without mention of other possible options as a solution to your insurance requirements, you have a right to become wary. Look for a career agent or broker. If they plan on being in the business for a long time, your chances of getting an improperly sold policy decrease.

- Let's assume the man of your dreams—let's call him Lance—comes into your life and sweeps you off your feet. He puts that incredible diamond ring on your finger. What is the first thing we are often compelled to do? We insure the ring. Forget the ring. Insure Lance.

DISABILITY INSURANCE

Oh, how I would love to say it was skiing. Or the ever-exotic parasailing. Or even a lowly car accident. Alas, I was clowning around, lost my footing and fell off a 15-foot ledge. As I was in the heyday of my youth when reflexes are sharp but judgement less so, I landed on my feet. And broke my ankle in three places. My ankle was rebuilt with the latest technology involving plates, pins, screws and wire. The whole ordeal meant emergency surgery, two weeks in the hospital, three months on crutches, nine months recovery and one ankle scarred for life.

I was 25 years old, working for a small dealership flogging photocopiers door to door in downtown Vancouver. It was a small operation, so there were no benefits and I was strictly on commission. I suppose I could have used the crutches and the cast to elicit sympathy and increase my sales, but the doctor wouldn't hear of it. This was most distressing because if I couldn't sell, I wouldn't have a job. So, I was now unemployed. I had no disability coverage, savings or means to earn an income. Ironically, my car was insured, as were my house and possessions, but not the income that paid for all these things.

Disability doesn't wait for a convenient time to strike. It seems to pounce at the worst possible moment. My relationship with the man I then shared a house with was deteriorating. We had been talking for some time about each getting our own address when this disaster struck. Nevertheless, he graciously offered to cover all expenses until I got back on my feet, as it were. The humiliating part of it was that, other than moving back to Mom and Dad, I had no options. It was hell. Two months later, we finally decided to call it quits. I may have been somewhat irresponsible with my own money, but my pride would not let me live off someone else. Parents, however, don't fall into the same category. After a phone call to the folks, I boarded a plane—cast, crutches and all—and headed home to an anxiously awaiting family. Bill Cosby says that human beings are the only species in the world who let their children move back home. Thank God.

Granted, there is no shortage of stories like mine and many that are much worse. People have lost homes and businesses because of an unprepared-for disability. Families dependent on a single income have suffered immeasurably when this income is interrupted. My accident is a good example of how easy it is to become sick or injured. I lost my biggest asset: my earning ability. My exciting adventure of living in a new city filled with career opportunities was abruptly called to a halt and I became dependent on the charity of others.

Usually, it is only after something happens to us or a loved one that we begin to pay attention to our own fragility. I had tons of clients who ignored reality until it came up behind them and bit them. The problem is we do not believe that it could ever happen to us. Evidence to the contrary abounds, however. Hospitals are overcrowded, wheelchair ramps and handicapped parking are available in most places. Yet we remain blind to the obvious. Great West Life Insurance Co. points out that almost half of all mortgage foreclosures in Canada occur because of disability. The Commissioners Disability Table illustrates this point:

IN A YEAR:
1 in 106 people die.
1 in 88 homes catch fire.
1 in 8 people become disabled.

It's not uncommon for people to insure their possessions but not the income that guarantees their lifestyle. It's foolish to spend your money on life insurance or Registered Retirement Savings Plans but not take into account what will happen if you become sick or hurt and lose your earning ability. While in practice, I saw a disconcerting number of women who owned life insurance that would take care of others when they die but have no disability coverage to look after them if they become sick or hurt. The vast majority of women's jobs are concentrated in the service sector that rarely provides company benefits. More and more women are leaving corporate Canada and the security of company-sponsored plans. As discussed earlier, women are opening businesses at three times the rate of men in this country; most of these are in the service field and rely entirely on the woman's skills. If she becomes disabled for a long period, the business will surely fail. Certain self-employed people, taxi drivers, estheticians, hairstylists and women who work unpaid in the home raising families do not qualify for either *private* or *group* coverage. Canada Pension Plan does offer a disability benefit for everyone but to qualify there can be no chance of recovery. This is not to be relied on except in the worst situations.

Consider the following: A 35-year-old woman is seven times more likely to face disability than death before she reaches 65. A man is three times more likely to be disabled than die before age 65. Whereas two out of every five men become disabled, one out of every two women will experience a disability lasting 91 days or longer.[18] If two women are out having dinner, these statistics suggest that one of them had better be very careful driving home.

Because women are disabled more frequently than their male counterparts, they pay significantly higher premiums. Those between the ages of 25 and 40 (childbearing years) pay an additional 30 percent (at a minimum) right across the board.

What happens to a woman's career possibilities and income level if she becomes disabled? The picture gets grim. The unemployment rate for physically challenged women is 16 percent;

for physically challenged men the rate is 13.2 percent. Physically challenged women are paid on average 47 percent of what their male equivalents are paid, 36 percent of what a non-disabled man receives.[19]

I had a client (and good friend) who owned her own computer consulting business. She had been in business for seven years. Jill had not escaped my haranguing about protecting herself, her family and her business. She was like everyone else; she saw the wisdom of income protection but "didn't have the time or the money at the moment." Besides, she was in no big rush. Jill said she was "unbearably healthy" to which I would invariably respond, "Yeah, but have you seen an empty hospital lately?" She called me one day at the office.

"Joanne," she started, "I swear, if you laugh when I tell you what I have to tell you, I'll never talk to you again. I might just have to kill you." We were very close. It couldn't be that serious if I was receiving death threats for laughing, so I relaxed. "What's up, Jill?"

"It's Michael," she said. "He, uh, hurt himself yesterday. Nothing too serious, but it looks like he could be off work for six to eight weeks. Maybe longer."

I sat straight up in my chair. "What happened?" Michael was a litigation lawyer and had recently become a new partner at a very busy law firm. He talked nonstop about this new partnership and was very proud of it.

Jill explained. "You and I both know that Michael's talent is his gift of gab in the court room. It's in everyone's best interest that I do the handy work around the house and keep him as far away as possible from a ladder or anything with sharp edges. But yesterday was such a beautiful day, he wanted to putter around in the yard. I thought to myself, 'Michael rarely gets a chance to work outside. What trouble could he get into trimming an odd hedge or two?' About an hour later, I heard a yell they are still talking about in Iceland! I ran out to the back yard and found Michael lying face down with that damned ladder beside him. He had lost his balance and fallen while cleaning out the eavestrough. I called an ambulance even though he was still conscious. I don't think I have ever seen anyone in so much pain."

"This is dreadful, Jill. What's the damage? Before you answer, I can't believe that you think I would find this funny. This is very serious!" I exclaimed.

"I haven't come to the punch line yet," she responded. "He will be fine, Joanne, really. His body is covered with bruises but none that rival the bruise his ego received. Oh, did I mention he broke his jaw and it has to be wired shut for several weeks?"

I completely lost it. As I struggled to regain my composure, I heard Jill sigh with resignation and quietly mumble, "I guess I'd better get used to this reaction." She continued, "The people at Michael's office were very sympathetic but also couldn't help laughing. You will be interested to know that Michael is covered for the time he is off with the insurance he has through the Canadian Bar Association. I want to come and talk to you next week about something for me."

After I hung up the phone, I sat back and thought about how shocking it is when this kind of thing happens even if you think you are prepared for it.... "Elaine!" I bellowed from deep within my office. "How do I find out how much the company pays me if I'm rendered useless and can't earn a living because I am hit by a runaway lawnmower or stressed out from being overworked?"

Elaine's response dripped with sarcasm. "You poor dear," she shot back in mock sympathy as I entered her office. "It's a serious consideration for people like you whose work schedule starts every day at the crack of noon!" (My alarm went off every morning at 5:45!)

Ignoring her, I plunked myself down in a chair and told her about the phone call. She was not surprised and commented that that was how most disability insurance policies are sold. The injury or illness of a close family member usually prompts people into action. "What a coincidence," she continued. "If you take a gander at your trusty priority pyramid, you will see this was next on our agenda." She pulled out a copy of the company's benefit plan from her desk drawer. "You were given this the day you were hired and told to read it carefully. I'm delighted to see that you follow instructions to the letter."

"Now answer the following questions," she continued. "Are you the owner of the plan or is the company? Do you pay tax on the monthly amount you receive if you are sick or hurt? How does the company define 'disability'? Is it flat out and down for the count or can a broken baby finger qualify? Will it pay anything if you are only partially disabled? How long will the company pay the monthly amount? Does it take into consideration inflation? What happens if you are well enough to work, but not at the job you had before your illness or injury took you out of the game? When can you start receiving the money? Can the benefits be reduced or cut off for any reason? Will the company help you become rehabilitated and how much will they pay you while you are on a program? I don't get it," she concluded. "Why is it that people only care about 'how much'?"

"OK! OK!" I cried. "Message received. I'll read the booklet." I snatched it out of her hand and headed back to my own office.

I had worked for many companies in my lifetime, but I don't think I ever knew the details of the benefits they provided. The only time I made the effort to become aware was during my experience of being hurt and unable to work, only to find out I had no coverage. On reading the booklet, I made a startling revelation. I did not have enough insurance. As I returned it to Elaine, I told her I'd better bump up my coverage in a hurry. If I couldn't work, the monthly benefit would be substantially less than my current income. Elaine was impressed I had found out earlier rather than later but promptly said, "You can't."

"Excuse me?" I replied.

"You're new to the business and you are classified as an independent contractor. This is like being self-employed but because your licences are sponsored by a company, you will have some company coverage. But as you found out, not enough. You have to wait a full year to be able to get some of your own insurance. In fact, anyone who starts up a new business has to wait a year. The only exception might be if you start up a business that is similar to your last job, but there are certainly no guarantees. The insurance company wants to be sure you're not a financial deadbeat and you have a modicum of stability. In the meantime, be thankful you at least have the company plan, such as it is."

I was stunned. The company plan might have been alright for some who worked there, but it certainly didn't cover my needs. Group benefits are pretty much the same for all who work at a company, regardless of how much they each earn. Some people may end up earning too much to be adequately covered. The most coverage you can expect to receive, whether from group, association, private or government plans like workers compensation, is from 60 to 85 percent of your total earnings. If you decide to buy private insurance in addition to a group policy at work, your benefits will be coordinated so as not to exceed your normal income. I was eventually able to take advantage of a privately-owned plan to make up the shortfall from the company plan and still be within that 60 to 85 percent range. Topping up your group plan is often hard to do, though, because this ceiling takes workers compensation and UIC into account. This reduces the amount you are able to buy on your own. Because I was technically self employed, I didn't have any government benefits to rely on so I had some breathing room. But then came another revelation. The amount of disability insurance you can qualify for depends entirely on how much income you earn. I couldn't go to the insurance company and say, "Give me coverage worth $8,000 a month," if I only earned $40,000 a year. Your income justifies the benefit amount.

I spent the next 11 months being extra careful about looking both ways before I crossed the street. When I was finally able to apply for additional coverage, I was surprised at the differences between my company plan and the one that I now owned personally. The good news about the group plan is that it costs very little. But if the company pays the whole shot or even part of the premiums, the monthly benefits are taxable. If I pay the premiums myself, the benefits are tax free. The other good news about company plans is that the state of your health is incidental, providing that you started with the company after the plan was implemented. If you can't get disability insurance privately for health or financial reasons, you can still take advantage of your group coverage through work. The major downside is that when you go, you lose it. It's like rented insurance. You are dependent entirely on the generosity of your employer.

The other pitfall to watch for with company plans is their definition of disability. This is the heart and soul of your plan. At one end are the private plans, which tend to have the most generous definition, at the other end is the Canada Pension Plan with its stringent and severe definition. Group plans may fall anywhere along the continuum but tend more toward the strict definition. Be very careful of the clause regarding "own or any occupation." If the policy says "any occupation," it can cut you off benefits once you are well enough to work in any job. If, for example, this had been the clause in Michael's policy, his benefits could be cut off (generally after two years) if he were fit to work as a gardener but not able to practise law. If you are buying a private plan, be sure it says "own occupation," which means you will continue to be paid until you can return to the job you had before. Also be sure this "own occupation," clause is not limited to two years, which is often the case for group plans. Get one that is good until you are 65. And finally, be sure your policy is guaranteed renewable and non-cancellable to age 65 at the same premium as when you bought it. Even if you become uninsurable or unemployed after you bought the policy, the insurance company cannot take it back. It's good for the length of the contract as long as you continue to pay the premiums.

Many professional associations, university alumni organizations and business groups offer disability insurance to their members. Association plans are often very useful for self-employed people or for people looking to top up their group benefits or to continue coverage if they are changing jobs (providing you are still a member of that group or association). It is important to realize, however, that association coverage is much like group or company plans. The association owns it, not you. Recently, certain associations experienced significant premium hikes because of increased claims. Because this type of insurance is not actually yours, the premiums can increase as you get older and the policy has to be renewed every few years. This means you will have to be "in the pink" healthwise or your insurance may be discontinued. Also, if you leave the association or group, your coverage stays behind. If you have become uninsurable during that time, you will be out of luck trying to replace it. Association coverage has more of a "group" flavour to it when it comes to the definition of disability. It tends to be more restrictive, especially with the "own versus any occupation" clause. Still an excellent option, however. Just be aware of the restrictions.

Having appropriate disability coverage through whatever means you choose is one of the first steps in creating a solid and responsible financial plan. It is disconcerting to me that so few people have proper disability insurance or know the details of their coverage if they are part of a company plan. Every birthday you celebrate increases the cost of disability insurance. If you are one of the few remaining souls bent on slow suicide who still smokes, brace yourself to pay up to 40 percent more.

The cost of disability insurance can itself give you a heart attack. So both Jill and I found out. However, insurance companies use an "unbundled option" approach that allows you to control the costs to some degree. There are several features available so you can build the plan most suitable to your own needs and budget. Jill was a 35-year-old non-smoker who earned $40,000 last year. She was given certain options that would reduce (or increase) her premiums. The biggest impact on cost was when the plan would actually kick in and start paying the monthly benefit. Jill could choose from having her benefit start 61, 91 or 121 days after her illness or injury instead of 31 days. These choices would significantly reduce her monthly premium. She opted to pay $95.00 for a $2,100.00 tax-free monthly benefit that will last until she reaches age 65. The $2,100.00 monthly benefit starts on the 31st day after the disability occurs. If she waited 61 days for the benefit to start, it would cost $69.00; 91 days, $58.00, and so on. I recommended that she stay with the 31-day option because her cash flow was so tight, her company wouldn't survive for 61 days without some income. She balked at the price as everyone does until I put it to her this way: She could live off of $40,000 a year and have no income if something happened or manage on $38,860 and receive a tax-free benefit of $25,200 if she got hurt or sick. It didn't take a rocket scientist to figure out the better option.

I was very lucky. Even while working for an employer, I owned my own disability and life insurance. When I left corporate Canada, my privately-owned plan came with me. I chose to own my own plan not because I knew I'd be self employed someday but because I like having control of my own affairs. Today I live worry free (as do my staff and creditors), secure in the knowledge that if I'm sick or hurt, there will be income to ensure the bills get paid.

Remember: Health buys insurance. Money only pays for it. Think of disability insurance as a parachute. You should always have one, but pray like crazy you will never need it.

Disability insurance is a very complex area. This is by no means a definitive discussion of the subject. It is designed only to give you some highlights and to get you thinking about it. Remember that whatever reason you may have now for not purchasing disability insurance will sound hollow when you're sick or hurt and unable to work.

Talk to a disability insurance expert, one who deals in it extensively, if not exclusively. These experts will be able to tell you the claim payment history of each company and describe the myriad options these policies offer. Furthermore, any financial advisor will be glad to sit down and review your group benefits with you. Spend 10 minutes rooting around in your desk to find your benefits booklet. You won't regret it.

DEMYSTIFYING MUTUAL FUNDS

> "When I was young, I thought *that money was the most im-portant thing in life; now that I'm old, I* know *that it is.*"
>
> Oscar Wilde

I was sitting in Elaine's office gloomily reflecting on the past few weeks. I had my estate planning and insurance needs under control. That had meant visits to lawyers, painful discussions of death, intensely personal questions on applications for life and disability insurance and the anxious waiting to see if I was insurable. I was beginning to think this whole idea of being financially responsible was far too depressing for such a free spirit. Elaine sensed my mood. She started off in a very chipper tone, "The road to building a solid financial base can be disturbing if you are uncomfortable with some of life's challenges, like death and disability. The good news is now that your nondeductible debt is paid off, your emergency fund is intact and your estate planning and insurance needs are looked after, your base of the priority pyramid is solid. You've done well, kiddo. We now get to move on to the rewards. You know, investments with a bit of sex and sizzle."

Finally, some real action. There was only one problem. If I had felt apprehension and bewilderment learning the basics of financial planning, the thought of investments like mutual funds instilled feelings of confusion and fear. I didn't even know what questions to ask. But I knew I had to do something. I began by relaying a story to Elaine to illustrate my sobering lack of knowledge in this area.

"Elaine," I began, "picture this scene: I'm at a dinner party. I'm surrounded by people chatting effortlessly about their investments. To my ears, it sounded like a foreign language. 'My bond fund did well last quarter thanks to interest rates dropping.'...'The European currency crisis sure had an impact on my international equity fund.'...'My Asian fund dropped after the securities scandal in Japan, but my Canadian resource fund netted a 45 percent return over the last six months.'

"As I stood there, I smiled brightly and intelligently and nodded my head but grimaced inwardly in panic for fear I would be asked a question.

"And as you can guess, Elaine, my worst fear was realized. Someone uttered the fateful words, 'So, Joanne, what is your money in these days?' I froze for an instant but recovered quickly. My response was divinely inspired. I stammered, 'The banks. Ah...yes, most of my money goes into, uh, banks.' I then smiled directly at my partner in triumph. I hadn't lied. Most of my money went directly to two banks. The ones that offered Visa and Mastercard.

"Elaine, it was then I realized I was becoming remarkably adept at faking knowing something when I didn't. Frankly, men had been teaching me this trick for years."

WHAT EXACTLY ARE MUTUAL FUNDS?

Elaine laughed generously at the vivid image of a grown woman squirming in public. Especially this particular grown woman. "I am always surprised at people's level of anxiety about mutual funds and the stock market," Elaine said thoughtfully. "Mutual funds seem to intimidate people and they often think that you need a fortune to get into them.

"Remember, Joanne, how I hammered home the importance of socking away that 10 percent of your after-tax income? You know, your palatial estate and lolling, dark, mysterious men fund?"

"I know exactly what you are going to say, oh wise one!" I quickly replied, anxious to impress. "Mutual funds. My money is going to find a nice, safe home in mutual funds, where it will go forth and multiply at a breathtaking rate, right?"

"In a word," she replied, "no. You know how your beloved priority pyramid is built according to risk. The base is the safest but the pyramid gets progressively more risky right up to the top where art enjoys the most speculative of positions. It's the same with mutual funds. You will be delighted to see that I have *another* pyramid that illustrates this point." Elaine pushed a piece of paper across her desk at me.

It looked like the priority pyramid except there were different types of mutual funds ranked according to their risk or volatility level. I groaned inside my head. "Elaine, you mean there are more than one type? This financial planning business is beginning to remind me of buying what used to be called 'running shoes.' Now you have to know in advance exactly what you need them for, how often you are going to be using them and if you would be using them for something other than 'running.' There are walking shoes, court shoes, long-distance running shoes, short-

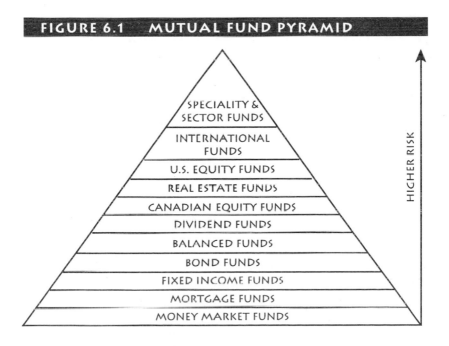

FIGURE 6.1   MUTUAL FUND PYRAMID

SPECIALITY & SECTOR FUNDS
INTERNATIONAL FUNDS
U.S. EQUITY FUNDS
REAL ESTATE FUNDS
CANADIAN EQUITY FUNDS
DIVIDEND FUNDS
BALANCED FUNDS
BOND FUNDS
FIXED INCOME FUNDS
MORTGAGE FUNDS
MONEY MARKET FUNDS

HIGHER RISK

distance running shoes, killer aerobic shoes, high tops, low tops, women's, girls', men's, boys', infants', with a gizmo pump, without a pump and cross-training shoes for those fools who want to do a bit of everything. Life used to be so much simpler!"

"Quit your whining, my little protégé," Elaine responded. "As with anything worth having, a little work must be done before you reap any appreciable gain. I suggest we let the education process begin."

Once I got over my initial fear of mutual funds through educating myself, I couldn't get into one fast enough. Mutual funds are a vital component of a solid, long-term financial plan. I believe every Canadian should be taking advantage of some form of mutual fund from the different families of funds. They are not hard to understand, but there is a lot to understand. Mutual funds have been around in Canada since 1932. To give you an indication of the explosive growth in this industry, in December 1992, there was 67 billion dollars under management. By December 31, 1994, it had grown to over 130 billion dollars. Experts forecast that the industry will grow to $300 billion by the year 2001. As the pyramid shows, there are many types of mutual funds to fit the many reasons people have for investing in them.

Simply put, mutual funds take advantage of the principle of shared resources and risk. For example, if you went into a bank with 50 dollars to put in a term deposit, you would likely get a paltry rate of return. If you had 50 thousand dollars, your interest rate would improve measurably. Now imagine having five hundred thousand dollars or five million dollars and what you could get as an interest rate.

You're right. Not even in my wildest dreams. But what I can envision is putting my 50 dollars in a pot with a large group of people and giving it to a company to invest as part of a much bigger sum. By pooling your money with other investors, you can take advantage of investments you otherwise couldn't afford in order to get that better rate of return. Not only do you get an expanded variety of investment choices, you do so more safely. If the money goes into term deposits and other guaranteed type investments, it is called a money market mutual fund. If it goes into stocks, it is called an equity mutual fund, mortgages, a mortgage fund and so on. This is the principle of mutual funds. You give your money, along with a zillion other investors, to a company that invests your 50 dollars a month in whatever type of investment you choose. You may choose from risk-free term deposits and mortgages to the more adventurous stocks and bonds, precious metals or specialty investments. Or, if you like, a combination of the lot. The wonderful part of these investments is that you may cash them in at any time (possibly at a loss, however!). They are completely liquid. Depending on the type of fund you choose, they may even get preferred tax treatment.

The mutual fund companies have experts on staff who know how to manage the money. These people are called money or portfolio managers. These professional managers do all the required selling and buying of stocks and bonds and make the investment decisions. The company does all the accounting paperwork and sends you quarterly or semi annual statements of the fund's performance. One attractive feature is that, through preauthorized chequing, the mutual fund company will automatically take a predetermined amount out of your account each month.

TYPES OF FUNDS

There is a wide variety of mutual funds as well as a choice of companies to buy them from. In Canada, there are over 1,200 funds available. It is important to have a clear idea of your investment goals before choosing. Some funds are more suited for certain ends than others. If you want to buy a business in six months, putting your cash resources into an equity fund would not be wise. If you want to retire 30 years from now in the lap of luxury in your country chalet, having your entire portfolio in a money market fund will not get you there.

There are two broad categories of mutual funds. The first offers long-term growth potential and invests in things like common stocks. When you see an investment described as a "growth" investment, that means it will be volatile. It will go up and down, sort of like a roller coaster. Stocks are particularly prone to this kind of movement. Common stocks are shares of ownership in a company. We are able to buy stocks because a company sells shares to raise the money it needs to expand. In other words, a share is a piece of ownership in a company. If the stocks you buy are from blue chip companies like the big banks and huge corporations, volatility tends to be less of a factor. These stocks, or shares (the two terms are used interchangeably), are more stable and don't fluctuate nearly as much as shares in newer, just emerging companies. Blue chip stocks are slower moving investments that are conservative in nature. If, on the other hand, the company is newer and just beginning to grow, there is likely to be much greater volatility. However, you have a better chance to be on hand for a wild ride to the top if the company flourishes.

This volatility is not a bad thing. It can actually be a very good thing. In her book, *Shifting Gears*, Nuala Beck talks about a new emerging economy. This economy includes medical technology, telecommunications and environmentally concerned companies. These companies are on the leading edge. By way of contrast, companies that are heavily involved in coal mining and beef cattle, for example, are undoubtedly on the decline, no matter how massive they may be. The smaller, leaner, progressive companies have nowhere to go but up, provided they are managed well and stay ahead of their competition. There may be lots of growing pains, but over the long term, they can be a good bet. In investing jargon, these companies are referred to as "small cap" (capitalization) companies. They are definitely much riskier but the growth potential can be very good. "Big cap" companies like the top five chartered banks and Bell Canada don't offer the same growth potential, but make up for it with slow, stable, secure growth. There are now mutual funds available that take advantage of the growth potential of these small cap companies. And, of course, there are and always will be the blue chip variety. Funds are also developing that offer a combination of the two so you can have both growth and stability.

Returns from mutual funds include interest and dividends earned on the fund's investments. They also come from the profits of the sale of stocks inside the mutual fund portfolio. This type of return is called capital gains. Returns are also earned when stocks increase in value (otherwise known as capital appreciation). This happens when the companies do well and the demand for their shares increases. When the demand increases, the share value increases. There is absolutely no way of knowing for sure how a growth-oriented fund will perform. It depends entirely on how well the stock market as a whole performs. You could enjoy a banner year and get 35 percent as a rate of return, then lick your wounds because of a minus five percent the next year. Because of their diversified nature, mutual funds don't tend to fluctuate wildly day by day unless there is some sort of hugely upsetting event. They don't tend to fluctuate as much as individual stocks with the exception of specialty funds.

I cannot emphasize strongly enough that growth-oriented mutual funds are long-term investments. You need to think of seven years as an absolute minimum, with 10 years being far more preferable.

The second category of mutual funds is more income oriented and provides not only income that you can use today, but stable, low to moderate growth for the future. These are *income mutual funds*. These funds invest in debt instruments like bonds and mortgages. Let's say the federal government (or a corporation) needs to raise money for something like modernizing a plant. It will issue a piece of paper called a bond or debenture. You give them your money which they in turn promise to pay back at the maturity date, with a predetermined amount of interest. In other words, you are loaning money to the government or corporation with the expectation of making a profit from the interest they pay you in return. That's why bonds are called debt instruments or securities. The income you receive from these kinds of mutual funds comes from the interest that has been generated. The exception is dividend funds. You get income from this type of fund from, you guessed it, dividends. Dividends are your share of a company's profit in a given year.

Balanced funds are a combination of growth-oriented and income-producing investments, but are still considered to be in the growth category. Give these types of funds at least five years to grow to roll with the ups and downs.

Historically speaking, growth funds have provided a better return over the long run than the more moderate income funds.

These, then, are the two broad categories of mutual funds. In addition, mutual funds are grouped into other categories depending on what they invest in and what they are designed to do. There are three major considerations when buying mutual funds: safety, capital growth and income-producing ability. Each type of fund offers one, two or all three of these benefits in varying degrees. The most common types of funds are Balanced Funds, Common Stock or Growth Funds, Specialty Funds and Fixed

Income Funds. In the '70s, a number of new funds evolved whose function is to take advantage of the new needs and developments in the securities industry. Examples include Money Market Funds, Mortgage Funds, Dividend Funds and Real Estate Funds.

INCOME-GENERATING MUTUAL FUNDS

MONEY MARKET FUNDS   These are the safest of funds. Why? Because they invest in cash. These funds invest in high-quality short-term investments like term deposits, treasury bills and high-quality corporate bonds that have a term of anything under a year. A money market fund is a great place for an emergency fund because it is completely liquid, yet will give you a higher rate of return than a savings account. Money market funds are very suitable for parking your money for short periods before deciding where it is to go for the long haul. Investors who believe that interest rates are going to rise will take advantage of this type of fund. The differences between money market funds are minimal but be sure to find one that has no load.

These are RRSP eligible.

There are also U.S. money market funds that invest in short-term U.S. securities like treasury bills and commercial paper. These are good for those who travel to the U.S. and require frequent access to American funds. International money market funds invest in international commercial paper and short-term securities.

MORTGAGE FUNDS   These are another low-risk form of mutual fund, though slightly riskier than a savings account or money market fund. On the other hand, they can offer a somewhat higher rate of return than a money market fund. However, that has not been the case over the last few years because of the general decline in the real estate market. As with all low-risk investments, however, you enjoy stability and security at the cost of a high rate of return. These funds invest primarily in residential first mortgages but some will invest in commercial and industrial mortgages. Mortgages are loans secured by property, so the house itself becomes the collateral. In commercial or industrial loans, the factory or office building secures the loan. Since these funds invest in first mortgages (which are safer than second and third mortgages), you don't have to worry about losing your blouse.

They don't tend to be volatile, either. Mortgage funds are increasingly investing in mortgage-backed securities which tend to be safer because they are government guaranteed. Mortgage funds are ideal for a novice eager to learn about the investing world. Investors who rate security, stability and moderate returns high in their investment priorities will also like these types of funds.

These are RRSP eligible.

BOND FUNDS   These funds invest mainly in medium to long-term bonds of federal, provincial and municipal governments. Quality corporate bonds might also be included. You may experience major swings in bond prices depending on how interest rates fare. In general, bond funds can be more stable than equity funds except when interest rates move sharply up or down. When interest rates drop, bonds will do well. When interest rates start to rise, steer clear. If you are conservative and want a steady monthly or annual income from your investment, bond funds are a good choice. They offer better than average returns and flexibility. They aren't like GICs that lock in your money for a set period of time. Bond funds are especially popular with people approaching retirement who want to move their investments from the more volatile equity funds to something possibly more stable and secure.

If you combine bond funds with mortgage funds you get what is called an *income fund* or *fixed income fund*. They get this name because of the income they provide in the form of regular interest payments. These funds are more volatile than a mortgage fund but less volatile than a bond fund. There are income funds that hold some stocks as well, say 25 percent stocks, and a combination of bonds and mortgages. These are then called balanced funds.

Bond funds and income funds are RRSP eligible.

You can also invest in international bond funds which invest in bonds from different countries.

DIVIDEND FUNDS   These funds invest in high-quality common shares, for example from blue chip companies like Bell, and preferred shares. Preferred shares have a guaranteed value attached to them unlike common shares which fluctuate according to a number of factors, including supply and demand. Common shares, though offering no guarantees, will most often provide a higher rate of return than preferred shares. Shareholders owning preferred shares are paid by the corporation before the owners of common shares.

Dividend funds are not as volatile as regular equity funds and are ideal for people with high incomes. Dividend funds are also good for those who need a current income. They offer good tax breaks for the well-heeled investor through the dividend tax credit and the fact that only 75 percent of the capital gains in these funds are taxable. The government likes it when you invest in Canadian companies. In order to encourage you to do so, they give investors a tax break in the form of the dividend tax credit which reduces the tax you have to pay. You'll end up in a better tax position with these funds than you would with interest-bearing investments like GICs and Canada Savings Bonds. On these investments, you have to pay the full tax. With dividend funds, you have the dividend tax credit at your disposal to relieve some of your tax burden.

These are RRSP eligible, but because of the tax breaks you get through the dividend tax credit it is usually recommended that you hold these funds outside your RRSP. However, because of today's low interest rates, people are putting them into their RRSPs to capitalize on the growth potential.

REAL ESTATE FUNDS   Income-producing real estate properties are the order of the day here. These funds allow Canadians to participate in another market from which they might normally be excluded—real estate. They invest in things like office buildings, shopping centres, medical facilities and apartment buildings. Unlike other mutual funds, these funds offer deferred taxation through what's called a *capital cost allowance*. This allowance tax shelters portions of the rental income that is distributed within the fund. These funds are designed for long-term growth through the increase in the value of the property in the fund and through having the rental income reinvested in the fund. They aren't very liquid as they are generally valued quarterly and can only be redeemed on certain days, with 30 days' notice often being required. Real estate funds are quite new in Canada and the recession has hurt their performance, especially those heavily invested in shopping centres. These funds are more risky than mortgage and bond funds and because of the current commercial real estate climate, have become more volatile than dividend funds. Because of the current real estate climate, there aren't many of these funds around anymore.

These are RRSP eligible, but because of the tax-preferred treatment of the capital cost allowance, it isn't generally recommended.

GROWTH-ORIENTED FUNDS

CANADIAN EQUITY FUNDS   Canadian equity funds specialize in stocks in Canadian companies. These funds are ideal for people wanting to invest in the Canadian economy. However, they can be volatile. The Toronto Stock Exchange annual rate of return varies widely. Over the 10-year period ending June 1, 1991, the annual return of the total return index of the Toronto Stock Exchange ranged from a low of -39.1 to a high of 86.6. This fluctuation is why equity funds are a long-term investment. If you choose an equity fund you will, at the very worst, compensate for the eroding power of inflation and taxation. That's why these funds are an essential part of financial planning. Moreover, equity funds ensure your money will outlive you if you plan carefully. Equity funds are designed for long-term investing, which makes them ideal for retirement planning. These funds are popular for RRSPs. People who hold these funds outside their RRSP will enjoy the tax advantages of the dividend tax credit and the fact that these investments are not taxed until you actually sell them. Even when they are cashed in, only 75 percent of the gain is taxed, unlike investments like GICs and Canada Savings Bonds whose interest is 100 percent taxable, every year, whether you receive it or not. Equity funds can include cash and bonds but are primarily stocks. They therefore can provide the three forms of income— *interest, capital gains* and *dividends*—in varying degrees. That's why they are a good bet.

However, equity funds make a lousy emergency fund. You can be sure that on the very day you need to access the money in your equity fund, the stock market will take a dive. It's called Murphy's Law. The depth of the dive will be directly proportional to how badly you need the money!

Canadian equity funds are very popular. But remember the importance of diversification. Mutual funds are, by their very nature, diversified, but you can take it one step further. Though an important market, Canada is considered small by world standards

FIGURE 6.2 WORLD MARKET CAPITALIZATION

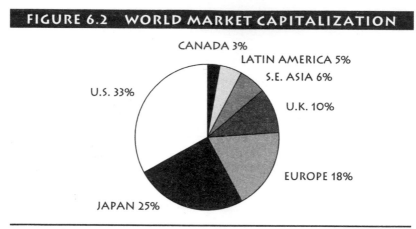

Source: RBC Dominion Securities. Reproduced with permission.

(see the chart above), representing only three percent of the world market. The Canadian stock market is also primarily natural-resource-based, which makes it more susceptible to market swings. A smart investor will expand his or her holdings to outside of the country to take advantage of opportunities internationally.

Canadian equity funds are RRSP eligible.

U.S. EQUITY FUNDS As the name suggests, these funds specialize in American stocks. The U.S. market is one of the world's largest and has more to choose from, including some of the biggest companies in the world. There are, however, certain considerations to be aware of when choosing a U.S. equity fund. The vast majority of American funds are not RRSP eligible and cannot take advantage of any of the Canadian dividend tax breaks, but can take advantage of the tax benefits of capital gains. They have performed better than Canadian funds over the long term and play an important role in a diversified portfolio. Generally speaking they cannot be used for RRSP purposes unless they fall under the 20 percent allowable foreign content rule.

INTERNATIONAL EQUITY FUNDS These funds take advantage of the entire world as a potential marketplace. The fund managers try to invest in parts of the world that have the best growth potential. Common stocks are purchased of growth-oriented companies located in different countries. Some funds invest only in a certain country or region of the world, like Japan or the Pacific Rim. These funds are for the well-established investor who is in the "accumulation" phase of their financial plan. They are also great for people who understand and want to capitalize on world market trends. International funds are a very aggressive part of your portfolio. They are riskier than Canadian or U.S. funds because you are also playing against the fluctuations of currencies in the different countries. The same tax and RRSP restrictions apply with international funds as with U.S. funds.

SPECIALTY OR SECTOR FUNDS   The concentration of specialty funds is on common shares of a group of companies in one industry or geographic location. For those people who are sure that a particular industry is going to do well, a specialty or sector fund is an option. Some examples of specialty funds are Asian funds, natural resource funds, gold or energy funds, technology funds and ethical funds whose investment decisions are based on moral criteria. These criteria might include not investing in companies that produce arms, tobacco or alcohol. A variation of this theme is a new fund started in the United States that invests only in "women-friendly" corporations. These companies must have a certain percentage of women in top management and must offer programs like job sharing and day care. The small cap funds referred to earlier fall into the specialty fund category.

These funds tend to be quite volatile since they don't have the benefit of diversification. They can provide stupendous rates of return but the reverse is also a real possibility. Specialty funds are a very "boom or bust" form of investing. They are highly speculative and not for the faint of heart.

With the exception of foreign specialty funds (which can be used only up to the allowed foreign content), these are RRSP eligible.

BALANCED FUNDS   These funds include a little bit of everything—stocks, bonds, cash, mortgages. The idea behind them is to maximize the growth potential of your investments while preserving the capital. This can be achieved by anticipating market conditions. The fund manager will adjust the asset mix or percentage of each asset according to the pulse of the economy. If the stock market isn't performing to expectations, then the manager may increase the cash portion of the portfolio. If interest rates are rising, the manager may minimize the bond portion of the fund and add equities. You will rarely see an even 50/50 split of aggressive and conservative investments. A higher percentage of fixed income securities like bonds and preferred shares tends to provide higher immediate income and reduces the price fluctuations of the fund. Though considered reasonably safe, a combination of poor market performance and rising interest rates will wreak havoc with balanced funds. As a general rule, they are less risky than pure equity funds.

Balanced funds are a relatively safe way to introduce yourself to investing. They are also recommended for the older investor who wants to start switching their equity investments over to less volatile or risky funds. They can help you have your cake and eat it, too. They will provide long-term growth possibilities with stability. They may not do as well as straight equity funds over the long term, however.

Balanced funds are RRSP eligible.

What fund should you invest in? It depends entirely on what you want it to do. The mutual fund numbers reported in July 1995 in *The Globe and Mail* put them in the following order in terms of rate of return for 1994: The largest gain by far was in the U.S. equity markets at 17.3 percent with Canadian bond funds a distant but respectable second with 14.2 percent. They were followed by special equity funds (14.1 percent), dividend funds (12.8 percent), balanced funds (11.6 percent), Canadian equity (11.1 percent), foreign bonds (9.7 percent), international equity (0.7 percent), resource equity (0.1 percent) and real estate (0 percent). This by no means tells you that U.S. equity funds are better than real estate funds. What it does tell you is that at the moment they are. Next year's numbers could look markedly different.

WHAT KIND OF FUND SHOULD I HAVE?

"Well, well," I announced with my usual enthusiasm. "I'm getting the general drift of things, Elaine, but how on earth am I supposed to know what I want or, worse yet, need? Remember me? The one who throws hissy-fits in sporting goods stores because they turned buying running shoes into a bloody science experiment?"

"That's what I'm here for, Joanne," Elaine replied. "That, and to listen to your bad jokes. It's all part of the sacrifice we make as financial advisors."

I brushed off her callous comment regarding my rapier wit and pressed on. "Give it to me quick then. How do I know what to do?"

"What do you want *it* to do?" she inquired. "Secure your retirement 30 years away or finance a trip to France six months from now? Do you want your fund to give you a regular income now or when you are in your prime at 65? The question to ask yourself is 'When am I going to need the money?' If it is under a year, your options are considerably narrowed. Forget about anything in the stock market. If you take your 10 percent which is reserved for long-term savings, say over 10 years, the stock market is perfect, providing the ups and downs don't keep you awake at night. You have to figure out your comfort zone."

My head was reeling from all these questions. "You will forgive me, Elaine, if I don't answer all hundred questions at once. One thing I do know for sure is that inflation and taxes are most proficient at sucking up my hard-earned money. If I understand what you have been saying, my GICs and Canada Savings Bonds are only a moderate hedge, if any, against inflation. If history repeats itself, the stock market will beat inflation by a much wider margin but I may have to sacrifice a few sleepless nights. Correct?" I inquired.

"Yes, ma'am" Elaine countered. "You need to tell me if you want safety and security, which means more modest returns, or if you want to devote your money toward higher returns, which means no guarantees. Or maybe something in the middle might be more to your liking. I'm afraid mutual funds are much like the rest of life; the more fun it is, the greater the chance you'll feel some pain. In other words, the greater the potential for a substantial return, the higher the risk. Similarly for the tax benefits of mutual funds. Are you willing to accept some risk to reduce the amount of tax you have to pay on your investments? That's an important factor if you own mutual funds outside your RRSP. If it is your retirement you are saving for, you must have a portion of your investments in equity funds. It is the best way to stay ahead of inflation. The number of years you have before retirement will have an impact on which fund you purchase."

"OK," I said, braced for the next step. "How do I know whose fund to buy? What separates the good from the bad?"

HOW DO I CHOOSE?

When I began my search for the right mutual fund, I discovered that if my neighbour starts talking about the hot, new fund she's picked up, it probably means it's too late and I've missed the bandwagon. You need to catch the fund on its way up, not when it is already at the top. It is important to find a fund that has steadily achieved good results over a long period. This can be a problem given the myriad of new funds popping up almost on a daily basis. In considering these funds you have to rely on other criteria such as the fund manager and economic philosophy. A good gauge might be to find a fund that is consistently a solid performer; around 10 to 15 percent over 10 years is quite realistic and respectable.

The reason you don't want to buy a big-time best-seller is pure and simple—cost. As the fund does better, the cost of the shares you purchase increases. In mutual fund lingo, the shares you purchase are called units and what they are worth is referred to as *net asset value per share* or NAVPS. Remember, the fundamental principle of successful investing is to buy low and sell high.

Watch out for the one-hit wonders. Anyone can have one stellar year. It is much more difficult to produce consistent results in bad times as well as good. When examining the performance of a particular fund, you need to look at a minimum of 10 years to get the real picture. The hard part about buying a mutual find is that the decision is based on what the fund has done in the past. No one can predict how it will do in the future. A certain amount of faith and a belief that "history will repeat itself" is necessary. The reasons for not buying a fund consistently positioned at the bottom of the heap are pretty self evident.

DIVERSIFY YOUR CHOICE OF MUTUAL FUNDS

Having all your money in any one thing is not recommended. There are many types of investments, all designed to do certain things, from retirement planning to helping you save for your first bungalow. Even though mutual funds are inherently diversified, each type of mutual fund still addresses a very specific need. Having your mutual fund portfolio moderately diversified is a very wise idea. But don't go overboard. Being overdiversified is no better than being underdiversified. It can also be important to diversify money managers, the people who make decisions as to the goings on in your mutual fund. They definitely do vary in philosophy and style.

Remember also that asset mix (what percentage of your portfolio is in equities, bonds or cash and T-bills) is more important in the long term than timing. People are generally poor at knowing when to buy and when to sell. (Most of us are adept at buying high and selling low.) This is a very good reason to be sure you review your portfolio on an annual basis. Your asset mix will change as you get older and as your life circumstances change. At the very least, however, I always recommend a Canadian equity fund for long-term growth and a money market fund for more immediate needs.

VOLATILITY

Another important question to ponder is how volatile is the fund? Volatility is a very polite way of saying you could lose your money. It is a term that is synonymous with risk. Money market funds have the lowest volatility factor and specialty or sector funds have the highest. This is another way of saying stocks are more volatile than cash, like T-bills, for example (see Figure 6.3). Really volatile funds tend to do exceptionally well when there is a bull (good) market and choke when there is a bear (bad) market. Even if you are a long-term investor, you need to be concerned about the volatility rating of your fund. The chances of losing a substantial part of your investment if there is a sudden downturn in the market will be minimized.

THE FUND MANAGER

There is usually a team of people involved in managing a mutual fund but, in most cases, the final decision rests with one individual—the fund manager. Who this person is should be an important consideration in your purchase of a mutual fund. When I was selling mutual funds, there was one in particular that was consistently doing extremely well. People were calling and

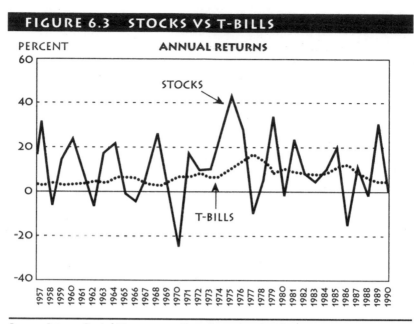

FIGURE 6.3   STOCKS VS T-BILLS

Source: Integra Capital Management Corp. Reproduced with permission.

placing orders over the phone! The manager of this fund was highly regarded and had an astounding acumen for picking winners. She was constantly in media headlines and many people invested in this fund specifically because of her. One day, she up and left and went to the competition. The mutual fund's performance since her departure has been lacklustre. Now, there could be other variables contributing to this, but you cannot ignore the importance of the person running the fund. You cannot, on the other hand, use the manager as the sole reason for investing in a fund. Long-term performance will always be an important part of the equation. When determining who the fund manager is (you can do this through your advisor or the fund's salesperson), be sure to find out how long they have been there. You want a successful long-term track record not only for the fund but for the person managing it.

But even though the managers are the experts, don't leave your financial future entirely in their hands. Don't assume they will guarantee your Italian villa at retirement. You still need to keep an eye on the fund's performance, bearing in mind the long-term nature of the investment.

LOADS AND FEES

Mutual funds were not created as a generous gesture by the investment community to give us poor, struggling novices a break. These companies are in it to make a profit. There are different types of fees associated with owning a mutual fund. They will vary widely from fund to fund so you need to develop your comparison-shopping instincts. Fees come in two categories: sales charges called loads, and administration and management fees. These fees can have a significant effect on your net rate of return.

SALES FEES

There are three types of sales charges on mutual funds. The ones you pay going in are called front-end load; those you pay coming out when you sell are called back-end load; and some funds have no load at all. A sales fee pays commission to the salesperson selling the fund. This commission covers the overhead costs of the sales person and the advice and services they provide. I never begrudge paying for any professional advice I receive. These sales charges can climb to a maximum of nine percent and most often are negotiable. There are exceptions, however.

Insurance companies will not negotiate but their commission fees are generally in the four to five percent range. You shouldn't have to pay more than five percent *anywhere*. If the sales charges are as high as nine percent, be sure you can justify that expense in your own mind. A common explanation you will hear is that you are paying for advice. You can get top-drawer advice for a lot less than nine percent. (I know because I used to give it.) Get in the habit of negotiating a lower commission, however. All the company can do is say no. Be aware that your fees will automatically go down the more money you invest with the company.

FRONT-END LOAD You pay the commission when you originally purchase the fund. If you invest $1,000 in a fund that charges five percent commission, you will only be purchasing $950 worth of fund units. The other $50 goes to pay the commission.

BACK-END LOAD These funds charge a redemption fee when you sell the fund. There is a declining back-end load which is becoming popular that enables you to pay a lower fee the longer you keep the money in the fund. Buying a fund with the back-end load is a good idea only if you plan on keeping your money in that fund for a long period. There will be no benefit if you plan to move it around.

NO-LOAD   No commission is charged going in or coming out. You buy the fund directly from the "manufacturer." Be aware, however, that the management fees with no-load mutual funds may be higher than funds with loads to cover the costs of sales. There is no such thing as a free lunch.

MANAGEMENT FEES

All funds have management fees, which can vary quite dramatically. As the investor, you need to pay for the salaries of the managers, researchers and administrative staff as well as the ongoing costs of running the business. Remember that these people do all the legal and accounting work for you as well. The idea behind mutual funds is to pool resources and this principle also applies to paying for the management of the fund. The costs of managing a fund are generally very high, but the costs are shared among the investors, so that as an individual, you pay only a small portion of the total. You pay in proportion to the size of your own investment into the fund.

Management fees are invisible to the investor. The rates of return published in the various newspapers have already taken into account these expenses. The fee structure is usually reported as a percentage of the fund's total assets. The average in Canada for equity funds is around 1.75 percent. This means that 1.75 percent of the fund's profits go directly to the managers and expenses. The remaining is what gets distributed to the investors. The management expense ratio expresses the costs of running the fund as a percentage of the total assets so you get a sense of how expensive it is. At the low end, money market funds will have an expense ratio of less than one percent of the asset value. Some international funds will charge up to three percent. If these numbers seem small to you, they're not. When you consider that mutual funds can be worth in the hundreds of millions of dollars, these fees amount to a sizable chunk.

The prospectus will tell you everything you need to know about the fund. It is illegal to sell a mutual fund without first giving the prospectus to the client. This booklet will tell you what the fund invests in, who the managers are, how much they are being paid, and what the sales and other charges are. Note that there may also be a fee for transferring funds out to another company or within the company's own family of funds. Read the prospectus carefully; it will give you the information you need. The prospectus will answer questions you didn't even know you had. It's not exactly scintillating reading, but it is mandatory nonetheless.

LOAD VERSUS NO-LOAD

When you are considering which type of fund to purchase, no-load is not necessarily the right answer. Commission should be a consideration, but ultimately the performance of the fund has to be the deciding factor. The majority of mutual funds in Canada historically have had loads, but that is beginning to shift. It seems no-load funds are gaining in popularity and will soon, if not already, equal the number of funds with loads. There is no correlation between a fund's performance and whether or not you had to pay a load to buy it. The advantage of a no-load fund, however, is that *all* of your investment (minus the management fee) is working for you.

A general rule is that if you are a savvy investor with no need for advice or have a solid awareness of what you need, look at the no-load funds. There are many excellent no-load funds especially in the money market and fixed income categories. When you get into the equity funds, however, it becomes tougher to find a quality no-load fund. The bottom line in choosing a fund is two-fold: Does the fund meet your objectives and what is its performance record. These should be your primary focus regardless of the fee structure.

WHO SHOULD I BUY FROM AND HOW?

Everyone is selling mutual funds these days. You can buy them through appropriately licensed people at your bank, trust company and insurance company. Of course there is always your stockbroker and mutual fund specialist. People who work for a bank or insurance company, or companies like Investor's Group, for example, will sell only their own family of funds. Stockbrokers and independent dealers offer a variety of choices. Though these people have access to a wider range of funds, some of the funds that are sold through a captive sales force have done quite well. No one company has a top performer in all the categories, so it is important to be sure you choose the company that offers you the best fund for your particular needs. This will be discussed in more detail in chapter 10.

There is a type of mutual fund called a *segregated fund* which is sold only by insurance companies. This fund looks and acts exactly like a mutual fund but offers what the industry calls a "money-back guarantee." If you keep your money in the fund for a minimum of 10 years, the insurance company will guarantee 75 to 100 percent of your *original* investment. They can do this because segregated funds are actually classified as an insurance policy in which the value fluctuates according to the underlying assets. There are also provisions which make these funds creditor-proof under most circumstances as long as there is a named beneficiary on the policy.

There is a need for reform in the mutual fund industry which is due in large part to the rapid growth it has experienced in the last few years. The rules governing it have not kept pace with this growth. Glorianne Stromberg, a retired securities lawyer and commissioner for the Ontario Securities Commission, has written a 256-page report to help guide the mutual fund industry through the necessary reform. The report is critical of some of the sales and distribution practices and inadequate disclosure guidelines at some companies. It suggests a strong need for improvement in education courses and standards for industry participants. This report is expected to lead to significant changes in the industry eventually, but not in the short term. In an article in *The Globe and Mail*'s Report on Business, in 1995, Ontario Securities Commission Chairman Edward Waitzer says there is no crisis in the mutual fund industry, but the industry's failure to update its practices could hinder its competitive edge and cause investors to swing to safer investment and savings products. Stromberg says that there is no urgent need for investors to pull their money out of funds and find a safe mattress as an alternative. People simply need to be far more aware of industry practices and the products they are buying. Most players in the industry support the need for reform. To get a free copy of the Stromberg report, write to: Monica Zeller, Communications Officer,

Ontario Securities Commission, 20 Queen Street West, 8th Floor, Toronto, Ontario M5H 3S8. Phone 416-593-8120.

DOLLAR COST AVERAGING

Elaine and I were having coffee in her office. I was attempting to digest all the choices I had. I was comfortable with the fact that I needed equity funds to save for my retirement. I was considering a money market fund to save for the down payment on a house. I had figured out what I was going to use for what, but I didn't have a clue how to go about getting these funds.

"Elaine," I began, "do I have to save a chunk of money before I can get into mutual funds?" I had visions of needing hundreds or even thousands of dollars before I could play in this league.

Elaine smiled patiently. "Got fifty bucks?" she inquired.

"You got me on a good day. I have fifty-two dollars."

"Can you come up with fifty dollars every month?" she asked.

"With the 'Iron Lady' as my financial advisor, that had better be the least I do," I replied.

"Then you've started your mutual fund." It was as simple as that.

You can get started in any type of mutual fund for as little as $50 a month and 15 minutes of your time. That's after you have decided what you will buy, of course. Not only will you see your investment program take shape, you will start to take advantage of a concept called dollar cost averaging. Let's say you have saved $1,200 to invest in a Canadian equity fund. You go to your institution of choice and make the deposit. If your luck is anything like mine, that will be the very day the stock market peaks and breaks all records. This also means the cost of the individual units of the fund will have gone up, so your $1,200 doesn't buy as much as if the units were valued at a lower amount.

The better approach is to take that $100 a month you were saving and put it directly into an equity fund on a monthly basis. We already know the stock market goes up and down. So one month, the value of the units might be lower than the following month. Or higher. The point is, if you put in the same amount of money every month, you are likely to end up owning more units at the end of a year than if you had made a lump sum deposit at the mercy of whatever the market looked like on that particular day. One month your $100 may buy seven units, the

TABLE 6.1 DOLLAR COST AVERAGING

As illustrated in the table below, your $600 invested over six months is now worth $662.91 – a gain of 10.5 percent.

Month	Unit Price	Units Bought	Amount Invested	Total Value
1	$13	7.692	$100	$100.00
2	$12	8.333	$100	$192.30
3	$15	6.667	$100	$340.38
4	$13	7.692	$100	$394.99
5	$14	7.143	$100	$525.38
6	$15	6.667	$100	$662.91
	Average Price	Total Units	Average Cost Per Unit	
	$13.66	44.19	$13.58	

Source: Reproduced with permission of Midland Walwyn Capital Inc.

following month it might buy eight. The month after that your $100 gets you six units and so on. On average, you will be further ahead than if you had made a single deposit. Hence the name "dollar cost averaging." (See Table 6.1.)

In a nutshell, the real reason dollar cost averaging works so well is that it forces the "buy low" part of the "buy low, sell high" equation upon you. It's only human nature to avoid in-

vesting in something that's going down in value. But that's not the way you should look at buying stocks or equity mutual funds. When they're lower in value, that's exactly when you *should* buy. Think of it this way: They're on sale!

To put dollar cost averaging into effect, all you

need to do is set up a preauthorized chequing program whereby your financial institution will take the $100 a month directly from your bank account. You simply fill out a form and give the company a "void" cheque. Usually there is a $50 a month minimum required. No muss, no fuss. Several objectives are met this way. You don't have to rely on your own initiative and discipline to make monthly payments. Since the money comes out of your account automatically, you are forced to save.

This is exactly how I set up my 10 percent "pay myself first" long-term savings program. Dollar cost averaging through PAC is also how I make my RRSP contribution to a Canadian equity fund. I divide my annual contribution by 12 and set up PAC to take that amount out each month. Not only is my RRSP contribution easily taken care of, I have also taken advantage of dollar cost averaging and started to earn a profit sooner than if I had waited until the last minute.

HOW CAN I TRACK HOW WELL MY FUND IS DOING?

I groaned at the thought of having to make sense of all those small numbers on the financial pages of the newspaper. But as usual, it proved to be far more difficult in thought than in reality. As mutual funds have become more popular, the newspapers have responded by making their reporting more accessible to the average Joe and Jane. I realized with chagrin that it took me approximately four minutes to figure out how to read the mutual funds section. The major financial newspapers such as *The Financial Post* and *The Globe and Mail* have guidelines on how to read these pages. Your financial advisor can also be helpful here. If you are computer literate, you can tap into mutual fund tracking services provided by brokerage houses and through Southam. This allows you to use your computer to keep track of your portfolio's performance through a disk which is updated monthly. You can even plug in benchmarks to see how well it is performing relative to, say, the TSE 300.

The company from which you bought your fund will send you statements (monthly if you are on PAC or quarterly) which will also tell you how the fund is faring. If you are investing for the long haul, however, don't be spooked by a bad month. There are likely to be many bad months over the span of 30 or 40 years of investing. When the statement for my Canadian equity fund (my long-term savings plan) appears each month, I give it a cursory glance to get a sense of whether it's up or down, then I mentally toss it. It's only if there is a general trend down, down, down over a long period that I might be inclined to get disturbed.

SHOULD I INVEST IN STOCKS AND BONDS DIRECTLY ON MY OWN?

In a word: sure. But not before your financial base is solidly established. Remember that mutual funds *are* a method of buying stocks, bonds, Treasury bills and real estate. You may not need to go at it directly yourself. If you do, make sure the following are in place before tackling the wilds of the market on your own:

- Have all your nondeductible debt paid off.
- Be sure your will, power of attorney and living will are set up.
- Look after your life and disability insurance needs.
- Have a proper accessible emergency fund.
- Make your maximum RRSP contribution every year.
- Once you have finally established a solid ground in mutual funds, particularly equity funds, you will have learned the general principles of how the market works. That's when it's a good time to take the plunge into the market on your own.

Investing in the stock market can be a very rewarding and exhilarating experience. You can realize more profit if you pick a stock that is a winner than you can from a mutual fund that is a winner. Because funds are diversified, you enjoy relative safety at the expense of really dramatic rates of return. However, for many including myself, the risk of the reverse happening is too high. I would never put into the stock market any money that I wasn't prepared to lose. If you have "found" money, or consider yourself a well-rounded investor, go for it, it can be a lot of fun. But make sure you have a relationship with a reputable broker who has *your* best interests at heart. Referrals from your friends and business associates are a good way to find someone you can trust.

There are ways of investing in the stock market directly that are especially appealing to the budding investor. Investment clubs are very popular. Many women have formed groups to pool their money and invest in stocks and bonds. They hold meetings to discuss their investing strategies. It is astounding how well many of these groups have done. The Canadian Shareowners Association is another excellent possibility. This is a non-profit organization that teaches you the basics of stock selection through a monthly newsletter and a library of educational materials. See the Appendix for their address.

WOMEN AS INVESTORS

Elaine and I were conversing over dinner one evening. "Why is it, Elaine, that when I talk to the most accomplished and proficient women, women who handle huge responsibilities at home and in the work force, the minute I mention the stock market or the word investing, they plead ignorance and fear? Now, what is really telling is that after I explain the fundamentals, they all, without exception, agree to the importance of investing and want to start right away. The fear evaporates and they turn into the most savvy investors I know! I think we women are far too willing to dismiss our natural expertise." I drew in a breath. "There. I'm over it now."

Elaine smiled and nodded in complete agreement. "I've noticed that as well. It might be something you want to pay attention to."

I remembered my own experience. I had had a job with serious fiscal responsibilities but was quick to admit that investing was out of my realm. This was pure, unadulterated horse-hockey. With appropriate knowledge, I have made my portfolio grow to a previously unimagined amount. While I was a financial advisor, I watched other women take tremendous pride in doing the same thing.

Over the next several years, I watched closely women's reactions to the world of investing. I saw some startling similarities in women's responses. After creating Women and Money Inc., I decided to take a more scientific approach to my study of women as in-

vestors. Through focus groups and seminars we talked to countless women to get a sense of their attitudes. There are as many different opinions as there are women who have them, but certain
patterns did emerge.

There is the beginning of some interest in the financial services
community, especially in the U.S., to determine the differences between women and men in their investing behaviours and attitudes.
I think this is an important area of study because it is made clear,
in the U.S. data and in what little research has been done in Canada,
that there are marked differences and similarities in how women
and men invest. If the financial services community wants to be sure
the needs of *all* their customers are met, it is in their best interest
to understand what makes women and men different and what
makes us the same—in investing, that is. For far too long, women
have been considered a secondary market, if they have been considered at all. Dealing with the women's market based on the male
model simply has not and will not work.

The problem with much of the research is that the surveys
were done in an attempt to prove an already established conclusion. Our research people took the North American studies
and put together a comprehensive report based on *everyone's*
findings, including our own. We then sent it to an independent research house that specializes in the Canadian financial services
market—Brendan Wood International—to attempt to Canadianize
and validate the information. The things we wanted to know included: Just how different are women and men in investing? What
are the stereotypes and what are the facts? Are women better at
investing than men? Are men better? Is there any difference at
all? Are women more conservative and afraid of risk than men?
What is women's general knowledge level of investing? Why do
so many women not see themselves as investors? What are
women's primary financial concerns? Are they different than
men's? Who makes the investing decisions in Canadian households? Do women need a different type of financial planning
strategy than men? What percentage of women who purchase
mutual funds also invest directly in the stock market?

These were just a few of the questions we put to the experts.
Combining their knowledge with our own research efforts, we
came up with some very interesting conclusions.[20] In the Brendan
Wood study, more women in households earning $35,000 to

$49,000 responded as co-equal chief financial decision maker. There was no difference at other income levels from the base rate of 54 percent male decision maker and 46 percent female decision maker. Single women in this sample were more likely to be divorced or widowed than single men (47 percent to 33 percent). There were no educational differences between single women and single men; nevertheless, the single women had lower incomes than the single men. Both single women and men saved or invested the same amount on an annual basis. Finally, the Brendan Wood study showed that single women switched or added mutual fund managers more often than men. The per annum rates were 33 percent and 26 percent respectively.

Women have the same financial worries and goals as men. Their reasons for saving and investing include:

- Income for retirement.
- Reduction or deferral of taxes.
- Desire for financial independence.
- Protection against inflation.
- Freedom to work or play when desired.
- Cushion in case of unexpected expenses.
- Provision of an estate for heirs.
- Desire to make money more quickly.
- Supplement to current income.
- Protection against unexpected threats to income or assets.

There is little difference between women's and men's attitudes toward investing on the following points:

- The best way to make money is to change investments as soon as performance starts to decline. Only 23 percent of the women and men surveyed believe this to be true.
- The best thing you can do is to buy a mix of investments that fits your needs, then stick with them. Seventy-seven percent of women went along with this.
- Good fund performance is more important than investment philosophy. Fifty-two percent of women and men agreed.
- Fifty-three percent of the women wished they could get better advice about the kinds of investments they should buy, though

they had a generally more favourable view of financial institutions than men did.

Regarding knowledge and risk:

- Men were more likely to say they understood financial planning than women were.

- Women rated their knowledge of financial products *lower* than men on 11 out of the 15 products that were rated: stocks, money market funds, stock funds, mortgage funds, balanced funds, segregated funds, sectoral or specialty funds, asset allocation funds, U.S. funds, global equity funds and global bond funds.

- Women rated their knowledge of the following financial products the *same* as men: term deposits, bonds, mortgage-backed securities, bond funds, GICs, mortgages, property and casualty insurance, personal lines of credit, and whole, universal and term life insurance.

- Despite the usual relationship between perceived knowledge and perceived risk, there were *no differences* in risk ratings for any of the 15 products.

- Men had more difficulty understanding disability insurance than women did (27 percent of men versus 19 percent of women).

- To better understand what "risk" meant to the respondents, Brendan Wood International asked them to rate six types of risk in terms of the importance to them. Five out of the six definitions of risk were ranked identically by women and men: short-term earnings, long-term earnings, loss of original investment, loss of investment gains and the possibility that another investment earns more.

- Women viewed swings in investment earnings as a substantially more important element of risk than men, although the rank order of risk elements was the same. Volatility was considered a highly important part of risk by 37 percent of the women and 25 percent of the men. Interestingly, volatility is the way that investment managers themselves define risk.

- Men review their investment portfolio performance more often than women. Some 64 percent of men review their portfolio every three to six months compared to 54 percent of women.

In choosing a mutual fund supplier, women attach greater importance to:

- One-time fees for buying the fund (front-end load).
- Ongoing management fees and expenses.
- Safety of their original investment.
- Convenience.

In choosing a mutual fund supplier, women and men attach equal importance to:

- Rate of return.
- Fees for early redemption (back-end load).
- Quality of service.
- Overall reputation.

There were no gender-specific preferences for any particular mutual fund supplier.

Service delivery areas that women judged more important than men:

- Accuracy of administration.
- Quality of communication with unitholders.
- Cost of management and administration.
- Ease of administration (sign-up, deposits and changes).
- Provision of other financial services besides mutual funds.
- Predictable rate of return.

The remaining service delivery areas (seven out of 13) were viewed as equally important by women and men:

- Speed of service.
- Ability to resolve customer problems.
- Handling of customer enquiries.
- Good rate of return.
- Telephone access to service representatives. (The rating was higher if the women were life insurance clients.)
- Quality of account statements.
- Variety of investment options.

Women typically have higher service expectations than men. They also express a higher degree of satisfaction with the service they receive. This is quite ironic considering that the financial industry has historically been remiss in its treatment of women as clients. Men tended to care about financial soundness whereas women felt personal attention was their most important priority.

Four other noteworthy conclusions were:

- Single men view rate of return as more important than single women.

- Despite viewing rate of return as less important than men, single women are less satisfied with their investment returns than men. Men were more likely to build up capital in order to gain income than women were.

- Women view the availability of a range of financial services as more important than men.

- Women were more likely to put money away for reasons of threats to income or loss of property.

- Women were more willing to buy insurance from banks.

- In order to make a large purchase, i.e. a house or car, women were more likely to save than men.

- Women are more likely to want more information and are more interested in how to use mutual funds to achieve their financial objectives. Men are less interested than women in gathering information. Women are predisposed to create an orderly plan to achieve their financial objectives.

Another interesting study commissioned by accounting firm Ernst & Young and done by Angus Reid shows how important mutual funds have become in the savings mix for Canadians. Thirty-eight percent of the people surveyed have purchased mutual funds and for those that haven't, half cite no money to invest as the main reason. A significant number (49 percent) said they would be interested in investing in mutual funds in the future. This indicates that the rapid growth the industry has been experiencing could likely continue. Other reasons for not owning funds were "do not have good understanding (18 percent)" and "prefer to put my savings in other options (10 percent)."

It makes sense that mutual funds were purchased in large numbers (41 percent) by people in the $30,000 – $60,000 income range. People seem to be looking for ways to diversify their savings. The survey also found, not surprisingly, that the top two reasons for purchasing funds were 1) safe way to invest in the market and 2) the financial returns. It also seemed that the number one influence in deciding whether to buy a fund was the financial advisor, followed by information on the fund's performance. This is why it's so important to have a reputable financial advisor whom you trust. People have come to expect a high level of service from the fund managers as well.

This survey showed that women were less likely to purchase mutual funds than men though no reasons were cited as to why. It is also compelling to note that my kindred folk down east in the Atlantic provinces, as well as people in Quebec, are less likely than folks in the rest of the provinces to purchase mutual funds. Go figure.

There are many stereotypes concerning women and money. Two frequently encountered ones are that women are afraid of risk and that they love to spend money. Neither is necessarily true. Since women want more information, they tend to be more careful before acting. This is not to say they won't dive into riskier investments. They will and they do if they have all the facts. Because of this desire for information, women make fewer investment mistakes than men do. Also, women are not afraid to admit when they don't know something. These two traits provide a good basis for developing investing savvy. As for loving to spend money, some women do, some don't. Women are expected to do the shopping for the entire household, then find themselves stereotyped as shopoholics.

When women are referred to as "risk-averse," there is the suggestion that they will only invest in GICs and Canada Savings Bonds. What risk-averse really means is that women don't expect their money to double overnight.

Part of the problem is that women don't see themselves

"Women want more information."

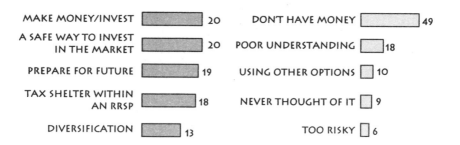

FIGURE 6.4 MUTUAL FUND PURCHASE (JUNE 1995)

(A) REASONS FOR PURCHASING OR NOT PURCHASING MUTUAL FUNDS

MAIN REASONS FOR INVESTING (%)   MAIN REASONS FOR NOT INVESTING (%)

MAKE MONEY/INVEST	20	DON'T HAVE MONEY	49
A SAFE WAY TO INVEST IN THE MARKET	20	POOR UNDERSTANDING	18
PREPARE FOR FUTURE	19	USING OTHER OPTIONS	10
TAX SHELTER WITHIN AN RRSP	18	NEVER THOUGHT OF IT	9
DIVERSIFICATION	13	TOO RISKY	6

(B) INCIDENCE OF MUTUAL FUND PURCHASE

HAVE YOU EVER PURCHASED A
MUTUAL FUND?

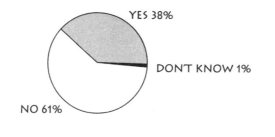

YES 38%

DON'T KNOW 1%

NO 61%

---

as investors. I know I sure didn't. Though women are sophisticated consumers, there is often a psychological barrier to investing. One out of every four men invests in the stock market,
but only one in eight women does. This is changing as women
begin to earn more and become more financially literate. The
rise of mutual funds as a form of investing is also having an impact. And the financial services community is beginning to take
steps to address women investors. Women-oriented seminars and

FIGURE 6.4 MUTUAL FUND PURCHASE (JUNE 1995) (CONT'D)

(C) INTEREST IN PURCHASING A MUTUAL FUND

HAVE YOU EVER BEEN
INTERESTED IN PURCHASING A
MUTUAL FUND?

ASPECTS MOST LIKELY TO INFLUENCE
DECISION TO PURCHASE FUND (%)

NO 70%

YES 30%

ADVICE FROM ADVISOR 47

PAST PERFORMANCE 38

QUARTERLY STATEMENT 9

TOLL-FREE SERVICE 4

(D) INCIDENCE OF MUTUAL FUND PURCHASE BY DEMOGRAPHICS

% PURCHASED MUTUAL FUNDS

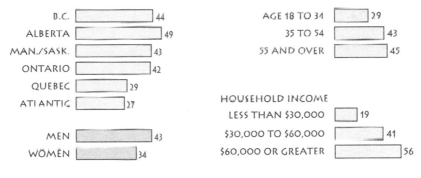

B.C. 44	AGE 18 TO 34 29
ALBERTA 49	35 TO 54 43
MAN./SASK. 43	55 AND OVER 45
ONTARIO 42	
QUEBEC 29	
ATLANTIC 27	HOUSEHOLD INCOME
	LESS THAN $30,000 19
MEN 43	$30,000 TO $60,000 41
WOMEN 34	$60,000 OR GREATER 56

Source: Reproduced from an Angus Reid Survey with permission of Ernst & Young.

marketing and advertising programs are making headway in over-
coming the perceptual problems women have in seeing themselves as investors.

THE GOLDEN YEARS

> *"Retirement means twice as much husband on half as much money."*
>
> My Grandmother

I was on my way to another session with Elaine. I started to think about the tremendous progress I was making in understanding personal finance. I was actually beginning to feel downright cocky. "Today," I thought to myself as I took the elevator up to the 26th floor, "the roof could fall in on my house, I could break a leg rollerblading or die in a daring rescue attempt and my financial affairs would be in order. Looking to the future, I'll be able to buy that cottage with my 10 percent savings or retire exceedingly wealthy. Life is so much less nerve-racking this way."

I had also begun to notice that the very vocal committee which had taken up permanent residence in my head was beginning to quiet down. The fast and furious internal debates brought on by anxiety about money were lessening to a noteworthy degree. Being financially organized resulted in some blessed relief from the interminable chatter going on in my brain.

Meanwhile, back at the ranch, Elaine was about to attempt another psychological breakthrough with me. She was going to try to get my head out of today and into the future—like, 35 years into the future. Considering that my definition of "thinking about the future" was deciding what to have for dinner, she had a daunting task ahead of her. As I settled into one of the comfortable armchairs, Elaine asked me one of her characteristically tough questions, one which I have subsequently asked many women. "Joanne, what is your greatest fear?"

"That Lance will find out about Steed," I said mischievously. This reply met with the standard lack of appreciation of my rapier wit. "Uh, that's not what you meant. OK, I would have to say being financially dependent on someone else, including the government. The general scuttlebutt is that Canada and Quebec Pension Plan will be a vague memory by the time I reach 65. Even if it isn't, it won't come close to supporting me in the lifestyle I plan on becoming accustomed to. As I understand it, it provides barely a meager existence now. The reality is, Elaine, I don't want to end up a bag lady—even if the bags are from Holt Renfrew."

Elaine nodded in agreement. "Too many women, particularly women our mother's age, married their retirement plan. The truth is that people die and people leave you. You need to be in complete control of your own financial present and future. It is my belief that retirement planning should start no later than age 30 if it is to remain painless. You're only a year behind. Ensuring your retirement dream starts today."

"Retirement planning?!" I exclaimed. "I'm just getting used to seeing a positive balance in my bank account. You want me to jump ahead and start to plan for something 35 years away?" I was incredulous.

"Get used to it, kiddo," Elaine replied. "Besides a house, your retirement is going to be the most expensive thing you will have to pay for. Remember, we want compound interest to do much of the work for you. In order for that to happen, you need time. And lots of it. Look at the priority pyramid. RRSPs are your next step. Actually, you take this step at the same time as or before you start your 10 percent savings plan, depending on your financial situation. In reality, Joanne, the entire base of the pyramid should be set up simultaneously. At the same time that you start your emergency fund, you should be starting your retirement fund."

I couldn't get over it. I was 31 years old trying to figure out how I wanted to live 35 years later. I had a hard enough time figuring what I wanted to do for the weekend. Still, I knew I had to follow Elaine's advice if for no other reason than that I was afraid of her. She had gotten me thinking. Visions of many women I knew intimately came to mind. I knew a dozen women who were over 65 who struggled for even their most basic requirements. My own mother will have a challenging time ahead of her. One of my closest friends is a 72-year-old woman who must work to stay financially afloat. She was a traditional stay-at-home mother who raised five children. Her husband died after a long, protracted illness, leaving her nothing. Not exactly an appropriate reward for her life's work. Maybe retirement planning at my age wasn't so far-fetched after all.

It wasn't until I had talked to hundreds of women of all ages as a financial advisor that I really began to understand the soundness of an early start. Though it is never too late, the earlier the better. Almost every woman I talked to shared the same concern: being poor at retirement. The comment I heard most frequently was, "I don't want to become a bag lady." Women need to be acutely aware of the reality of what their lives could be like when they get older. It's not a pretty picture. It is alarming to see that statistically, the older many women get, the poorer they are liable to be. Many of these bag ladies whom we so often

Reprinted with permission from *The Globe and Mail.*

glibly refer to are wives and mothers who were left destitute by the death of their spouse or abandonment by spouse or family. At the turn of the century, Elizabeth Cady Stanton astutely pointed out: "Woman will always be dependent until she holds a purse of her own." The statistics show that women haven't been able to follow this advice.

According to Statistics Canada, by age 65, fully one-third of women living in Canada are living alone. Compare this to 13.6 percent of men over 65 who live alone. My mother works with senior citizens in the Ottawa area. She shocked me one day when she told me that three out of four nursing home residents are women. Women over 85 comprise nearly 70 percent of the total population in these homes. At this end of the age spectrum, it is literally a woman's world. Half of these women have incomes averaging $19,396. This is only 60 percent of the average elderly man's income. Because of women's longer life span it is entirely possible that their retirement will last longer than their careers. This can be quite a problem because many women don't earn enough to be able to save for retirement. Women are still predominantly responsible for both child and home care which means they must often work in the service sector or that part of the labour force which allows for occasional work. These jobs typically do not provide pensions and pay significantly less than the average income that men receive. Even in the professions, such as law, women are frequently paid less for the same job. Of women who are already retired, 80 percent are not eligible for pension benefits.

TABLE 7.1	AVERAGE EARNINGS BY MARITAL STATUS, WOMEN AND MEN AGED 45–54, 1990	
Marital Status	Women	Men
Single	$30,756	$35,116
Married	25,059	43,350
Other	31,161	42,198
Total	26,501	42,847

Source: Reprinted with permission, Status of Women Canada.

TABLE 7.2	WOMEN'S MEMBERSHIP IN EMPLOYER PENSION PLANS*						
	1982	1984	1986	1988	1989	1990	1992
Number of Pension Plan Members (thousands)	1,477	1,525	1,621	1,763	1,869	1,981	2,189
Percentage of Total Labour Force	30.4	30.1	30.2	31.0	31.9	33.1	35.3
Percentage of All Employed Workers	36.2	37.3	37.0	37.2	37.8	39.0	42.5

* An age breakdown is not available for these data.
Source: Reprinted with permission, Status of Women Canada.

There are financial penalties affecting women's retirement that derive from the fact that we are the child bearers. RRSPs, Canada and Quebec Pension Plan and private company pensions (which are only available to people in the paid labour force) are diminished or, worse, eliminated while you are off having children since they are income based. Women have this fact as well as the actual interrupted earnings to contend with. If you look at the situation of a woman in the paid labour force as compared to that of her husband, you will see quite a difference in the C/QPP payout. Let us take, for example, the case of a woman who earns less and has lost five years in total due to child rearing. Her C/QPP at age 65 will be $345.39 per month. His will be $543.06.[21] (The contributory period for Canada Pension Plan is based on earnings between 18 and retirement age. It is important to note, however, that the months of zero or low earnings while caring for a child under the age of seven are excluded or dropped out in calculating pension benefits. This can positively affect the benefit paid to some mothers since the low to no income earning years won't pull down the overall average. The mothers who work in the home after the child is seven will not benefit from the drop out. This system tries to balance out some of the inequities women experience as the primary caregivers. For that matter, with anyone who experiences periods of zero or low earnings, up to 15 percent of that person's contributory period may be dropped out in calculating the retirement pension. This 15 percent drop-out feature does not replace, but is actually in addition to, the child rearing drop-out provision.) Although these two contributors worked in the same industry, the woman's contributions were erratic because of child rearing. Also, because she earned less than her husband, her contributions were less. As you can see, the effect on her pension is dramatic. Women also leave the work force more frequently, not only because of child rearing, but to relocate with their husbands. It is very sobering to see how interrupted careers can severely affect your pension payout.

A Registered Retirement Savings Plan is an option for anyone who earns an income but the amount you can sock away depends on how much you make. Since women on average earn less, they have smaller RRSPs. The good news is that women comprise the fastest growing group in Canada taking advantage of RRSPs. According to Statistics Canada, in 1979 women contributed 700 million dollars to RRSPs. In 1993, that had increased to nearly 6.6 billion.

The other factor which may have a negative effect on retirement planning is divorce. For the most part, women fare much worse financially after divorce than men do. The divorce rate is close to one out of every three marriages. Statistics Canada recently released a report based on tax returns that shows that fewer than 20 percent of single-parent families, of which two-thirds are women, receive financial support from their departed partner. Sixty percent of single-parent families live below the poverty line. How do these women plan for retirement? They don't. They are too busy trying to stay above water.

The reality can be pretty grim for many older women. But the news isn't all bad. Women today who are approaching retirement are healthier and more affluent than they were even 10 years ago. They are certainly in a better economic position than the previous generation of women. Women are beginning to gain significant economic power since they are working long enough to be entitled to some pension benefits. Their longer life span can also mean ultimate control over the family's assets, if there are any. Women are beginning to grow older in a financially more active and positive way. Statistics Canada says the number of women receiving the full Guaranteed Income Supplement benefit, which is for people with little or no income, fell 50 percent between 1979 and 1989. The number of women receiving Canada and Quebec Pension Plan benefits, which are based on earned income, rose from 22 percent to 45 percent between 1979 and 1989. As shown in Table 7.3 below, this is mainly because of the growth in the number of women in the paid work force. In 1979, fewer than 14 percent of the women who paid income tax contributed to an RRSP. By 1993, that rate had increased to 36 percent. The percentage of women participating in company pension plans (Registered pension plans or RPPs) also increased four percentage points to 36 percent during the same time period.[22]

The older women of the future will have much more financial savvy and be more knowledgeable about money than many older women are now. Society is beginning to encourage women to think and talk about money. The old adages "Never talk about money. It isn't lady-like" or "Money is toxic and immoral" are, thankfully, dead and buried. If she were alive today, my grandmother would be having a tough go in her retirement. My mother will also be challenged, but her situation is a shade better than was her mother's. At least Mom recognizes where the buck stops. As for me, I have no intention of depending on anyone, Lance or the government, to ensure that I will live with dignity and integrity in my twilight years. Fortunately, I have many more options than the previous generations of women in my family, and for that I am thankful.

TABLE 7.3	LABOUR FORCE PARTICIPATION OF WOMEN			
	1961 age 15–24	1971 age 25–34	1981 age 35–44	1991 age 45–54
Total Population ('000)	1,450	1,422	1,462	1,457
Number in Work Force ('000)	565	579	943	1,018
Participation Rate %	39.0	40.7	64.5	69.9

Source: Reprinted with permission, Status of Women Canada.

In looking at my own family, I see the trend line moving in a positive direction. My grandmother Pearl was a full-time mother and homemaker right up to the day she died at age 70. She was never able to qualify for QPP (she lived in Quebec) since she hadn't received an income for her labour at home. (QPP is essentially the same as CPP except that the Quebec government administers the pension plan for its workers whereas the federal government administers the plan for the rest of the country.) Pearl certainly didn't have a private company pension plan and she depended almost entirely on my grandfather for her retirement needs. At 65 she did receive a small sum from the Old Age Security program, but that basically was it.

Now my mother, who represents the next generation, has fared somewhat better. Though Mom stayed at home until she was 40 before taking her first paid full-time job outside of the home, she will be able to receive some Canada Pension Plan benefit. It won't be much since she was in the paid labour force for a much shorter time and was paid far less than was my father, for example. My mother is able to take advantage of RRSPs, but cannot contribute much because her income is low. But it will help. She is in the middle generation between women like my grandmother who are living below the poverty line because of non-existent retirement planning options and women of my generation who are beginning to have significantly more control, income and choices. I will qualify for CPP providing it's still around when I retire. Because I work in the paid labour force there is a better chance that I have access to, or could have in the future, a company pension plan. (At this time I am self-employed so I don't have access to a company plan.) I can also make RRSP contributions. I earn more money and have been in the work force longer than my mother. These factors will have a favourable impact on what my retirement will look like. As we will see later, women still have a long way to go, but things are definitely looking up.

THE RETIREMENT CHOICES

There are three principal sources of retirement income in Canada—the government, your company and you. There is a great debate going on at the moment as to whether the government will even be part of the picture by the time the baby boomers reach retirement age and get through and exhaust the system. The odds are that if you were born after 1950, you will have to count exclusively on your own resources for a secure retirement. It is estimated that in the year 2015, six million Canadians will reach 65. That's a lot of baby boomers hitting retirement age at once. It is expected that Canada's social welfare system is going to be greatly affected by this wave and that it will be hit the hardest between the years 2015 and 2045.

Many of our existing social programs were developed during the time when Canada was experiencing high birth rates, from the beginning of the baby boom after the Second World War up to the '60s. Because of costly benefit enhancements over the years and a subsequent baby bust, the cost of continuing to provide C/QPP is going to have to rise dramatically over the next 30 to 40 years. One factor that has helped keep the cost of C/QPP from escalating through the roof is women's relatively recent increased participation in the labour force. They have added a whole new raft of contributors to the C/QPP net and they are still too young to be drawing off any of the benefits. At this point, the contributions they make are higher than the cost of paying the benefits.

The Canadian Institute of Actuaries states in a report called *Canadian Retirement Income Social Security Programs* that C/QPP offers important advantages that should provide an incentive for Canadians to keep it around. The report says C/QPP offers "virtually full coverage of the working population." (My grandmother and mother who worked unpaid in the home might object to not being considered part of the so-called "working population." Watching soaps and eating bon-bons were not high on their list of priorities.) The report goes on to explain that the benefits are portable and indexed against inflation as well as having relatively low administrative costs. But here is the basis of the C/QPP controversy: In 1994, the combined employee/employer C/QPP contribution level was 5.2 percent of your earnings up to $34,400. By the year 2035, it is estimated that the C/QPP contribution will rise to 13.25 percent.[23] Will Canadians be prepared to pay this? Only time will tell. If they are, then C/QPP should continue.

Nevertheless, it has always been my advice that you should never count on the government's ability to fund your retirement. One thing is for sure, C/QPP is not likely to be around in its present form. Government-sponsored pension plans only provide a small part of your total retirement income, on average 39 percent, as the Canadian Institute of Actuaries' report points out. C/QPP was a much better deal for our grandparents and parents than it will be for baby boomers and those younger. A recent study done by the QPP Actuary is quite interesting. He concluded that a male born in 1920 would receive benefits worth seven times what was contributed on his behalf. A man born in 1960 would receive benefits with a value of 2.6 times the total contributions. A male contributor born in 1980 could, at best, expect to break even. The actuary also projected that someone born in the year 2000 would receive only 80 percent of the value of total projected contributions. It is a good idea to plan for your retirement as though government benefits won't be an option for you. If C/QPP is around, consider the income you receive from it as gravy.

A quick, easy guideline is that you need to set aside 15 to 18 percent of your salary for 35 years. Increase that to 20 percent, if you are like most people and haven't started thinking of retirement planning until your 45th birthday. Don't panic. This does include your RRSP and company pension plan contribution. If you are using your house as part of a retirement plan, its value can be included as well. The ideal is to be sure you will have 70 to 80 percent of your current income coming in and sustained during the length of your retirement to maintain your existing standard of living. This is no small feat. The following are your possible sources of retirement income to ensure your future security.

OLD AGE SECURITY

Established in 1952, Old Age Security is a universal program that applies to everyone, whether they work in the paid labour force or not. The Old Age Security program consists of the Old Age Security pension, the Guaranteed Income Supplement (GIS) and the Spousal Pension Allowance (SPA).

The OAS pension is for anyone over 65 who is a resident of Canada (subject to length of residence). The GIS is for people receiving OAS who have little or no income. The SPA is given to spouses aged 60 to 64 of OAS pensioners or to widows or widowers whose family income does not exceed a certain limit. You do not have to be a member of the paid labour force to qualify for these plans.

Despite pension reforms to programs such as RRSPs, women still rely to a large extent on the government for their retirement needs. Government programs such as Old Age Security and the Guaranteed Income Supplement are extremely important for women in the unpaid labour force or who have only sporadic paid employment. The maximum amount available from these two programs is considerably below the poverty line for an individual. Based on current increases in the Consumer Price Index, in 1994 the maximum OAS benefit is $4,647 a year. At best, these plans reflect only 14 percent of the average annual lifetime earnings. The GIS maximum is $3,597 a year for a married person and $5,523 for someone who is single. For single elderly women, OAS and GIS make up 40 percent of their total income. The comparable figure for single elderly men is 25 percent. For those at or below the poverty line, OAS and GIS represent 75 percent of their total income; this figure increases to 87 percent when you factor in C/QPP. When your income reaches a certain level (over $53,215), you have to start paying your OAS back at tax time. Full repayment of the benefit is required when your income exceeds $83,800. This is what is referred to as a *clawback*.

CANADA/QUEBEC PENSION PLAN

You contribute to these plans according to your earnings. You must be salaried or self-employed, aged 18 to 70, and have an annual income that exceeds a minimum threshold which is adjusted each year. It is important to note that while Canada Pension Plan provides for mandatory credit-splitting upon divorce, this splitting is not automatic. Historically, fewer than one in 20 divorced women ever exercise their legal right to their share of their ex's C/QPP credits. This failure to claim what is rightfully theirs was the result of a lack of education. The story is much different today. It's nearly 100 percent today because of greater awareness.

REGISTERED PENSION PLANS

These are tax-advantaged plans and are available to you through your company.

REGISTERED RETIREMENT SAVINGS PLANS

These are privately-owned pension plans which you control. RRSPs came into being in 1957 and were designed to help those people who don't have a pension plan through work.

REGISTERED PENSION PLANS

Employer-sponsored pension plans are far from homogeneous.
Some are very generous, some are not. Pension plans are far more
prevalent in some industries than in others, and are more common
in the public than in the private sector. Full-time and unionized
workers are much more likely to have pension plans than those
who are part-time and non-unionized. Big companies offer pension plans more frequently than do small- to medium-sized companies. We begin to see, then, why women do not do as well at
being covered by an employer-sponsored plan as men do. Women
concentrate more in the business and service sectors that typically

TABLE 7.4   PENSION COVERAGE BY INDUSTRY, 1992

(Pension plan members compared with the number of employed paid workers in each industrial sector)

Industry	Employed paid workers*	Pension plan members	Coverage %
Agriculture and Other Primary Industries	728,000	116,787	16.0
Manufacturing	1,865,000	992,745	53.2
Construction	695,000	321,945	46.3
Transportation and Communication	916,000	444,495	48.5
Trade	2,169,000	451,640	20.8
Finance, Insurance, and Real Estate	760,000	348,867	45.9
Community, Business, and Personal Service	4,376,000	908,645	20.8
Public Administration	832,000	1,731,665**	100.0

Source: Reprinted with permission, Status of Women Canada.

Note: These data should be interpreted with caution due to the limitations in
the allocation of multi-industry plans. They are presented here only as an indication of comparative coverage in different sectors.

* Excludes self-employed (unincorporated business) and unpaid family workers.
** Pension plan members include armed forces personnel, although they are not
included in labour force data.

don't offer pension coverage and women are far more likely to work part-time. Even though the coverage rate in these areas is only 20 percent, the increase in employment in these areas increased 40 percent in the 10-year period between 1981 and 1991. This increase reflects the trend of women entering the work force at a significant rate in these particular sectors. On the other hand, during the same time period, significant job losses occurred in manufacturing and other industries that have always had high pension plan coverage.[24] The world is indeed changing.

That is why group and individual RRSPs have experienced such dramatic growth in recent years. They provide a way to compensate for the inadequacy of pension coverage. The late '80s did bring about certain long-awaited and significant pension reforms. One of the most significant changes is that pension benefit legislation has now expanded the definition of spouse to include a common-law spouse for the purpose of designating survivor benefits.

Traditionally, there have been two main types of company pension plans: 1) defined benefit and 2) defined contribution plans.

DEFINED BENEFIT PLANS

This type of company pension plan is the most common. It promises to pay a specific amount of pension income based on your years of service to the company and how much money you earned. A typical example might be as follows: Your employer pays you two percent × the number of years you have been on the plan × the average of your best three to five years of earnings. Let's say you have been with Bell Canada as a telephone operator for 30 years. Your best three years of income averaged $30,000. Using the above formula, your pension will be $18,000 a year. You figure this out by taking two percent times 30 years, which comes to 60 percent of $30,000.

Sometimes these pension plans are indexed, which means they attempt to keep up with cost of living increases (inflation). You should also check to see if your (or your partner's) pension plan has survivor benefits. If you die, wouldn't it be appropriate for your partner to continue receiving at least a portion of your pension? Survivor benefits are often worth only 60 percent of the original pension.

DEFINED CONTRIBUTION PLANS

These plans are also known as money purchase plans. You and your employer make a specific contribution to an account each year based on your earnings. What you have accumulated over the years through these contributions and the interest they generate is what you use to buy your pension. Your income is actually unknown until the day you retire.

There used to be only these two choices. Nowadays, companies are becoming infinitely more flexible and are beginning to offer one, the other, a hybrid of both, or none at all. The idea behind this new-found flexibility is to give people more room to contribute to their RRSPs. With RRSP contribution levels going up so much (they have doubled in the last few years), people want the freedom to control their own pension planning. Some employers will set up a group RRSP in lieu of a pension plan. A group RRSP is essentially a combination of individual RRSPs. Under these plans a single trust or contract is established for employees of a company. Individual RRSP contracts are registered for all participants but their contributions are pooled and invested accordingly.

Here are some key questions to ask when investigating if you have a pension at work and, if so, what kind:

1. Is the plan comprehensive enough to include benefit indexing? Will it attempt to keep pace with inflation?

2. What happens in the following situations: you die, your partner dies, you divorce, you retire early, you become disabled or you quit or are terminated? It can be quite a shock to the system to discover that since you decided to retire at 55, you now get only 50 percent of the pension. Or your spouse dies and you discover that 60 percent of his pension isn't enough to live on. Almost half (46 percent) of the men who participate in pension plans are in plans that have no reduction to benefits to the surviving spouse. It's a good policy to know for sure. Also, be sure to find out if you can take the pension with you if you quit or are terminated.

3. If your company offers a variety of plans, ask if you can transfer between plans and how often.

4. Usually you have to be with a company for two years before you are eligible for the pension plan. As part of your initial

negotiations for employment, you might consider asking if you can join the pension plan right away.

REGISTERED RETIREMENT SAVINGS PLANS

After doing some research, it was easy to conclude that Elaine was right about the prohibitive cost of retiring. "O.K. Let's do it then," I said to her shortly after our retirement discussion. Quite frankly, I wasn't entirely sure what *it* was.

Elaine picked up the ball. "What we need to do is start an RRSP for you. As a self-employed person, you don't have access to a company pension plan so you are on your own. That's why RRSPs exist in the first place, to give people like you a chance to secure your future. They are like personal pension plans. What type would you like it to be? I have a suggestion, but you go first."

Puzzled, I replied, "Type? Like it to be? Like what to be?"

"Your RRSP," Elaine stated matter of factly.

"Oh, brother," I thought. "Are we back to the running shoe school of finance again? I have to choose a type?!" I finally answered, "Elaine, I thought when you bought an RRSP, you bought an RRSP. You have lost me here. What do you mean by *type?*"

Like thousands of other unsuspecting Canadians, I fell into the trap of assuming an RRSP is a product unto itself. I was quick to learn that it is not. The key component in *registered retirement savings plan* is the word *plan*. You can open more than one. In fact, it is advisable to diversify your RRSP portfolio just as you do with the other elements of your financial plan. You also get to pick and choose from a variety of investments what you will put into your RRSP. The investments you can choose from include daily interest savings accounts, guaranteed investment certificates, mutual funds, a variety of bonds including Canada Savings Bonds, municipal, provincial and federal bonds, treasury bills and certain types of mortgages, including your own (if certain conditions are met). You can also have limited partnership units that are available on Canadian stock exchanges, certain warrants and bankers' acceptances, shares of a qualified small business corporation up to a limit of 100 percent of your RRSP, debt instruments issued by public corporations not listed on

Canadian stock exchanges, and debt instruments of foreign governments. There are other options that you can discuss with your financial advisor.

Once you have made your decision as to which investment or investments you want inside your RRSP, you fill out a form with your financial advisor, if the advisor sells financial products, or at the financial institution of your choice. This form will be identical to the form you would fill out if you were buying a regular GIC, mutual fund or opening a daily interest savings account. The only difference is that when you get to the box that says, "Do you wish this plan to be registered?," you check off *yes*. If you say yes, your GIC now becomes part of your RRSP. Now that it is part of your RRSP or, as we say in the business, *registered*, you get to enjoy watching your investment grow in value and you don't have to pay any tax on that interest. If the plan wasn't registered but was just a regular GIC or daily interest savings account, you would have to pay tax on the interest it earned every single year whether or not you cashed in the GIC. If you don't pay tax on an investment until you cash it in, presumably years down the road, you will end up with much more money in your pocket than if you pay tax on it every April. This is why it is important to defer your taxes whenever you can. The retirement income option you choose after collapsing your RRSP will determine when the money will be taxed.

The way it works is pretty simple. If you are in a 50 percent tax bracket (for simple math purposes) and have $1,000 in a GIC earning 10 percent interest (again for simple math), you will earn $100 in interest in a year. But because your tax bracket is what it is, you will have to give $50 of that $100 interest to our friends at Revenue Canada. Therefore, the following year you will be investing only $1,050 since you had to pay $50 in tax on the interest. Now, if that $1,000 GIC were in an RRSP, you wouldn't have to pay tax on the interest until you cashed the RRSP out at retirement. The entire $100 of interest will be reinvested the following year. In other words, you will be investing $1,100 instead of $1,050. Even though you will have to pay tax on the investment at whatever rate your tax bracket is when you collapse (cash in) your RRSP, you will be much further ahead than if you had paid tax on the interest every year, even if you are still in a 50 percent tax bracket. The fact that the interest is tax sheltered is one reason why an RRSP is an essential part of your tax and retirement planning.

You can also put mutual funds inside your RRSP. They work much the same as other investments, but because most mutual funds are already tax advantaged, the reasons for having them in a tax-sheltered retirement savings plan are different than the reasons for having a GIC, for example, in your RRSP. Perhaps it seems redundant to put an investment that is already receiving tax-favoured treatment into a tax shelter. But remember that guaranteed products like GICs don't experience the growth one needs in the long run to counterbalance the impact of inflation and taxes. Even though the interest on your guaranteed investments will accumulate tax sheltered, balanced funds and, in particular, equity funds can provide a more significant growth opportunity. The idea behind an RRSP is long term: to provide for retirement. Equity funds are also long term. It seems to me they form a perfect marriage since their goals are essentially the same. Ideally, what people need is to do both: have a portion of their RRSP portfolio in equity mutual funds for maximum growth potential *and* invest in equity mutual funds outside their RRSP, say, in their 10 percent savings plan, to take further advantage of the tax benefit these funds offer. If you have only a limited amount of money to invest, putting equity mutual funds inside your RRSP definitely makes sense.

Eighty percent of the stocks and bonds that make up an equity fund in your RRSP have to be Canadian. This rule is in place because it's a *Canadian* tax break you're getting. Be sure that

TABLE 7.5 ACCUMULATED VALUE OF ANNUAL RRSP CONTRIBUTIONS OF $1,000 INVESTED AT DIFFERENT RATES OF RETURN				
	After 10 Years	After 15 Years	After 20 Years	After 25 Years	After 30 Years
8% Return	$15,645	$29,324	$49,423	$78,954	$122,346
10% Return	$17,531	$34,950	$63,002	$108,182	$180,943
12% Return	$19,655	$41,753	$80,699	$149,334	$270,293
Cumulative Investment	$10,000	$15,000	$20,000	$25,000	$30,000

you take advantage of the 20 percent foreign content which you are allowed to have.

At time of writing, I am 38 years old. My RRSP is predominantly in Canadian equity mutual funds. This strategy reflects my goals and risk tolerance level. My plan is to diversify into other types of investments, including guaranteed investments, for the additional tax benefits by the time I'm 55. Some suggest that as you approach retirement, say in your early 60s, you should begin to shift out of the more volatile mutual funds entirely and start converting to guaranteed investments like GICs. I absolutely disagree. We are living, on average, to over age 80. If you retire at 65, there's still 15 years plus to plan for financially. You still have to make your money work hard. Shifting the mutual fund portion of your RRSP to a balanced fund might make more sense. A balanced fund will still give you the growth you need but in a more stable pattern. The guaranteed investment part of your RRSP should have staggered maturity dates so you are always able to take advantage of the best investment opportunity at the time of their maturity. There is a very loose rule of thumb called the age rule. If you are 35, 35 percent of your portfolio should be in low-volatility, more stable investments like GICs and mortgage mutual funds. Sixty-five percent should be in growth-oriented investments like equity mutual funds. If you are 50, then it should be 50-50, and so on. This is by no means totally accurate since asset allocation depends on such things as individual goals and risk tolerance. But what it does do is illustrate how important it is to continually monitor your portfolio, RRSP and otherwise, as you age. You cannot make an investment choice and assume it will serve your purposes for the duration of your lifetime. You need to diversify on an ongoing basis. A financial advisor should review your plan every year and recommend any changes that may be in your best interest.

Your retirement plan should be set up in phases. Phase one is what money you use at 65 if that's when you choose to retire. This phase would include the cash assets you have accumulated. Phase two could start at 71 when you begin accessing your RRSP. You can't, by law, hold RRSPs past 71. At this point you can convert your RRSP into a Registered Retirement Income Fund or an annuity, both of which can pay out income on a monthly basis. Phase three, perhaps at age 75 or 80, could be the proceeds from the sale of your house. (It is interesting to note, however, that the majority of Canadians do not sell their home the day they retire.) These phases suggest a very loose guideline, but the point is, you don't have to cash in your RRSP the day after you retire. The longer you let your money sit in a tax-sheltered investment, the more powerful the effects of compound interest will be. Be sure, before you decide what goes where, to talk to a financial advisor to help you determine what you want to do.

The other significant advantage to RRSPs is that the amount you contribute is tax deductible. This simply means that your contribution will reduce the amount of income tax you have to pay. Having an RRSP may make the difference between paying more taxes and getting a tax refund.

A case in point: Sybilla is a physician in the 50 percent tax bracket. She decides to invest $5,000 a year in an RRSP. She is consistent and carries this on for 25 years, earning eight percent interest each year. On the other hand, Nada, also a physician, invests her $5,000 a year in a non-tax-sheltered investment, like a GIC, which earns the same interest rate as Sybilla's. Because Nada's $5,000 is not tax deductible as is Sybilla's RRSP contribution and she is in the same 50 percent tax bracket, she really ends up investing only $2,500. Now the double whammy: The interest she earns on this $2,500 is also taxed at 50 percent every year. So much for the eight percent interest. In reality, Nada is only earning four percent. At the end of the 25 years, Sybilla will end up with $286,493 more than Nada. Even if Sybilla cashed out her entire RRSP in a lump sum in the 25th year and had to pay 50 percent tax on the entire amount of just under $400,000, she would still have almost $190,000 or 82 percent more than Nada's savings of $108,279. It's pretty easy to see why RRSPs make sense.

RRSPs have evolved, almost by default, to become the most important tax and retirement plan-

Non RRSP
$108,279

RRSP
$394,772

ning tool available. The government has, for all intents and purposes, choked off just about everything else. RRSPs do have a drawback, however. Remember, they are a tax deferral mechanism. If an emergency arises and you find yourself with no other option than to cash in your RRSP, expect a hefty tax bill upon collapsing the investment. You will have to pay tax on the amount you take out, the tax you haven't been paying all along. As emphatically stated earlier, RRSPs should not be considered as a source of emergency funds.

WHO CAN BUY AN RRSP?

Anyone earning an income who is under the age of 71. There is no minimum age as long as you are earning an income. That means your eight-year-old's financial empire from her paper route is eligible income for an RRSP.

WHAT QUALIFIES AS EARNED INCOME FOR AN RRSP?

Here is a list of types of income that qualify for RRSP contribution purposes:

- income from employment, whether you work for a company or are self-employed
- net rental income
- child and spousal support payments
- disability benefits
- supplementary unemployment insurance benefits
- royalties
- research grants

The following *do not* qualify but are often assumed to:

- investment income
- unemployment insurance benefits
- pension income

HOW MUCH CAN I PUT IN?

As stated earlier, RRSPs were developed to help give people with no company pension plans a break. The idea was to try and equalize retirement savings opportunities. Therefore, people with pension plans at work can't contribute the same amount to an RRSP as those who don't have one. That wouldn't be fair. Let's say Nada has a pension plan through the hospital where she works. After reading this book, she realizes she is missing a significant opportunity and decides to start investing in RRSPs. Sybilla, on the other hand, is in private practice and doesn't have access to a company plan. Though they earn the same income, it wouldn't be right for Nada to be able to put the same amount into her RRSP as Sybilla. For Nada to determine how much she can contribute to her RRSP, she (actually her employer) needs to calculate a value of her pension benefit accrued under the hospital pension plan in the *previous* year and subtract that amount from 18 percent of her earned income or $13,500 (the maximum contribution level), whichever is less. This is called a *pension adjustment* and is used to determine your contribution limit.

Now back to Nada. Her RRSP contribution limit for 1995 is calculated by taking her pension adjustment and subtracting it from $13,500 or 18 percent of the previous year's earned income, whichever is less. Sybilla, who does not have a private pension plan, gets to maximize her contribution of $13,500 or 18 percent. To illustrate, let's say Sybilla earned $100,000 last year. Eighteen percent of that is $18,000. The government will say, "Sorry, friend. All you can put in is $13,500. That's this year's maximum." It's the lesser of the two amounts up to a maximum of $13,500.

Now that I've gone to great pains to help you understand how your RRSP contribution is calculated, you can promptly forget about it. Revenue Canada does all this for you. They will send you a Notice of Assessment that tells you exactly what you can contribute. They have taken all the guesswork out of this exercise. It's one less task for our already overworked gray matter to contend with.

There are situations in which you can contribute more than your basic contribution limit. You can transfer payments of certain types of pension income to an RRSP. If you leave your company or it folds and you have accumulated a pension, these funds may be transferred into a locked-in RRSP. These funds are available by age 55, at which time the RRSP must be taken as a life annuity. In certain provinces, you can choose a life income fund. The latter gives you more flexibility over your investments, but it must be converted to a life annuity by age 80.

You can also *overcontribute* up to $8,000, which will be reduced to $2,000 in 1996, over the course of your lifetime. This cushion is for the mathematically challenged who accidentally contribute too much. It can also help those whose defined benefit pension plan has been upgraded retroactively which may mean they overcontributed inadvertently. Revenue Canada watches overcontributions carefully. If you overcontribute to your overcontribution, there is a one percent per month tax penalty on the amount by which you have exceeded your limit.

WHAT IF I DON'T WORK OR HAVE A SPORADIC WORK HISTORY?

Spousal RRSPs are an excellent way of addressing the situation of women who are working unpaid in the home or who earn less than their partner. Spousal RRSPs can be the great financial equalizer. If you don't have a pension plan but your partner does, this is another reason to consider a spousal RRSP. The main purpose of a spousal RRSP is to split retirement income more evenly between partners. Women who would otherwise have little or no retirement income will enjoy some peace of mind through this arrangement.

A spousal RRSP is essentially the same as a regular RRSP except that it is registered in the name of the spouse who owns the investment part of the plan while the contributing spouse takes a full deduction for all the contributions made to the spousal plan. The total contribution cannot exceed the personal contribution level. You also have to be sure that there were no withdrawals made in the previous two years or these withdrawals will be taxed in the contributor's hands. The chances are that the tax bracket of the spouse owning the spousal RRSP will be lower than that of the contributor, so there will be less tax to pay when the spouse takes the money out.

Remember Lynn's story. She was a stay-at-home mom who had no income. Stan earned a substantial living as a lawyer. This would have been the ideal scenario for a spousal RRSP. One year, Stan did take out a small one ($2,500) for Lynn. Lynn owned the RRSP (which she eventually had to use to pay legal fees). Stan got to use his contribution to the spousal RRSP as a tax deduction. If he had done this regularly, Lynn could have been guaranteed a dignified retirement with some security. However, had their separation been finalized before Stan's death, in the division of their property, Lynn and Stan would have had to divide the assets inside the spousal RRSP evenly. If withdrawal from the plan had been necessary, they would have split the tax between the two of them. Where no alternative to collapsing the plan exists, each partner can roll his or her share over to a new plan without incurring taxes.

The Canadian government has decided to enter the 21st century. As of January 1993, common-law spouses are treated, for tax purposes, the same as traditionally married couples. What this means is that common-law spouses now qualify for spousal RRSPs. You have to have been living together for at least a year or have a child together. One other point: It is always wise to name your partner as the beneficiary of your RRSP so the money can automatically roll over tax free into your partner's RRSP when you die. This is to avoid having to pay probate fees on the value of the RRSP.

WHAT ABOUT NON-CANADIAN INVESTMENTS?

You can have 20 percent of each RRSP portfolio in foreign stocks and bonds. You can put your RRSP in mutual funds that invest in international stocks, currencies or bonds. Investments outside of Canada have often outperformed Canadian investments so it is a good idea to take advantage of the bigger pond and diversify to the extent that you can. The Canadian market is such a small piece of the pie, representing only three percent of the total world market. I made sure the mutual funds I hold in my RRSP take advantage of the foreign content rules. This 20 percent limit is based on the book value or *original purchase price* that you paid when you acquired each investment. Since you are receiving a Canadian tax break, you can't go above this percentage without incurring a hefty penalty.

CAN I CHANGE INSTITUTIONS?

No problem. You can transfer from one institution to another by filling out a special form provided by the institution to which you are transferring. This way the RRSP isn't collapsed and you don't trigger any of the tax implications. There is no limit on the number of times you can change. Some institutions will charge an administrative fee in the neighbourhood of $30 for doing this, however. Check first.

SELF-DIRECTED RRSPS

These are typically for the well-heeled investor. You make the ongoing investment choices for your plan yourself with the help of a financial advisor. There is an annual administration fee for handling a self-directed RRSP, which ranges from $90 to $200 and is tax deductible. I have seen it recommended that you have anywhere from $10,000 to $75,000 in your portfolio before going the self-directed route. If you have a multitude of plans in a multitude of institutions, a self-directed plan will organize them all into one statement by one financial institution, for example a brokerage company. You don't have to deal with several financial institutions in order to have several investments in one plan. Self-directed RRSPs tend to be more flexible but you had better be sure you are comfortable with the principles and language of investing before taking one on.

WHAT IF I CAN'T AFFORD TO MAKE MY CONTRIBUTION?

I had a client, a 30-year-old woman, who tried to beg off a particular year's contribution of $5,000. I have heard it so often: "I can't afford it this year. I've got a car bill to pay...." When I explained to this woman that postponing a $5,000 contribution at age 30 meant taking as much as $85,000 out of her pocket at retirement, she capitulated.

If you are financially short and find yourself unable to make your contribution, you do have an option. It used to be that if you missed your contribution, you *missed* your contribution—there was no way to make it up. Recently, the rules were changed to give us folks a bit of a break. And none too soon with this recession. Sybilla was unable to make her RRSP contribution in 1994 because her office overhead was much higher than she had expected and her billings weren't what she had anticipated. She is, however, able to make up that missed contribution. When she gets her Notice of Assessment in 1995, her contribution eligibility will include her basic contribution *plus* what she didn't use during the previous year. If she has a banner year, she can make both years' contributions at once. This is called *carry forward.*

WHAT ABOUT BORROWING TO MAKE MY CONTRIBUTION?

For most people it makes sense to borrow to make your contribution even though the interest on the loan is not tax deductible. The benefits of tax-sheltered compound interest will outweigh the costs of borrowing if you pay the loan off within the year. In fact, in most cases I would recommend that you borrow as opposed to carrying forward your unused contributions. Many of us find it hard enough to save for retirement without tempting fate by postponing our contribution. Procrastination is the greatest enemy of financial and retirement planning. If it was hard to come up with $5,000 this year, how much easier will it be to come up with $10,000 next year? We have already seen what postponing our contribution one year can mean in terms of tax-sheltered compound interest. Some institutions offer one-year interest-free RRSP loans if you purchase your RRSP through them. This is an option certainly worthy of serious consideration.

THE RRSP HOME BUYERS' PLAN

It's around for good now. Part of the reason is home buying stimulates all kinds of spin-off industries, like the furniture and construction business, so it goes a long way to getting people back to work and paying taxes. Royal LePage Real Estate Services did a study that showed first-time buyers are fuelling the residential market, accounting for almost half of sales in some cities. The extension of the plan helps to support this continued activity. That, as well as low interest rates and needing only five percent for a down payment. Another interesting point about this plan is that it will likely get a lot more people interested in RRSPs if they can be used to save tax sheltered for a home. Even if the RRSPs aren't technically being used for actual retirement savings, greater exposure to this vehicle by young Canadians can only be beneficial. For these reasons, making the Home Buyers' Plan permanent has been applauded by the real estate industry and, naturally, most first-time home buyers. However, I, like many financial advisors, feel somewhat wary about the concept of this plan, for no other reason than that it is hard for people to save for their retirement. This plan creates an additional incentive to deviate from your RRSP's original intent, which is to save for retirement. That is, of course, unless you plan on using your home as part of your retirement savings program. In fact, part of the rationale behind the federal government's decision to continue this plan was their recognition that owning a home is often a form of saving for retirement. But one should be careful when considering accessing your RRSP to buy a house. If you don't pay back the money borrowed from your RRSP, the chances are good that you will likely *have* to sell your home at retirement, since you will likely have no other retirement savings. Again, that may be perfectly acceptable, but remember, *choice* is what you are after in your retirement years. You don't want to be forced to sell your home if you don't want to. A proper retirement portfolio should be diversified. It is also going to be difficult, if not impossible, for most people to make mortgage payments, maximize their RRSP contributions each year *and* pay back the required annual installments from the RRSP loan. Also, be sure that if you use this plan, you don't access the investments that are earning high rates of return, say in the 8 to 10 percent range. Real estate isn't appreciating that fast these days. Make sure you weigh the pros and cons carefully. Details on how the RRSP Home Buyers' Plan works are covered in chapter 8.

WHAT HAPPENS TO MY RRSP IF I DIE?

If I die tomorrow and I am single, my RRSP proceeds will be counted as income in the year of my death and will be fully taxable. If I am married or have moved in with Lance (by the way, Lance *is* mythical), the money would be rolled over into his RRSP and continue along just as it did in mine. Lance, however, gets to pay the tax when he accesses the money. If Lance predeceased me and I have a child or grandchild who is financially dependent on me, the money from my RRSP can be rolled over to the child and taxed in her hands instead of my estate. If my daughter is a minor, a special annuity will be purchased which will pay equal annual payments until she is 18.

HOW TO BUY YOUR RRSP

Here is the typical Canadian scenario: It's the RRSP deadline, March 1. The lunch-time crowd at the bank is immense. The line-

ups stretch around the block as last-minute procrastinators con-
verge on frazzled bank tellers. The tellers' eyes have glazed over
and their voices have a monotonous, robot-like quality. Bank
managers, sequestered at the back of the branch, are rapidly dart-
ing about putting out numerous administrative fires. People are fid-
geting under the weight of their heavy winter coats and standing
in little puddles of grimy water as the snow melts from the body
heat. Kids are squalling, mothers are shushing and business people anxiously look at their watches every two minutes. Everyone
has been standing in line at least 30 minutes. Sound familiar?

The banks do their best to prepare for the inevitable onslaught of last-minute contributors, but at the last minute you
won't get the advice you need. If you go in advance and talk
to one of the mutual fund representatives, maybe. But not the last
day of RRSP season. You don't have to subject yourself to this
cruel and inhuman punishment, you know. You can buy an
RRSP in a way that is reasonably painless and effortless. *You*
can be the person walking smugly *past* the bank at 12 noon on
March 1 as you make your way to a nice, quiet restaurant for a
relaxing lunch, shaking your head and tsk-tsking at the swelter-
ing mass of humanity waiting impatiently to do what you have
already done.

Where can you buy an RRSP? Anywhere, everywhere. Banks,
credit unions, insurance companies, trust companies, mutual fund
companies, stockbrokers, they all offer them. You might be able
to get an RRSP through work if your company offers group RRSPs.
They are the same as regular RRSPs except that your employer
deducts your contribution directly from your salary. Be sure,
however, that you agree with the investment philosophy of your
company. Some companies will offer a choice of investments for
your RRSP. Don't sign on the dotted line until you know where
your money is going.

For those of you who work for an employer, there is a little
known but highly effective way of making your RRSP contribution. You have to go through your local Revenue Canada
Taxation district office, but it's well worth the effort. You need
to get a *Request for Reduction of Deduction at Source* or *Tax
Deduction Waiver.* You fill out this form and bring a copy of the
form you filled out to open your RRSP as proof of purchase.
You then submit these directly to Revenue Canada. The tax de-

duction benefit that you usually don't get until after your taxes are filed is available immediately and appears regularly on your paycheque. Let's say you make a $200 a month contribution to your RRSP and you are in a 50 percent tax bracket. This means you will in effect receive a refund of $100 for every $200 you contribute. Instead of having to wait until May or June for Revenue Canada to send back the tax refund they owe you, you will see an extra $100 every month on your paycheque! Not only will you end up with extra money every month, you will also enjoy the advantage of having your RRSP bought and paid for by the time the deadline rolls around. I think this is a superlative idea for those who contribute to their RRSP monthly.

However, one of the best ways to take the maximum advantage of your tax-sheltered savings is to make your annual contribution as early in the year as possible. Eighty percent of RRSP owners make their contributions in the last two weeks of February. But if you contribute on January 1, 1996 rather than March 1, 1997 for the 1996 tax year, the money will be in your RRSP an extra 14 months. Because of the power of tax-sheltered compound interest, you could earn almost $60,000 more in your RRSP if you contributed $5,000 on January 1st of each year for 30 years (assuming an eight percent interest rate) rather than on March 1st of the following year. This is one situation where sooner is definitely better than later.

We have already talked about the power of dollar cost averaging in purchasing mutual funds. Since I'm self-employed, what I do with my RRSP contribution is to divide the annual amount by 12 and make monthly deposits into my plan. That way, by March 1, my contribution is taken care of in full and I have enjoyed the benefits of dollar cost averaging.

STATISTICS THAT SPEAK VOLUMES

As wonderful as they may be, RRSPs are not as common as one might expect. Hubert Frenken, Senior Analyst with Statistics Canada, recently released an in-depth analysis of who contributes how much to RRSPs. In a nutshell:

- Only one-third (4.5 million) of all tax-filers contributed to an RRSP in 1991.

- The most contributions were made by people in the 35 to 54 age group. Eighty-three percent of the male and 70 percent of the female taxfilers in this group have an RRSP.

- Fewer women than men had earned income and their average earnings were lower as well. (Two-thirds of the 1990 taxfilers with income below $5,000 were women.)

- The likelihood of participating in an RRSP increases with age with people in their 50s showing the highest participation rate.

- Not surprisingly, the higher the income, the higher the participation rate. Eighty percent of those earning more than $80,000 made RRSP contributions.

- In the last decade, the growth rate in the number of women contributing to RRSPs outstripped that of men. In 1981, 31 percent of the contributors were women. By 1993, that had increased to 42 percent. The amount women contributed increased significantly as well. In 1981, women's contributions made up 26 percent of the total but by 1993, that had increased to 34 percent.

- However, in 1993, some 650,000 Canadians under 65 cashed in a total of almost $3.5 billion of their RRSP savings. Since total 1993 RRSP contributions were $19.2 billion, it would appear that for every $5 contributed, nearly $1 was withdrawn by people under retirement age. In 1991, RRSP contributions rose 22 percent from 1990, but the total amount withdrawn rose 27 percent. A striking 53 percent of the withdrawals were by people under 45 and they withdrew 42 percent of the total. Compared with 16 percent of men, 24 percent of women under 65 who withdrew savings had neither employment nor UI income. Of the 3.5 billion dollars cashed in 1993, women withdrew 44 percent. This number is way out of proportion to the number of contributors when you consider that only 34 percent of the 1993 contributors were women. Frenken concludes that women seem to have a greater dependence on RRSP income.

- This statistic is interesting: It seems that only 25 percent of taxfilers who didn't have a company pension plan filed with an RRSP contribution, yet 45 percent of the people who *had* a pension plan filed *with* an RRSP contribution.

- Women were less likely than men to have a company pension and were also slightly less likely to contribute to an RRSP in the absence of a pension. Women's participation in company pension plans continues to lag behind that of men in 1991 (31 percent of women as compared to 36 percent of men with earned income).

- Frenken suggests that even though women do not have the same level of access to pension plans as men do, which should be the incentive to make RRSP contributions, women's lower average earned income inhibits them from doing so. Women's average income was $18,360 as compared to men who averaged $30,000.

- Fifty-four percent of the women filing did not report savings in RPPs and RRSPs as compared to 47 percent of the male tax-filers.[25]

The trend *is* moving exactly where it should—up. Everyone, especially women, should be taking advantage of RRSPs to help overcome the financial challenges of lengthy retirements and less income to provide for them. Statistics Canada shows that 48 percent of women between the ages of 60 and 65 live on $10,000 a year or less. Only 18 percent of men fall into this category. RRSPs can ensure that our golden years will, indeed, be golden.

8

YOUR QUANTUM OF SOLACE

> *"Women constitute half the world's population, perform nearly two-thirds of its work hours, receive one-tenth of the world's income and own less than one one-hundredth of the world's property."*
>
> United Nations Report, 1980

One day Elaine remarked, "Joanne, I think you're ready to consider buying your own home." I was already trying to recover from the shock of discovering that Elaine, who was only in her mid 30s, owned three houses. She owned one in Burlington and when she decided to accept a job offer in Toronto, she bought another one here. She then met her life partner and proceeded to marry him. She co-owns and shares a house with him north of the city. Her example boggled my mind. There was only one word to describe my feelings on home ownership: terror.

I terminated further discussion with, "Thank you for your concern, Elaine. No." Blinking with surprise at my abrupt answer, she asked, "Uh, no?"

"No, nada, no way José, nein, NOT!" I clarified for her. In keeping with her usual style, she ignored me. "That's ridiculous, Joanne. Give me one good reason why not."

"Because," I answered, trying to avoid the real reason, "experts say a house is not as great an investment as everyone thinks. I can do just as well by renting and investing the difference." I thought to myself what a remarkably quick recovery that was. Unfortunately, Elaine didn't buy it.

"You're afraid," she said quietly. "Yeah, yeah, so what?" I replied, my pride just a little hurt at being found out. Elaine was sympathetic. "Tell me what you fear. Twenty bucks says I felt the same thing."

I took a deep breath. "The whole idea is too big, too adult; there's too much debt, it's too locked in and it takes too long to save for; a house is too much trouble and I hate shovelling snow." Elaine looked at me and smiled. "Don't hold back, Joanne. Now, tell me how you really feel." I made a face at her as I continued, "I never thought it was possible that I could own my own home. Unless of course I did it with a significant other. I suspect I have always thought that my knight in shining armour was going to ride into my life and bring the castle with him. It never occurred to me to buy my own castle. Besides, I have a hectic lifestyle. I travel and I'm impulsive. I once drove a friend to the airport and on the spur of the moment ended up boarding the plane with her to go to Victoria, B.C. for the weekend! I like to move around a lot. I've lived in almost every major city in this country. I love the freedom of a nomadic lifestyle. And I'm not sure how intellectually stimulating I'd find fixing roofs and unplugging toilets."

"How long have you lived in Toronto, Joanne?" Elaine asked. "Thirteen years now. Why?" I queried. "How long ago was that stunt that took you 3,000 miles across the country for a weekend?" she asked. "I don't know," I said, shifting uncomfortably. I didn't like where this was heading. "Maybe 11 years ago."

Elaine pressed on. "Have you ever heard of carpenters and plumbers? Maybe you even know high school kids who earn extra money shovelling snow and cutting grass? My dear, fear is the only reason you don't want to buy a house. And a darn fine one at that. There is not a person on the planet who hasn't experienced serious anxiety at the thought of buying their first home. And I must say that buying a house isn't for everyone. It is as much an emotional decision as a financial one. Never lose sight of that. A home is your quantum of solace, your safe haven from the world. A home should not be bought as an investment, although it can turn out to be quite a good one."

"I guess that's why you own three?" I asked smugly.

"I happen to own three because in two cases the market turned against me as a seller," she countered. "This can be the downside to owning a house. The housing market took a serious dive and, had I sold the property, I would have taken a bath! I had to rent the house in Burlington to cover the monthly mortgage payments. The house in Toronto, well! This one really hurts. Like so many others bitten by the real estate bug, I bought when prices were exceedingly high in 1988. It astounds me how grossly inflated house prices were in the '80s. People weren't buying houses for shelter. Speculators would buy them and 10 minutes later put them back on the market and watch people kill each other trying to up the ante. People had an irrational fear that prices were going out of sight and they would never be able to afford to buy a home. They rushed out to buy whatever they could, however they could."

"I know this to be true, Elaine," I offered. "I have friends in the most precarious of financial positions today because they pushed their lines of credit and credit card limits to the maximum and borrowed well beyond their means to jump on this bandwagon. The pressure I got from so many people to buy a house during that period was unbearable. Most of my friends did. I do not glory in their misfortune, but look who's laughing now."

Elaine chuckled. "My house in Toronto was bought strategically at the top of the market. I watched in horror over the next two years as it dropped $60,000 in value. And when the housing market went down the drain, so did the rental market. There was such a glut of houses for rent that people were negotiating 25 percent off the rent and first and last month free! People like me who had the choice to sell and take a huge loss or try to carry the monthly payments as best we could on the rental income were in a terrible bind. My choice was to try to hold on until the market turned around or the rental income increased enough to cover the expenses. This is why I find myself with such vast land holdings today; I have a strong belief that real estate is a wonderful investment but poor judgement in timing. It's a deadly combination if you are in only for the short term."

"Well, knowing my luck, I'd buy a house and a heavy metal band would buy the place next door. I don't know, Elaine. It sounds like a lot of trouble and risk," I said.

"That's a good point, Joanne," Elaine answered. "Many people believe that buying a house is risk free. As the '80s demonstrate, that's not true. One thing is for sure, it is low risk if you are in for the long term and buy prudently. Historically real estate has had stable and secure growth and is a good hedge against inflation. The national average growth rate has been 10 percent a year. Some neighbourhoods have performed well above the average, with values rising as much as 20 to 25 percent. That isn't the reality in today's world, though. It is safe to say the growth rate will be much less for the foreseeable future.

"Location is critical to the equation. A good rule of thumb is to find a neighbourhood not often frequented by heavy metal bands. Here's the best reason why real estate is a great idea. Let's say you bought your house for $175,000, decided to sell it a few years later, and cleared $50,000 after the sale was completed. Revenue Canada won't require you to give them a share. The beauty of this profit is that it is completely tax free, as long as the house is your principal residence. Since we Canadians are one of the highest taxed people in the world, I would suggest to you that it is in your best interest to take advantage of whatever tax breaks exist. And there isn't much to choose from."

"I see your point. But what if I wanted to take off for six months or move to Paris or buy a convertible? Or what if there is an emergency and I need cash and it's all tied up in the house? I can't sell the bath tub and buy it back later when I have the money again. As an investment, a house doesn't strike me as being very liquid." I lived for freedom of choice.

"You're right," Elaine said. "You don't take off for six months, you can't buy the convertible and you sell the house when you move to Paris. You also never let yourself get so house poor that you can't take care of day-to-day emergencies. That's a big mistake many people make. However, you can take advantage of home equity lines of credit which make it possible for you to tap into cash right under your own nose, the profit built up in your home. You don't have to sell it or worry about rigid repayment schedules. Mind you, you do have to own your house for an appreciable length of time to build up equity of any significance. Buying a house is a lifestyle choice. Unless you are one of the rich and famous, you give up certain things to gain others—things like pride in the home you own and a forced savings program since it is somewhat difficult to sell pieces of the house to raise cash. A house is an asset which will appreciate tax free over the long term. Owning your own home can also contribute to securing your retirement. Even if you don't sell your house when you stop working, there is much to be said for enjoying your last quarter in a paid-up home. Owning your own home can alleviate much of the uncertainty of old age.

"Joanne," Elaine continued, "I am not suggesting you *must* do this. You can, in fact, rent and, if you consistently and wisely invest the difference, for example by maximizing your RRSPs, you will do as well as and maybe even better than homeowners. Renting is a perfectly acceptable alternative as long as you save the difference. Don't let people tell you that by renting, you are just throwing money out the window and paying someone else's mortgage. You see, most people realize that the monthly amount they put into their house is going toward building tax-free equity, so they immediately assume that it is better to have their money going into something that is building capital. Renting, at first glance, looks like money going into the air. The mortgage payments for the house I live in are $2,100 a month. It's a dandy fine house and I believe worth the money. How much do you pay in rent, Joanne?"

"Nowhere near $2,100, I'll guarantee you that. And my place fits my needs perfectly," I replied. "Also I don't worry about utilities, property tax, insurance, upkeep and hydro."

"There's my point," Elaine said. "You are paying less monthly than I am and as long as you continue to invest for the long term and in a vehicle that is tax sheltered, you will be absolutely fine from an investment point of view. But this is where a house has the advantage. It *forces* you to save. You can't be tempted to forego your savings program this month or year because of your cockamamie travel behaviour. The bottom line is that we all have to pay living costs one way or the other. That money can never be viewed as wasted."

"So I am right after all?" I asked in disbelief.

"You could very well be and that's for you to decide. You know, Joanne, if home maintenance doesn't appeal to you, there is another option," Elaine said. "I figured as much," I sighed.

"How about a condominium? Often the costs are similar to or only marginally higher than renting, especially if you settle in

CHAPTER 8   YOUR QUANTUM OF SOLACE **233**

a comparable neighbourhood. No muss, no fuss," Elaine summed up.

"That means I use all my hard-earned savings for a down payment. I don't know why I don't like that, I just don't. I get a warmer, more secure feeling from having a variety of investments, not just one. I know the 'it's my own pad and it's tax free' argument. I agree that real estate is an excellent investment, barring periods of political and economic havoc. I can't help but think of those people in Calgary when the economy virtually collapsed in the early '80s. I know people who locked their front door and walked away. It was like the Great Depression. Granted, Calgary was a one-industry oil town, but its collapse sure made me realize how sensitive the housing market can be to outside influences. I'm sure I don't have to tell *you* that. Nevertheless, I know that as a long term investment, owning your own home has all the elements an investor should look for. But I'll have to mull the idea over. I'm not sure it suits me, not today anyway. I'll tell you, Elaine, I'll gladly put my investment portfolio on the line and in 10 or 20 years compare my net worth with that of a person who uses her home as her savings. We could very well be in the same place, or I could even be ahead. And I will have flown to Bora Bora on 24 hours' notice."

"You're hopeless," Elaine groaned.

I did take Elaine's advice and started to think about buying a house. I decided to "feel the fear, but do it anyway." The one thing that helped me move forward was being firm in my commitment to take all the time I needed. If I was going to spend my nest egg on a down payment and go into debt for tens of thousands of dollars, I was going to be very, very sure about my decision. Since I was in no hurry and content with my lifestyle as it was, I browsed on and off for four years. I looked in the country, in the suburbs and downtown. I looked at houses, condominiums and townhouses. I looked at all the price ranges to get a sense of what the different prices would buy. By far my favourite was a $500,000 job on a quiet tree-lined street. (That should come as no surprise.) Since I was attempting to find a place to live in for a long time, I needed to figure out what I would be most comfortable with.

I discovered a number of things about the housing market. The further away from the city, the less expensive the house.

The "fixer upper" can be a good deal if you are inclined to be handy and are meticulously careful in what you buy. I took a pass. Elaine and my real estate agent stressed the three key points in buying real estate: location, location, location. Depending on what you want in your home, schools, public transportation and shopping are important considerations as long as they aren't parked immediately in your backyard. Since I had no children, drove my own car, and was averse to shopping of any sort, I didn't care about any of these things. However, in her inimitable style, Elaine insisted I begin to care about them for two reasons. One, life can change in an instant and what if I decided to actually go out on a date? What if I ended up marrying some poor bloke and having a family? Schools and shopping would then mean something. I needed to consider all the possibilities, short and long term, no matter how remote. The second reason was the resale value. Being near to these things makes a house more attractive to a wider range of potential buyers. I told Elaine that all I cared about was that my house have a fireplace, a big backyard with a stellar view, and three large bedrooms so I could set up an office and an exercise room. The kitchen was optional. Elaine reminded me that these features are attractive for most people so having them could only increase the house's value. She did mention, however, that she had never seen a house without a kitchen, so I might have to compromise.

As time went by, I became very good at sizing up almost instantly what I liked and what I didn't. Eventually I only went out to view specific houses in a certain price range, in the kind of neighbourhood I wanted and with certain features. I actually began to enjoy the exercise. I mastered the art of walking casually through a house that made my heart pound with excitement and my head spin with anticipation. But my excitement would be known only to me. The real estate agent could no more guess that I liked this particular house than fly to the moon. The more noncommittal I was about the house, the more bargaining power I would have.

As with everything else that I had undertaken in financial planning, the fear of the unknown was the worst part. Again, I demystified the process by becoming part of it. As I became more comfortable, I started to think about the financial end of purchasing a house. How much could I afford? How much would closing fees and insurance and taxes be? What should I put aside for hiring someone to move me, shovel snow, cut grass, clean out eavestroughs, garages, furnaces and chimneys, repair roofs, caulk windows and install the new shower. Rumour has it there is more to securing a mortgage than going to your bank manager and saying, "Please can I have one?" Elaine was a great help. She emphasized that I wasn't to spend more than 30 percent of my gross income on mortgage payments, energy costs and taxes. I instructed my real estate agent to stay as close to this figure as possible when looking around for a house for me.

WHAT DO ALL THESE TERMS MEAN?

I now started to turn my energy toward educating myself about mortgages, rates and terms and that word that sounded to me like a dreaded operation of some sort, amortization. The first thing I had to do was find out exactly what these words all meant. I also had to figure out a way of getting this information without admitting my total ignorance to Elaine. My *sense* of what they meant was mostly guesswork based on the odd snippet I would pick up here and there. I knew enough to know that I wanted a pre-approved mortgage. As I would later discover, lenders will give tentative approval for a mortgage amount based on an assessment, with final approval depending on an appraisal of the property you want to buy. All kinds of financial institutions offer pre-approved mortgages, so I had the freedom to shop around for the best financing terms and not feel obligated to deal with anyone in particular. This put me in a better bargaining position to make an offer since I knew, not only that I could get the financing, but how much I could get. However, I was only guaranteed an interest rate for a short period of time (usually no more than three months). I shopped around and didn't stop at the first place that approved me, which tends to be human nature. People are generally so pleased they have been approved that they don't look any further. This works well for the lenders, but not necessarily for the borrowers.

We were having lunch at our favourite crepe joint when, out of the blue, Elaine asked, "Are you able to handle a conventional mortgage or are you going with a high-ratio mortgage? You also need to think about whether you want a closed or open mortgage.

Oh yes, I'm curious, what term are you interested in and over what amortization period? I guess that depends on what you think interest rates are going to do. Are you going fixed or variable?"

This was the moment of reckoning. Struggling not to look completely stupid, I said, "Elaine, when did you learn to speak Spanish?" My cover was blown. Elaine laughed all the way back to the office. My education in house-buying jargon began at that moment. And, as usual, it was all remarkably straightforward.

It was embarrassing how basic I needed to get. Like, beginning with what a mortgage actually was. When real estate, which is immovable property, is used to secure a loan, the borrower signs a contract called a *mortgage*. This is different from a chattel mortgage, discussed in chapter 2, which is generally used for movable goods. Although a mortgage is simply a large loan, the magnitude of the sum borrowed, how long it takes to pay back and the nature of the security make it somewhat complex. Your property may have more than one mortgage on it, which will be ranked as first, second, etc., according to the order in which they were recorded at the local Registry Office. If the first mortgage is paid off or discharged, the second automatically becomes the first. This is rare, though, because first mortgages are usually for larger sums and longer terms than second mortgages.

The distinguishing characteristic between first and second mortgages is who gets what, when, in the event you can't make your mortgage payments. If the property must be taken back and sold, the holder of the first mortgage gets first crack at the proceeds of the sale. After they have been satisfied, then the holders of the second mortgage would have their claim settled. If there isn't enough to settle the second mortgagee, tough luck. They have to accept a loss. This is precisely why second mortgages carry a higher interest rate. They are higher risk.

Mortgage payments are set up as a combination of interest and principal so that by the end of, say, 25 years, the balance will be zero. The 25-year period you use to pay off the house is the amortization period. Simply put, it is the term during which the debt must be fully paid back. In the early years, you are paying off mostly interest. You don't actually begin to wear away at the principal until several years later. This is why it is a good policy to pay off as much of your mortgage as you can so you start to pay down the actual principal as soon as possible. This will dramatically lower your interest costs over the years. The shorter the amortization period, the less interest you have to pay. Remember the power of compounding. It works the same way with debt. By shaving off some of that debt in the early years with extra payments, you will save significantly by cutting back on the compound interest on your debt. But don't cut off your nose to spite your face. It isn't wise to gamble on short term periods if you are struggling to make your payments now. If interest rates go up even one percentage point when you have to renegotiate your mortgage, the impact on your monthly payments will be great because of the size of the loan. It doesn't take a rocket scientist to figure out that it is a wise policy to pay off your mortgage as quickly as you can, but without killing yourself in the process. I have seen many young couples who have given up any semblance of a normal life because they are so consumed with paying down their mortgage. Moderation is important. After all, we are only young once. Paying your mortgage biweekly instead of monthly can make a sizable difference. Let's assume you have a $200,000 mortgage amortized over 25 years with an eight percent interest rate. If all you do is pay biweekly instead of monthly, you will reduce the length of time you have to pay to 20 years instead of 25. In terms of savings in interest costs, instead of paying $257,926 in interest, you will reduce your interest charges to $195,430. That's a saving of almost $63,000!

The payment term you choose is often confused with the amortization period. They are two different things. The term you negotiate with the lender can be anywhere from six months to five years. What you choose will depend on your view of which way interest rates are going. You will need 50 six-month terms or five five-year terms for a 25-year amortization period. When you renegotiate your mortgage at the end of its term, be sure you adjust the amortization period accordingly or the debt will last forever.

TYPES OF MORTGAGES

Financial institutions are becoming very competitive and remarkably innovative in the mortgage lending world. It used to be pretty simple, like back in the days when running shoes were running shoes. (I think you've heard this story before.) We only shopped around to compare interest rates. It has now become mandatory to shop around to see what new ideas they have come up with to lure us through their doors. Today's world of mortgages is mind-boggling. Financial institutions want your mortgage business very badly. When I saw some of the numbers, I began to understand why. Even a one percent difference in the interest rate can make a huge difference because of the size of the principal.

CONVENTIONAL AND INSURED MORTGAGES

The first step is to decide whether you qualify for a conventional or a high-ratio mortgage. Like most people, I went the conventional route. To get a conventional mortgage, I needed at least 25 percent of the purchase price of the house as a down payment and my debt load had to be manageable and meet certain criteria. Thinking about this is when I discovered what really frightened me about owning a home—the amount of money it is necessary to borrow. We are talking serious debt here. Even though it is investment debt and a wise debt, a necessary debt, or whatever else the lenders tell you, it is still a ton of money to owe to an institution. Don't minimize the feeling of apprehension you will experience. Almost every homeowner I have talked to feels exactly the same way.

At one time, all mortgages were conventional mortgages, but in 1954 the federal government established a system to guarantee mortgage loans made by approved financial lenders as a way to increase the mortgage money available to home buyers and builders. This legislation is the *National Housing Act* and the crown corporation that looks after everything is known as the *Canada Mortgage and Housing Corporation,* or CMHC. A lender making a mortgage loan that is approved by CMHC can extend a mortgage that is more than 75 percent of the value of the property. These insured mortgages allow the buyer to obtain the mortgage with less than 25 percent of the value of the property as a down payment. If you default, the lender can go back to CMHC to attempt to recoup their losses.

To finance this mortgage insurance program, you, as a buyer, pay a fee, from one-half of a percent to 2.5 percent of the total mortgage loan, which is added to the principal at the outset. It is built right into the payment schedule. At a glance, this insurance seems like it only benefits the lender. But without it, mortgages with low down payments would not be available, or you would have to resort to a more expensive second mortgage. These insured first mortgages are sometimes referred to as high ratio loans.

OPEN AND CLOSED MORTGAGES

I was openly confused about open and closed mortgages because of the degrees of openness and the fact that few are completely closed. A fully open mortgage allows me to pay off the loan whenever I wanted, free of penalty, but I would have to pay a higher interest rate for the privilege. A totally closed mortgage, on the other hand, doesn't allow any prepayments. They are impossible or, at best, very costly, to get out of before their term expires. In practice, however, most closed mortgages have prepayment options of up to 15 percent of the original principal, usually on every anniversary date. In reality, then, some mortgages may be called open, but may be only partially open and some mortgages that are called closed aren't, because they may allow prepayment without penalty under certain conditions. Nothing is simple anymore.

VARIABLE RATE MORTGAGES

I then needed to decide on a variable versus fixed rate mortgage. Variable rate mortgages offer an interest rate that is generally adjusted monthly to keep in line with what is happening in the economy. A payment schedule, based on a 20-year or 25-year amortization, is drawn up for a specific period, usually one year, during which the borrower is committed to regular payments of a predictable amount. The interest rates on variable rate mortgages may be half a percent lower than for other types because you run the risk of the rate increasing. You should also remember that the interest is compounded monthly rather than semi-annually.

While I contemplated what type of mortgage to get, it occurred to me that while the lenders get to sleep better at night, variable rate mortgages could disrupt my blissful sleep patterns by making it harder for me to know what my future costs will be. If interest rates rise, I may find myself in the not-so-enviable position of my fixed monthly payment being composed entirely of interest with no reduction of the actual principal. It is conceivable that some of my payments might not cover all the interest due, and that the balance of the interest owing could be added to the unpaid principal. Then, I end up increasing liabilities instead of assets. I had to consider carefully what I believed interest rates would do over the next while in order to decide what type of financing to get. Frankly, this gave me a headache. I'm not convinced anyone really knows for sure, so it's a bit of a crap shoot.

In times of stable interest rates, people tend to be less interested in variable rate and flock more toward fixed rate mortgages. These are short term, fully open mortgages with a guaranteed interest rate for a period of, say, six months. These are good for people who have strong opinions that interest rates will go down or, at least, stay the same. However, people generally shouldn't speculate on their mortgage's interest rates. If you play the short rates, you need to take a very proactive role in the monthly management of your mortgage.

PREPAYMENT OPTIONS

There is a distinct difference between *repaying* your loan and *prepaying* your loan. Repaying means you follow a predetermined payment schedule to end up at ground zero, while prepaying is a way to accelerate your arrival at ground zero. You can repay your mortgage faster than the original schedule by making lump sum payments to reduce the principal. Whether you can do so depends on the type and terms of the mortgage.

With a prepayment option, you can increase your monthly payments, once a year or on any payment date, by as little as 10 percent or as much as 100 percent. Making mortgage payments weekly or bi-weekly will also shorten the amortization period, in essence by allowing you to make extra payments over the course of the year.

RRSP HOME BUYERS' PLAN

This plan allows first-time home buyers to withdraw up to $20,000 tax-free from their RRSP and pay it back in installments over 15 years. If you default on the payments, the amount you borrowed becomes taxable as income that year. You are considered a first-time home buyer if neither you nor your spouse owned a home and lived in it as your principal place of residence in any of the five calendar years before the time of withdrawal. You can only participate in this program once. You are able to make a tax-deductible contribution up to 90 days before the money is withdrawn.

WOMEN AND REAL ESTATE

Royal LePage conducted a study in 1993 which highlighted some interesting trends. Out of 50,000 home buyers in Canada in 1992, 37 percent were first-time buyers. Falling interest rates and government incentive plans, like the Home Buyers' Plan which allows you to use money from your RRSP, were contributing factors. But what encouraged me was the increase in women buying homes. In 1992, 23 percent of all homes purchased were purchased by single people. Of that total, almost half, 48.1 percent, were women. In several cities including Vancouver, Toronto, Calgary and Ottawa, single female buyers outnumbered single male buyers and the trend is continuing. It looks as though we are becoming our own knights.

As I was going through my education in real estate jargon and the mortgage pre-approval process, something happened which changed the course of my life. I was participating in a financial trade show in Toronto. As I stood in the booth kibbitzing with the other exhibitors, I was approached by an intense, yet good-humoured young man. He passed me his business card and asked if I would join him for a coffee. As we walked toward the cafeteria, I looked at his card. He worked for a well-established Canadian publishing company. "What could he possibly want with me?" I wondered as we sat down. I was soon to find out. "Joanne," he began, "have you ever considered writing a book on personal finance for Canadian women?"

The rest, as they say, is history. I didn't end up buying a house after all. In fact, my down payment and the publisher's advance supported me during the year it took to write this book. My RRSP is still intact and I have the experience of publishing this book as a major accomplishment under my belt. One thing is for sure, though. Buying a house is a state of mind. As I get older, the desire to nest grows stronger and the urge to have my own quantum of solace is becoming quite pronounced. I'll have to play catch-up, but the goal of owning a home by the time I'm 40 is firmly in place. Besides, who really needs to go to Bora Bora on 24 hours' notice?

9

THE RUBBER HITS THE ROAD: WHAT EVERY WOMAN MUST KNOW ABOUT TAXES

> *"The art of taxation consists in so plucking the goose as to obtain the largest amount of feathers with the least amount of hissing."*
>
> Jean-Baptiste Colbert, French aristocrat, 1619-1683

It was the middle of April. Everywhere people carried an air of anxiousness and looked about with furtive glances. I was no exception. Other than bringing the first signs of a much-anticipated spring to winter-weary Canadians, April has not a single redeeming feature. This is the dreaded income tax season. April 30, midnight to be exact, is the time by which Canadians must cough it over to Revenue Canada.

Elaine dropped in on me one afternoon during tax season. At least she must have assumed it was me. There was *some* form of human life buried under the mountains of receipts who was issuing a litany of wildly imaginative curses. "A little tense today, Joanne?" she queried. A pair of unamused eyes peered over the paper version of Mount Everest. "Dare enter only if you are an accountant or seriously injured," I answered, glowering at her. I detested the chore of getting ready to file my tax return. "Elaine, why do they call Revenue Canada 'the taxman'?" I asked, feeling very irritated. "A friend of mine who works for the government found out for me how many women work at Revenue Canada. Half the staff are women—50.33 percent, to be precise. You know, this really bugs me. It looks like I'm going to have to put this so-called 'taxman' to death." It was evident I was bucking for a fight. "If you want to know what God thinks of money, look who she gives it to!" I muttered, feeling totally exasperated as I pushed a path through the paper on my desk.

"There you are!" Elaine exclaimed brightly. "Now I can see your shining countenance. Ah yes, the dreaded income tax season. You shouldn't complain, my dear. The only thing that hurts worse than paying income tax is not having to pay income tax. By the way, I've received my refund already." With that, she flounced out of my office.

I really needed to hear that. My assassination plan for the taxman shifted momentarily to Elaine. Elaine had been emphatic that taking financial control of one's life included getting one's tax life in order. The whole tax scene not only intimidated me, but it had a sedating effect on me as well. I had always rebelled against any suggestion of taking on the tax monster. Elaine had the gall to tell me not only that it wasn't difficult, but also that tax planning could be done properly with minimal effort and maximum results. She declared that she would have me tax literate before I knew it. It seemed inconceivable; this stuff was for the rich and famous. My version of tax planning was figuring out how I could drop off the shoebox stuffed with receipts at my accountant's without her being there. This was to avoid the harassment I inevitably received from her.

The simplicity of tax planning was revealed to me during my first annual financial review which Elaine and I conducted over chocolate crêpes one day. I had come into the financial planning exercise debt free. In one year I had done my will, power of attorney and living will. I had secured my life and disability insurance, maximized my RRSP contribution and had started an emergency fund. I had my own personal line of credit established and was investing in a mutual fund outside of my RRSP as part of my 10 percent savings plan. I was even entertaining the idea of buying a house. Though it sounds like I must have had to rob a bank to afford all of this, that simply wasn't the case. This financial planning game is largely a matter of *getting organized*, one step at a time, one month at a time. My life and disability insurance, my RRSP contribution, the emergency fund and mutual fund were all paid for and building up each month through preauthorized chequing. I hated to admit it, but Elaine had been right. In retrospect, financial planning was easier than I had expected it to be.

"Congratulations, Joanne. I am very proud of what you have accomplished in such a short time. I'll let you pay for lunch today." Elaine was beaming. "You are pretty organized, my friend; even your tax planning is respectable."

"Excuse me?" I stared back at her blankly. "Tax planning? I don't think so. I don't do numbers, remember? Tax or any variation thereof is a four-letter word in my vocabulary."

"Well, sweet thing, surprise. You *are* doing it. If you have a will, you own life insurance or are saving for your child's education through an RESP, you're doing it. Anyone who contributes to an RRSP through work or on their own is tax planning. If you're splitting your income with your spouse through a spousal RRSP, you're doing it. If you own an equity mutual fund outside your RRSP, you're doing it. Ha! I fooled you. And you thought it was going to be so complicated." Elaine rubbed her hands back and forth with glee. Tax planning is something everyone needs to do regardless of how much or how little wealth they have acquired. If you earn $28,000 a year, any dollar above that is taxed at 40 percent. Canadians are so heavily taxed that it has become our civic duty to do proper tax planning. In 1994, every woman, man and child in essence was in debt $17,000 because of Canada's huge debt and deficit problem. Thirty-one cents of every dollar Revenue Canada brings in goes to paying just the interest on the country's outstanding loans. It just keeps going up. If you combine provincial and federal debts, every man, woman and child owes $127,000, according to TD Bank president Richard Thomson speaking at the 1995 annual general meeting. In an attempt to bring in more revenue, the government has had to choke off almost all of the tax shelters in its 'anti-avoidance' campaign. I guess that makes tax planning easier because there are fewer choices, but it also makes it a critical exercise for all Canadians.

"Tax planning can be as complicated or as simple as you want to make it, but for the average Canadian, the whole process is remarkably straightforward. But a word of advice, Joanne. I know people who have become so tax conscious that they invest solely on the basis of the tax benefits. This can lead people into some pretty high-risk and off-beat stuff like Arabian horse farming. Find an investment you like, then worry about the tax consequences. Never let the tax tail wag the dog."

"Arabian horse farming!?" I joked. "I'd like that. Where do I sign?"

"Before you go riding off on that horse," Elaine continued, "I want you to learn the basic principles of taxation. Forget the high-end or business-planning angles. My main point is that you should *never* pay more tax than you have to and yet we do it all the time. You should also have a reasonable working knowledge of tax language and a few tips to help ease the load. I'm not interested in teaching you how to fill out your tax return; that's why God made accountants."

KNOWING THE LANGUAGE

TAX PLANNING

A critical disclaimer: Like buying life insurance, tax planning is an individual process. The concepts discussed in this chapter are *very* general and are intended to provide a starting point only. There are almost 2,000 pages in the *Income Tax Act*. Be sure to consult with an accountant or a tax planning specialist.

If you noticed Jean-Baptiste Colbert's quote on taxation at the beginning of the chapter, you will see that tax planning is nothing more than making sure you keep as many of your feathers as possible. It should include such long-term goals as retirement planning, protecting oneself and one's family in the event of disaster, in addition to minimizing what goes to Revenue Canada at income tax time. It is an ongoing challenge because the only thing constant in tax planning is change.

It seems pretty silly to pay more tax than the government requires you to. Incidentally, proper tax planning is not tax evasion. Tax evasion is deliberately and intentionally offering misleading or inaccurate information. Tax planning is becoming knowledgeable about the legally available tools which will reduce the tax you have to pay. There is a term that was used a lot in the past—loopholes. Eliminate it from your vocabulary along with the term tax-free. Loopholes are errors in the structure of the law that benefit the taxpayer. They have gone the way of the dinosaur since the government has cracked down aggressively in its attempt to increase tax revenues. Tax incentives, on the other hand, are programs which the government wants you to use, like RRSPs. The bottom line in tax planning is to keep as much money as you can in your pocket and away from Revenue Canada.

TAX DEFERRAL

Do it! Do it! Do it! Postpone paying taxes on income whenever you can. RRSPs and a pension plan at work are the best examples of deferring tax payments as long as possible. The longer you put off having to pay tax, the longer you will have money in your pocket to do other things. Examples of tax deferral plans are RRSPs, RESPs, your company pension plan and *exempt* life insurance policies.

TAX SHELTERS

A tax shelter is an umbrella under which your investment will sit warm and dry away from Revenue Canada's rain—taxation. As long as it stays under the umbrella, you won't have to pay tax. When you close the umbrella, baby, the rain must fall. Tax shelters use government-approved incentives to maximize your deductions and minimize the income you have to pay tax on. They have to come with a tax shelter identification number before you can use them as a tax write-off. RRSPs are the best example of a tax shelter and they are available to anyone earning an income. Then there is the other end of the scale, things like oil and gas ventures, limited partnerships, mining exploration investments and Canadian film productions. If you are anything like me, these types of investments will make your heart race and palms sweat. These are definitely for those with iron nerves. This book is written for people who are getting started on their financial journey. This high-end and risky form of investing is beyond the scope of what we are trying to achieve, which is showing you how to build a solid financial base. These investments should never be considered until you are a financial expert and are making truckloads of money.

TAX-FREE

Dream on! The only thing that is tax free in this country is the profit on the sale of your principal residence.

TAX AUDITS

Tax audits exist to protect the integrity of Canada's self-assessment method of income tax filing. Audits encourage compliance. According to the government, in the 1992-1993 tax year, there were 73,000 income tax forms reassessed (read: audited) and Revenue Canada recovered an additional 2.8 billion dollars for their coffers. During the same time frame, a GST audit of 100,000 tax-fillers generated an extra one and a half billion dollars of unclaimed GST.

Who gets audited is determined by very sophisticated software and very knowledgeable staff who are keenly aware of regional, industry and business inconsistencies. Also, if a tire company gets audited, for example, there is a reasonable chance that the subcontractors, shareholders and other affiliates may also be audited.

Once the notice of assessment goes out, the government has three years to audit you. You can be guaranteed that sooner or later Revenue Canada will catch up with you if you subscribe to the school of creative accounting and tax planning. Most financial advisors suggest that it is in your best interest in the long run to stay above board. Sensible advice.

HOW WILL YOUR INVESTMENTS BE TAXED WHEN THEY GROW UP?

Canadians love their CSBs and GICs. They are right up there with our love for maple syrup and hockey. CSBs and similar investments are fine for older or low-risk investors and as a source of emergency funds, but we tend to rely on them for everything. They appeal to our essentially conservative nature, but the problem is that the interest from these investments is taxed at our marginal (or top) tax rate. (There is, however, a major shift toward investing in mutual funds as interest rates remain low.) This creates a paradox for Canadians because the more conservative we are with our investments, the more we are taxed.

There are basically three forms of investment income—*interest, capital gains* and *dividends*—and they all get different tax treatment. As shown below, stocks, bonds and certain mutual funds which take advantage of capital gains and dividend income receive preferential tax treatment at the hands of Revenue Canada. For the most part, riskier investments, those in the top third of the priority pyramid, get tax relief. Anything at the bottom of the pyramid gets fully taxed, such as any interest you earn on your GICs or Canada Savings Bonds.

As described earlier, let us imagine, for simplicity's sake, that you are in a 50 percent tax bracket. You earn $100 in interest on a GIC. Revenue Canada will squirrel away its share of $50 out of that $100 interest for its pocket. This happens for anything on

FIGURE 9.1 AFTER-TAX RETURN ON INVESTMENT INCOME

INTEREST INCOME
EARNED ON:
T-BILLS, MONEY MARKET FUNDS, MORTGAGE AND BOND FUNDS, GICS, CSBS AND BANK ACCOUNTS

TAX PAYABLE ON: 100% OF THE INTEREST AMOUNT, AT THE SAME RATE AS EARNED INCOME.

CAPITAL GAINS
EARNED ON:
EQUITY AND GROWTH FUNDS AND POSSIBLY ON BOND AND MORTGAGE FUNDS

TAX PAYABLE ON: 75% OF THE CAPITAL GAIN, AT THE SAME RATE AS EARNED INCOME.

DIVIDENDS
EARNED ON:
STOCKS, DIVIDEND AND EQUITY FUNDS

TAXES PAYABLE: CALCULATED USING A GROSS UP AND DIVIDEND TAX CREDIT FORMULA.

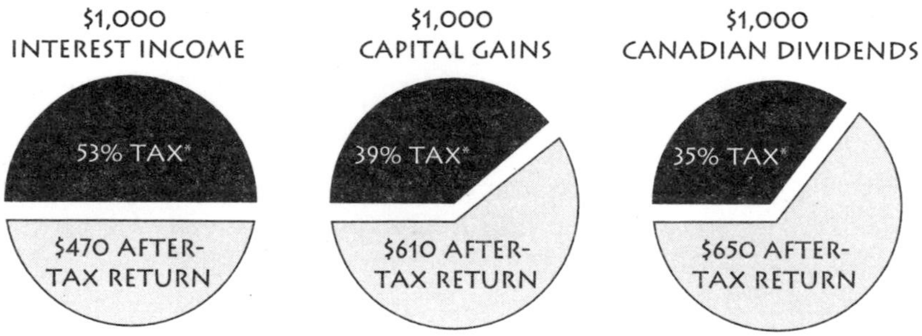

$1,000 INTEREST INCOME — 53% TAX* — $470 AFTER-TAX RETURN

$1,000 CAPITAL GAINS — 39% TAX* — $610 AFTER-TAX RETURN

$1,000 CANADIAN DIVIDENDS — 35% TAX* — $650 AFTER-TAX RETURN

* TAX PAYABLE, ASSUMING THE HIGHEST APPROXIMATE COMBINED 1995 FEDERAL AND PROVINCIAL (ONTARIO) TAX RATES.

Source: Royal Bank *Report On Investment Planning*. Reproduced with permission.

which you earn a guaranteed interest, things like daily interest savings accounts, CSBs, term deposits and GICs. So if you stay in the base of our beloved pyramid, you will get chewed up in taxes (the exceptions being your principal residence and RRSPs). The higher you travel up the pyramid, the better the tax picture looks. For example, stocks, bonds and certain types of mutual funds are not subject to this high form of taxation. It's the government's way of creating a little incentive for Canadians to invest in themselves and the Canadian economy.

CAPITAL GAINS AND LOSSES

If you bought something for $15 and sold it for $20, you have made a $5 capital gain. If, however, you bought something for $15 and sold it for $5, you have experienced a capital loss of $10. It's not a whole lot more complicated than that.

THE DIVIDEND TAX CREDIT

Dividend income from Canadian corporations gets better tax treatment than does plain, old interest income. If you own shares in BCE Inc. (Bell Canada) and receive $500 in dividends, you will pay less tax than if you receive the same amount in interest from Canada Savings Bonds. The way in which the dividend tax credit is calculated is complex, to say the least. Although the main reason for the complex calculation is to avoid what is called "double taxation," I laughed out loud (from disbelief that they could make something so complicated and cumbersome) when I saw how it was done. Elaine Wyatt explains this concept in her book *The Money Companion* as simply as I've seen it explained anywhere. I can't improve upon her explanation so I'll quote it here: "Because the corporation in which you've invested has already paid taxes on the dividends it has paid to you, there is a dividend tax credit you can use to reduce your taxes. To claim this complicated credit, you must 'gross-up'—a peculiar phrase meaning 'increase'—the dividend you've received by 25 percent and then calculate your federal tax on this increased amount. You then subtract the dividend tax credit of 16.67 percent of the dividend you actually received. Finally, you add your provincial tax."[26] Your accountant or financial advisor will explain this to you in more detail. But as a starting point, it is important to be aware that this credit can be of benefit to your overall after-tax picture.

MARGINAL TAX BRACKETS

Throughout the book I have used examples based on a 50 percent tax rate. One of the fundamentals of tax planning is knowing what marginal tax bracket you fall into. The tax system is divided into levels or brackets that are based on how much you earn, how you earn it and what province you live in. The federal tax rate, not including provincial tax, works out to 17 percent on anything you earn up to $29,590. It then increases to 26 percent on anything you earn between $29,591 and $59,180. Finally, anything you make over $59,180 is taxed at 29 percent.

When you add the provincial share, your tax rate can go as high as 70 percent. This includes the surtaxes, which are taxes on taxes. The highest tax rate generally hovers somewhere around 53 percent, however. The provincial tax rate tends to be pretty similar from province to province, so I will use my home province as an example. The combined federal-provincial marginal tax rates in Ontario work like this:

- If your salary is between $6,757 and $29,590 a year, the government takes 25.8 percent of anything you make over and above $6,750. The interest you earn on your Canada Savings Bond is taxed at 27.4 percent at this income level. Any dividend income is taxed at 7.4 percent and any capital gain you receive is taxed at 20.5 percent.

- Once your paycheque starts to read from $29,591 up to $33,400, Revenue Canada whittles away 40.3 percent of your salary, 41.9 percent of the interest on your CSB, 25.5 percent on dividend income and 31.3 percent on any capital gain.

- Between $33,401 and $40,560, the government will take 41 percent of anything earned in this range. Interest income is taxed at 41.9 percent, dividends and capital gains again at 25.5 percent and 31.4 percent respectively.

- There is no appreciable increase in the tax rate until you hit the $59,181 mark. Anything you make over and above this amount, including the interest on your guaranteed investments, is taxed at 50.1 percent. Dividends are taxed at 33.8 percent and capital gains at 37.5 percent.

- The final marginal tax bracket is for all those lucky sods earning $66,653 and over. Revenue Canada will quietly relieve you of over half the income you earn, up to 53.2 percent. The interest on your GIC will automatically get taxed at 53.2 percent since interest income is always taxed at your highest bracket. Dividends get a better break at 35.9 percent and capital gains at 39.9 percent.

Your marginal tax bracket also tells you how much you will save if you use a tax deductible investment such as an RRSP. If you are in a 41 percent tax bracket and you deduct one dollar from your taxable income, you will save yourself 41 cents in taxes. So when you hear people say they are in a 50 percent tax bracket, that doesn't necessarily mean the government takes exactly half of *everything* they earn, though it may feel like it. It simply means that everything they earn in excess of a certain amount is taxed at that level. Where this becomes very important is in choosing your investments. As we have seen, the interest you earn on GICs and Canada Savings Bonds is taxed at your *highest tax bracket.*

INCOME SPLITTING

Spousal RRSPs allow you to split your income with your partner who earns less money than you do. RESPs allow you to split your income with your children who earn less than you do. The idea is that since they earn less, there is less tax. For example, Mom, who is in a 52 percent tax bracket, can split some of her income with Dad who is in a 26 percent tax bracket or with her daughter Sally who is in the lowest possible tax bracket because she is still in school. Once Sally starts to work and earns an income, her tax liability will go up. This family is saving money on every dollar of taxable income transferred over. This is because the investment will be taxed in Dad's or Sally's hands, at their lower tax rate, when they cash it in. What's a little tax among family, right?

INCOME DEFERRAL

This is great for self-employed, commissioned, or professional people who control their billing cycle or for self-employed women planning to have children. Income deferral means taking income from a high rate tax year and shifting it forward to a lower rate tax year. Consider a woman who earns a good income this year, but knows she will be off next year having a baby. Next year's tax rate will be lower because her income will be lower. She can shift some of her earnings from the high year to the low year when she will be on maternity leave. This strategy will balance out the tax burden. It works with deductions as well. She can shift any deductions she has in the low rate tax year to a high rate tax year when they will serve an infinitely better purpose.

TAX DEDUCTIONS

The great Canadian dream is to reduce the tax one has to pay. If you earn $29,591, you will have to pay 26 percent on $29,590 and 40 percent for that one dollar which is into the next bracket. This is where tax deductions come in. The idea is to reduce your taxable income so you won't have to pay at such a high rate. If I can come up with a deduction, say an RRSP contribution, that will reduce my taxable income, I won't have to pay 40 percent on that dollar. I've just dropped myself down into the lower tax bracket. If I have a $100 tax deduction and I am in a 40 percent tax bracket, it will save me $40. If I'm in a 26 percent tax bracket, a $100 deduction will save me $26. Some examples of expenses that may qualify as deductions are child care expenses, interest on loans made for investment purposes, fees paid to accountants and other financial advisors, credit card fees (if you use the cards for business) and moving expenses.

TAX CREDITS

Tax credits are different from tax deductions, which are part of the calculation of taxable income. Tax credits are subtracted directly from the amount of tax due to Revenue Canada. If you have a tax credit of $100, it will result in a $100 tax saving regardless of your tax bracket. Tax credits are available for things like being married and working unpaid in the home, and for medical and education expenses.

Tax credits are considered to be fairer than tax deductions. The benefit of a tax credit is not dependent on the income you make, but is the same for everyone. With deductions, on the other hand, the more income you make, the more benefit you derive. Low income earners do not benefit from deductions to the same extent as higher income earners. That is why tax reform has converted many deductions to credits, which is supposed to make the system fairer. However, two areas that have remained deductions and have not been converted to credits affect women squarely in their pocket books. RRSPs and child care expenses.

WHAT IF YOU'RE SELF-EMPLOYED?

I discovered the tax implications of being self-employed the hard way one year. I was used to having my employer take off the necessary deductions for income tax. This particular year I underestimated my income and subsequent tax requirements. My accountant called me at home one evening and insisted that I sit down. It was good advice. I had a heart attack when I realized that for the first time in my adult life I would have to pay Revenue Canada instead of the other way around. This was because I had not properly planned for the payment of my own taxes now that I was self-employed. I immediately opened a tax account wherein I deposited a set amount each month to pay my tax bill. As a self-employed person, you are obligated to make quarterly payments to Revenue Canada for which they will bill you directly. These payments are based on your previous year's income. The good news about being self-employed is that you can choose your own year end as long as you maintain consistency in the following years. This allows for regular tax deferrals, like income shifting. Revenue Canada is also more liberal in the tax deductions it makes available for those gutsy individuals who choose to go it alone. Remember that since you are now your own employer you also have to provide for all your own benefits such as pensions and insurance.

WOMEN AND THE TAX SYSTEM

THE GENERAL ISSUES

It is sobering to see that much of our system is still based on the free services of women as caregivers and on the family as traditionally defined—"mommy and daddy and baby make three." Contradictions surface because women are more and more becoming an integral part of the labour force. There is tax legislation in place that was initially designed in the '40s to encourage women to work unpaid in the home. We need policies that reflect the fact that it has become the norm for families to have two income earners, policies that acknowledge that the vast majority of Canada's poor are single mothers, children and elderly women. Why is it that women earn on average only two-thirds what men earn in this country and therefore have a harder time taking advantage of tax breaks designed for higher income earners? What about the fact that more and more Canadians are living common-law? What about same-sex couples and their invisible treatment by the system? Why does the tax system assume that the income brought into every family is shared equally? Why are women financially penalized in their later years for choosing to work unpaid in the home? Why do divorced women pay tax on their support payments while men get to deduct the costs of support from their taxable income?

Until recently, the system has also assumed that everyone gets married in the customary sense. The traditional family is no longer the norm. Single parent families are normal. So are common-law families. Gay and lesbian families are struggling for their right to be recognized in the eyes of the government and the legal system.

Much has been accomplished. But close examination of many of today's tax policies will show there is still much work to be done. These policies continue to reflect the values of the '40s and '50s. Many of the tax laws that affect women haven't been changed since they were implemented in a very different world over 50 years ago.

The number of Canadian women living below the poverty line is on the rise. Between 1971 and 1986, the number of women living in poverty in this country grew 110.3 percent. During the same period, men's poverty level increased by 23.8 percent.[27] As discussed earlier, women are breaking out of the pink collar ghetto and now represent 50 percent of those graduating from law and medical schools. Once they graduate, however, they find circumstances not unlike those facing their sisters in the secondary or service labour force. Consider, for example, the difficulties encountered by women in the law profession.

Even though women make up half of the enrollment and the graduating classes in law and medical schools, they represent in disproportionate numbers those leaving these professions. In 1991, the Canadian Bar Association conducted an in-depth study of gender-related issues amongst its members called *Transitions*. Here are some of the highlights:

- Women lawyers bear almost twice as much responsibility for childcare as male lawyers.

- Fifty-eight percent of the male lawyers reported that their partners did most of the housework as compared to five percent of the women lawyers. Thirty-nine percent of the women lawyers took on most of the household responsibilities compared to four percent of the men.

- Three times as many women as men rely on paid caregivers.

- When asked about balancing career and family, six times as many women as men say they have lost income because of their child-rearing responsibilities.

- Many more women report child-rearing responsibilities as a reason for leaving the law profession than do men.

- A strong support system is lacking for people with families. Sixty-four percent of members reported disability insurance as part of their benefits package while only seven percent had paternity leave and job sharing.

- Women deal with a higher degree of questioning and testing of their commitment to their law careers as a direct result of being child-bearers and caregivers.

- The report demonstrated that substantial differences in the income levels of male and female lawyers continue to exist, particularly within the private practice of law.

A spokesperson for the Canadian Bar Association was quoted in *The Globe and Mail* in February 1993 stating, "If existing business culture had not been based on a gendered division of labour, child-care expenses would have been seen as business expenses. If men had been responsible for child care and had not had access to the unpaid labour of their spouses, child-care expenses would manifestly have been seen to have been expended 'in the ordinary course of business'."

So the controversy rages. The issue of gender inequities in the tax system is profoundly difficult and complicated. There is a wealth of proposed solutions from a variety of sources reflecting the whole range of political beliefs. Some suggestions leaning to the left would see a state supported, universal child care implemented and abolishment of high income earners preferred tax deduction programs like RRSPs. Some opinions leaning to the right, on the other hand, believe the answers are outside of the tax system and some may suggest that child care should remain an individual or family responsibility. One thing is for sure, there is no shortage of opinions. However, one cannot have an opinion unless one knows the issues.

CONSUMPTION TAXES

It is very important to have equity in a *progressive* tax system. There are two ways to achieve this fairness. One is *horizontal equity* which means that those sharing a similar financial picture are taxed in more or less the same manner regardless of the source of income. As the Canadian Advisory Council on the Status of Women's publication called *Tax Facts: What Every Woman Should Know* suggests, "A system that taxes investment income at lower rates than earnings from paid employment is not committed to horizontal equity."[28]

Vertical equity, on the other hand, means that people in different situations are treated accordingly, i.e., that you are taxed according to your ability to pay. Under this kind of system, those in the high income range pay more tax. A system is said to be progressive if the tax burden is the lightest on those who can least afford to pay.

A progressive tax system should also be simple and relatively inexpensive to administer so that the government can levy taxes that will maximize its financial gains. *Tax Facts* suggests that Canada's tax system has become less progressive and more regressive. The whole concept of "those who can, pay" has been undermined by the introduction of consumption taxes. Consumption taxes are based, not on your ability to pay, but on what you buy or consume. In 1992, 23 percent of the government's tax revenue came from this form of taxation. Though almost all industrialized countries have some kind of poll or GST-type tax, that still doesn't change the fact that it is the low income earner who is hurt the most. And who makes up a disproportional percentage of low income earners in this country? Women. Women generally find themselves having to spend most of their paycheque on essentials like food, shelter and clothing. Here is an example of how consumption taxes affect the low-income earner. Let's assume an eight percent sales tax. Indra and Bryan both buy $5,000 worth of goods and services a year. Indra is the low-income earner making $15,000 a year. The tax on her purchases represents 2.7 percent of her salary. Bryan earns $80,000 a year. The tax on his purchases is only 0.5 percent of his salary. Hence the term *regressive tax system* because it penalizes the low-income earner more dramatically. However, the government has introduced a GST credit for the lower-income taxpayers, but the tax credit isn't indexed for inflation so its value will diminish over the years.

INDEXING FOR INFLATION

Inflation has a major impact on fair taxation. Before the tax reform of 1986, our tax system was fully indexed for inflation. Tax brackets, credits and deductions were adjusted each year according to cost of living increases. This is no longer the case. The federal government will only adjust the tax brackets, credits, deductions and repayment of Old Age Security benefits for inflation over three percent. Therefore, there is some protection, but not for the full amount. This means that the long-term value of credits and deductions will be eroded over time. Since women live as long as they do, anything that affects the policy on inflation is of grave concern. The failure to restore full indexing has been viewed by critics as one of the most serious omissions of the mid '80s tax reform.

TAX TREATMENT OF WOMEN WHO "DON'T WORK" AND WOMEN WHO DO

I'm curious. Just who are these women who "don't work"? It is a term I hear frequently and yet I do not know who these women are. I have posed this question to both women and men. Many respond: "You know, like my mother and grandmother. They *just* stayed at home and looked after us."

After my temper cools, I am inclined to do a little explaining. My great-grandmother, grandmother and mother were women who "didn't work." In order to get a sense of what life was like for the rural women on her side of the family, I asked my mother to write about their lives. My mother wrote a wonderful letter which vividly detailed aspects of the work load of three generations of farm women. The letter described making laundry soap from the fat of animals, sewing sheets, pillowcases and undergarments from bleached flour bags, scrubbing, rinsing and wringing every item of clothing by hand on wash day, canning, churning butter and slaughtering livestock. I was exhausted by just reading the letter. Furthermore, the letter depicted only a small part of the daily routine. Add to those chores maintaining the house, garden and livestock *and* caring for children. My grandmother Hazel was an exceptional seamstress as well as cook, butcher, nurse, doctor and veterinarian, teacher, mortician (women often undertook the task of preparing bodies after death) and midwife. Yet Census Canada listed farm wives as well as other women who worked in the home as "no occupation." Modern conveniences have eased the load considerably, but the work remains. I have always believed that the most automated appliance in the household is my mother. The 1993 United Nations Human Development Report stated that if economic value was put on the work women do in the home, the *world's* gross domestic product would increase by over 30 percent.

You would be hard pressed to find anyone these days making their own soap or washing sheets and blankets by hand, but I use this example to illustrate a point. Today's women who "don't work" but stay home to raise families are doing the unpaid work of nurses, cleaners, cooks, psychologists, seamstresses, chauffeurs, diplomats, managers, planners and educators. In today's world, money is the way society shows that it values what you are doing. These jobs acquire an entirely different status the minute a wage is exchanged for the same services. It is my personal mission in life to eliminate the phrases "women who don't work" and "just a housewife" from our vocabulary. I once heard Roseanne eloquently proclaim, "I don't like the terms 'housewife' and 'homemaker.' I prefer to be called 'Domestic Goddess'... it's more descriptive."

The 1970 Royal Commission on the Status of Women, The Fair Tax Commission in Ontario and various women's groups such as The Canadian Advisory Council on the Status of Women all share a common vision—that women's unpaid work in the home get some kind of economic recognition. Over the years, there have been demands for provisions in the tax system that would recognize this unpaid work, not only in tax treatment, but also in provisions for retirement.

The Fair Tax Commission evaluated tax systems from different countries, including the U.S. It decided that Canada's "modified individual tax unit" was the best system for supporting women's economic independence and autonomy. This modified individu-ally-based system states that while the *individual* is the basic unit of taxation, marital and family status are relevant in some instances. Even though using "the couple" as a unit of taxation has been touted as a measure of equity and fairness, there is evi-dence to show this isn't the case. The argument states that the proper measurement of "ability to pay" should be total family in-come. Even if income isn't split equally in the household, the tax payable by couples with the same total income should not vary. Some arguments also suggest that since it is cheaper to live as a married couple than as a single person, the tax payable should reflect this reality.

Critics of this system accurately point out that recognition of the *marriage unit* instead of the *individual* can, in many cases, make it more advantageous from a tax point of view for the woman to stay out of the paid labour force. This can work against women's autonomy if it is their choice to work outside the home. The rate of participation of married women in the paid labour force has increased over the last 20 years. Nevertheless, studies have shown that a married woman's decision to join the paid labour force is more wage and tax sensitive than a man's. Women are not recognized as separate and distinct from their relation-ship with their mate when couples are used as a tax unit.

PENSIONS AND RETIREMENT SAVINGS PROGRAMS

You will remember the story of Lynn and Stan, their messy sep-aration, and Stan's untimely death. As dreadful as this may be to say, had Stan not died when he did, Lynn could have become one of the poverty statistics in her retirement. She couldn't contribute directly to an RRSP. Stan was not receptive to the idea of setting up a spousal RRSP. She didn't qualify for Canada Pension Plan benefits since she worked unpaid in the home. Stan was self-employed and had no company pension from which Lynn could get survivor benefits. She would have been entirely dependent on Old Age Security and whatever Stan had arranged for her. She was very vulnerable.

RRSP contribution levels have almost doubled since 1990, which is good news to high-income earners. The old rules al-lowed $7,500 as a maximum contribution if you didn't have a pension plan or 20 percent of your total net income, whichever was less. Today, you can contribute $13,500 or 18 percent of your total net income, whichever is less. Do you notice what I notice? The high-income earners get a better tax break. You need to earn in the neighbourhood of $75,000 to take advantage of the maximum allowable contribution. This is almost four times the average income of women who filed tax returns in 1992. The low to middle income earner gets to contribute less: 18 percent instead of 20 percent.

These tax policies aren't *intended* to discriminate specifically against women. They are, however, detrimental to the low-income earner. We don't need to be reminded who makes up the majority of this group.

CHILD CARE EXPENSES

Suitable child care is essential to women's economic independence. The Fair Tax Commission notes that "the lack of child care is one of the greatest barriers to self-reliance facing sole-support parents. The absence of affordable child care of adequate quality is also a major obstacle to equality in the workplace for mothers."[29] The average cost of child care outside the home ranges from $13,000 a year for an infant to $4,200 a year for a school-aged child. A domestic worker providing child care in the home will cost the employer on average about $18,000 a year.[30]

Sixty-six percent of mothers in families with pre-school children were in the workforce in 1991. Many women, particularly single mothers, are unable to afford child care and have to rely on informal arrangements with friends or relatives. In Ontario alone, it is estimated that 80 percent of the children receiving non-parental care are in unlicensed child care. The women providing this service are paid at the lowest end of the wage scale and often prefer to deal in cash. It then becomes impossible to provide the necessary receipts to qualify for the income tax deduction. It is estimated that in Ontario, only 40 percent of the women who qualified for this deduction actually claimed it in 1992.[31] Again, it seems that those who earn higher levels of income are the major beneficiaries. Parents who provide receipts can deduct up to $5,000 a year per child under seven or over seven if that child has a severe disability. For those in the 50 percent tax bracket, that works out to a tax savings of $2,500 a year. The maximum annual deduction is reduced to $3,000 for children between seven and 15. Lower-income parents who don't claim the deduction are able to claim a $213 credit for each child under seven.

Tax Facts points out that the deduction for child care expenses was retained as a deduction and was not converted to a credit as were most other deductions during the last tax reform. The amount of the deduction was increased, and so the high-income taxpayer benefits even more. The suggested solutions to the various problems associated with the child care expenses deduction have ranged from creating universally available, publicly funded child care facilities to abolishing the tax deduction and using the resulting tax revenues to fund child care programs. One thing I'm fairly certain of—my grandchildren will still be waging this battle.

CHILD SUPPORT PAYMENTS

In 1990, child support orders were issued in only 68 percent of the divorce cases involving dependent children and averaged only $250 per month per child. Until recently, in a great many cases the enforcement of these support orders was difficult or impossible. Fifty-seven percent of single parent families headed by women in Canada live below the poverty line.

In a discussion with Hubert Frenken of Statistics Canada, I was alarmed to discover that, in 1991, there were 90,000 unpaid support orders representing 470 million dollars in delinquent payments. As a result, Ontario's Bill 17, which came into effect in March, 1992, implements strict measures for collecting delinquent payments from the wages of employees. Employers are obligated to withhold amounts of support payments from wages and these deductions are as obligatory as UI and CPP deductions. In 1994, this Family Support Plan Act of Ontario collected $367 million from deadbeat dads. Before the legislation (i.e., before March 1992), child support receipts averaged $14 million monthly. By March 1995, they had jumped to $36.8 million as a result of mandatory remittance. This is legislation whose time has definitely come. As well, according to 1989 tax returns, the average amount of child and spousal support payments received was 15 percent of the total income of the recipients (mainly women) whereas the amount paid represented 9 percent of the average income of the payors.

The issue of child support payments and how they are taxed is a very contentious one. The situation is that the men (and it usually is men) who make these support payments can use them as a tax deduction, while the women who receive the income have to pay income tax on it. This is not typical tax policy, which takes great pains to define tax deductions as *expenditures made in earning an income*. Critics of this practice state that money used to raise children should be outside of the tax system completely. Similar deductions are not available for parents living together or for the custodial parent. There seems to be a complete absence of horizontal equity in this instance.

Proponents of this tax arrangement consider it a form of income splitting. Men earning higher incomes off load some of it, and the resulting tax liability, to the lower income spouse. The wife is often in a lower tax bracket so will pay less tax. The original legislation was designed in the 1940s to create significant tax savings but it was based on a very traditional view—that after divorce or separation, the husband would continue to be a high-income earner and the wife to work unpaid in the home. Today, most single mothers *have* to work outside the home, and not all husbands are high-income earners. The number of tax brackets has been reduced since the '40s, which means that support payers and recipients may be in the same tax bracket even though one earns more than the other.

The view that child support payments should be included as income in order to be fair from a tax perspective seems to me an unusual one. I wonder why these payments are even considered as income when they are simply reimbursements of costs incurred by the custodial parent to raise the children. Most believe that both parents have an obligation to share these costs equally. Critics of the existing system state that it would make more sense to take child support payments out of the tax system entirely, so that they are neither deductible nor included as income. Such a policy would result in equal tax treatment for parents who live together or apart.

Suzanne Thibedeau was catapulted into the limelight when she took her case to the Supreme Court of Canada arguing that she was being discriminated against because she was required to pay tax on the $1,150 in monthly child support she receives from her former husband, who was not taxed on that income.

Thibedeau won her case, but the federal government appealed the decision in order to buy time to look at this complex issue in more detail. Though the government won the appeal, there was a compelling element to the May 1995 court ruling which stated that it was not unconstitutional to require the custodial parent who receives child support to pay tax on that money while the payor (predominantly men) can use it as a tax deduction. The decision was split 5-2 by the country's top judges—with the three men arguing for continuing with the status quo and the two women on the bench dissenting.

Although the government may appear to be the bad guy here, in fact it is not unsympathetic to women's problems with this issue. Despite the Supreme Court's ruling against Thibedeau, the government continues to work to restore fairness to the system. The Justice Department is finalizing a guideline to increase settlements by introducing a standard formula to help judges calculate the impact of taxes and decide how much should be awarded. The government also plans to crack down on non-custodial parents who don't make their payments. Passports and driver's licenses may be denied to those whose child support payments are in arrears.

Until some of these initiatives are adopted as law, the following suggestions can be used:

- Many people I know stick to a verbal deal. Though the payor loses out on the tax deduction, the payee doesn't have to pay the tax. But you have to be able to trust the person not to renege—you don't have any legal ground to stand on if they do bail out. And in divorce, trust is a rare commodity. Revenue Canada will likely seek to ensure some predictability to these payments, however, but this will end up making the income taxable. It's always best to be completely above board.

- Do as Lynn attempted to do: Get your payments grossed up to reflect the tax liability. Pray that your spouse doesn't slam the door shut on negotiations, as Stan did. If he does, you won't have to pay tax on any money you receive from him since there is no legal agreement. Grossing up your payments is, for the moment, likely to be your best recourse.

- Things are different, of course, if you have a wealthy spouse who can afford to pay you a lump sum. This isn't taxable because it's not categorized as a periodic payment. An ex of mine gave his former wife a lump sum—unfortunately she went out and blew the whole bundle in less than five years. She's in dire financial trouble now, and has been for several years. So there are risks in this method if you don't have financial savvy or know someone else who does, who can help you. It's also tough to know how much is enough to carry you through till your financial obligations end.

- Some people organize it so that each is responsible for specific expenses in raising the children. He would pay for field trips, for example, while she pays for the Nikes. You'd better have an open line of communication should certain expenses discontinue and new ones come up. These ongoing money discussions are fertile ground for additional animosity.

- One of the best tips I could give you is to cover this issue in your prenuptial agreement or marriage contract long before divorce becomes a reality. Even restating the existing laws in the agreement will encourage couples to think before they leap. No contract can override the tax law, but one could, possibly, improve the protection available under family law. Be sure to talk to a lawyer about the matter—it's easier to walk away from a lawyer than from your partner.

SPOUSAL SUPPORT PAYMENTS

In the old days these payments were called "alimony." The assumption again was that in a marriage the woman was dependent on her husband's income. She was entitled to continuing support if found blameless in the breakup of the marriage until she remarried and became financially dependent on another man. Nowadays, spousal support payments are based on what women have contributed to the relationship through actual income, personal property and work done in the home. An important discrepancy in the tax treatment of such payments is that lump sum support payments and those that aren't court ordered are neither tax deductible nor included in the income of the recipient. However, those who receive periodic payments do have to pay tax on those payments. There is a distinct lack of horizontal equity here. At the very least, most tax commissions suggest that there should be a distinction made between support paid to wives and that to children. There isn't at the moment.

CHILD TAX BENEFITS

January 1993 saw the demise of three social programs—Family Allowance, credit for dependent children and the refundable child tax credit which provided benefits to families with children. These were replaced by an integrated child benefit. The new benefit is income-related, which means the more you make, the less you will receive. A low-income family with one child could receive $85 a month while a middle-income family with two might get $70 a month. The number of children you have does also have an effect. The idea is that the more children you have, the less discretionary income is available to pay taxes. Even families earning $85,000 will receive some benefits if both mom and dad work outside the home and have three children to care for.

The new integrated child benefit was put in place to assist people who really need help in raising their families. Since so many of our children live in poverty, this was seen as a direct anti-poverty measure. While in theory, and to some extent in practice, this seems fair, what begins to happen is that the concepts of horizontal equity and universality become eroded. The old "credit for dependent children" recognized that people who have families do not have the same ability to pay taxes as those who don't and they also are making a social contribution. In designing the new tax system, however, the government took away benefits from some families with children to give to other families with children. This benefit, therefore, ceased to be enjoyed by *all* taxpayers with children. Eliminating the old benefit also eliminated the principle that couples with children do not have the same ability to pay taxes as people without children who earn the same level of income.

Another bone of contention is the special supplement for low-income earners with both parents in the paid labour force. As *Tax Facts* points out, "These families can receive an increase in child benefit (up to $500). But parents without paid jobs are excluded. This means a single mother on social assistance would actually receive lower child benefits than a low income woman working outside the home." The new child benefit is not taxable, but like other social benefits, it is only partially indexed and will lose much of its teeth over the years.

I remember a conversation I had with Lynn shortly after these changes to the new child benefit had been made. Because of Stan's income, they would not have qualified for these benefits to any significant degree. She commented that she understood the rationale behind the changes, but she still felt disturbed. Intellectually, she supported the notion that those who need it the most should get it, and she knew that the country could no longer afford to pay Family Allowance to everyone. What disturbed her, however, was that the Family Allowance was the only income, nominal though it was, that she received in her own name and that she could control. More importantly, it was some kind of recognition for the work she was doing in the home. I was flabbergasted when I heard it put in this context. Even though this benefit didn't make a significant financial contribution to her household, it did recognize the special contribution to society that women like Lynn make who work at home bearing and raising our children.

TRADITIONAL MARRIAGE VERSUS LIVING COMMON-LAW

Another concept that is important to a fair tax system is neutrality. The tax system should not determine your choice of lifestyle or economic activity. In reality, however, it does. Because the government needs people to save for their own retirement, it has created incentives like Registered Retirement Savings Plans. The tax treatment of married couples as compared to common-law couples is another area where the tax system has had an impact. In the '80s, the number of people opting to live together instead of getting married actually doubled. I know of several couples who chose living together instead of marriage because of the favoured tax treatment offered to common-law couples.

That all changed in January 1993, however. As of this date, common-law spouses are "deemed" to be married in the eyes of the *Income Tax Act*. For *all* purposes. This change reduced and eliminated child tax benefits previously enjoyed by non-traditionally married couples with children. Single parents with common-law partners lose the ability to claim a special credit called the equivalent-to-married credit for dependent children. Since mothers have custody of the children in significantly greater numbers than fathers, this change will affect them more. The new amendments also mean that only one principal residence is allowed per "family unit" for purposes of the principal residence exemption. Two unmarried spouses living together are now considered a "family unit." Common-law couples are now able to make spousal RRSP contributions and to transfer property between them on a tax deferred basis.

There has also been a human rights tribunal declaration that the definition of "spouses" should include same-sex partners. No one can guess when and if the *Income Tax Act* will ever be amended to reflect this decision. It is generally agreed by most advocacy groups that one's marital status plays too important a role in the tax system, which therefore loses its neutrality. Many believe that one should be free to choose how one will live without tax consequences having to be a part of that choice.

In my capacity as a financial lecturer, I am frequently surprised at the low level of awareness by both women and men as to how the tax system affects women differently. These issues have been in the social consciousness and on the political agenda since the 1966 Royal Commission on Taxation, and the subsequent commissions on the Status of Women and the more recent Fair Tax Commission. That's almost 30 years of hounding various governments to revamp tax policies to reflect more accurately the realities of women's lives. Awareness by a critical mass has always been the first step to social change—the operative words here being *critical mass.* The more people know and are disturbed by the status quo, the greater the chance for change.

It's up to us as women to educate ourselves on how the tax system works, despite its complexities, so we can change it.

WHO IS RIGHT FOR YOU?: GETTING THROUGH THE FINANCIAL SERVICES MAZE

> *"If you educate a man, you educate a person, but if you educate a woman, you educate a family."*
>
> Ruby Manikan, writer

One of my major pleasures is my StairMaster. Not only is it wonderful for the physical health benefits, but it is powerfully effective as a stress buster. I can get on it and lose myself for long periods of time. My leg muscles would put Hulk Hogan to shame. Some of my best ideas are born while I am exercising. One day I was furiously climbing the stairs to nowhere and enjoying the freefloating thinking process that always results. I was contemplating how much more secure I felt. It wasn't because I had won the lottery or had amassed an unimaginable fortune. Not even close. But I *was* organized, educated and responsibly saving for things that mattered in my life.

"Wow!" I thought, as I wiped the sweat from my forehead. "Can this actually be me? Has this financial reprobate crossed over from the dark side!?" I certainly hadn't skipped and leapt joyously down the road to a fulfilled and prosperous financial future. It was a definite trudge, sometimes fearful and reluctant. I let my mind roll back to that pivotal day of my thirtieth birthday. Life had definitely taken a turn somewhere. "It's amazing I managed to do this!" I thought to myself in awe. Then, with lightning speed, another thought intruded. "Elaine. That's how I managed to do this," I thought as I leapt off my StairMaster to cool down. My turnaround resulted from a combination of my dedication and desire to get on track and her common sense and understandable approach. Elaine had given me the road map to follow and had acted as tour guide when I needed her. She could be a financial advisor one minute and a psychologist the next. She was a friend all the time.

How easy it would have been to succumb to the allure of seminars or books whose titles scream out "Financial Planning Made Easy" or "How To Become A Millionaire Without Risk or Sacrifice, With Little Money, In Five Minutes." Elaine's gift to me was her "Get Rich Slow" style—one step at a time, building a solid foundation, with just enough sizzle to keep my interest. I have been able to pass on this approach to my own clients.

As I towelled off, I pondered what kept me so focused. Undoubtedly, considering financial services as a career was a major motivating factor. But it was also, in large part, my financial advisor. I needed someone I could trust, someone who would make the journey interesting and "doable." When I became a financial advisor, I stayed very connected with the part of me that knew what people needed from a financial "expert." I drew on my experience with Elaine. I asked my clients what they expected of me 10 minutes after they walked in the door. Many of my clients became friends. There is a lot of empirical data to show that women are relationship-oriented in their business dealings, more so than their male counterparts. Women want to feel a connection with the person they are dealing with. That was certainly my experience both as a client and as a financial advisor.

I have given advice to both men and women, together and separately. I can state unequivocally that men come to the task of financial planning differently from women. How they receive the information (especially if the advisor is a woman), how much information they need and how many questions they ask does vary from man to man and woman to woman. But the differences between men and women—in a word, *unbelievable!* Men challenged my statements much more frequently than women did. Often, when I have spoken privately to the woman after planning for both her and her partner, she has commented on and even apologized for the adversarial tone of her partner. There is no doubt that I needed to "prove" myself more to men than I did to my women clients. Women ask a lot more questions to obtain information and aren't prone to act as if they know something when, in fact, they don't. This has led to one of the greatest criticisms of the financial planning industry: Many advisors prefer the responses and quick action of their male clients to the slower, more detailed process that is involved with women clients.

I was recently a guest on a radio phone-in talk show in Montreal. I was billed as an expert on the topic of women and money and the host encouraged the women of Montreal to call in to ask questions about money. Over the course of an hour, we received 15 calls. The host and myself were astounded by the fact that three women called to ask questions and 12 men called to answer them. No kidding. Every male caller that we spoke with didn't have a question for himself, but began by saying, "That lady's question about trusts? She can do this..." or "I don't think the lady who wants to start saving for her son's education should use mutual funds. They are far too risky and one should never gamble with your kid's education." And so it went.

There were times during the broadcast when the host and I intentionally avoided each other's eyes for fear of completely breaking up with laughter. At one point, he felt compelled to say on the air, "Look guys, this is the woman's time. Let's give them a chance to call in." Afterward, the host said he would never have believed it had he not seen it with his own eyes. He learned a lot about the male sex that day.

So, what do you need to be aware of when looking for a financial advisor? Ask yourself the same question I asked myself: How do I know if I need one? To figure this out, ask yourself: Am I confused about conflicting financial advice from several sources? Do I pay too much tax? Do I have time to look after my financial affairs on my own? Am I having trouble making ends meet or saving money? Has there been a major change in my financial life recently such as job loss, retirement, an inheritance, a new baby or loss of a partner? Then ask yourself: What do financial advisors or planners do exactly? How much do they cost? Is one enough? What qualifications should I look for? Should I avoid people who are paid commission? What about these "women only" places? Will the advisor answer all my questions without being impatient or making me feel stupid? How do I know whom to trust?

I have worked on both sides of the street—on a fee-for-service basis and for commission. I have also had both women and men as advisors. (Elaine eventually moved up the corporate ladder.) I have dealt with new people just starting out and with veterans in the business. It all comes down to this: Once you are comfortable with how they are paid, do you trust the person? Can you envision forming a long-term *relationship* with them? Is this advisor aware of the financial obstacles women face and do they offer appropriate solutions? There is no magical secret. It comes down to asking the right questions and then trusting your intuition, that inner voice everyone has. I have learned to cultivate, listen to and depend on my inner voice. It guides and serves me very well in day-to-day living and has been particularly helpful in determining comfort zones when planning my finances. Although everyone has some form of it, women have been especially blessed with what is commonly referred to as "women's intuition." Authors, poets and scientists have been writing about this phenomenon for centuries and remain baffled by this highly developed gift that women possess. This intuition must be respected. World renowned anthropologist Margaret Mead said, "Because of their age-long training in human relations—for that is what feminine intuition really is—women have a special contribution to make to any group enterprise." It's important to remember that the buck stops with you. Ultimately, you make the decisions even though you are acting on the advice of your advisor.

Lately, there has been a rash of interest in women and their money, from how women invest to how they are treated by financial planners. Trimark Investment Management Inc. launched a successful marketing program targeting women. Scotia McLeod has introduced gender awareness training and "How to Reach The Women's Market" seminars as part of their new broker training program. Other brokerage houses like Midland Walwyn are joining in. In my view, this is good news if for no other reason than that women are finally being acknowledged by the financial institutions in their drive for business. Women do not want special treatment from their advisors or financial institutions. They want to be treated equally and in many cases have not been by the financial services industry which was, until recently, a male bastion of monolithic proportions. Today there are a lot more women selling stocks, life insurance, mutual funds and banking services but, in general, they are sparsely represented in executive suites. As a result of my experience in the computer business, I knew only too well how intimidating financial institutions could be for women. I hadn't dealt with a single woman unless she was an administrative assistant, a clerk, or in human resources. Financial services excluded women as a target market unless they were older wealthy widows. It was a netherworld for women—unless you were part of the 75 percent of the financial industry's lower paid, female labour force. In all my dealings with these financial institutions while in the computer business, I had not been approached by a single person to buy an RRSP or mutual fund—with one exception. A stockbroker called once and asked to speak to my husband. When I told him there wasn't one, he promptly thanked me and hung up. I was aware that certain segments of the financial services industry claimed to be behind the women's movement. It was becoming clear to me that they were. About a hundred years behind. Thankfully, today most of the financial planning industry is beginning to change. Now that I am a part of this industry, I am quite intrigued by some of the studies' findings.

The U.S.-based magazines *Working Woman* and the prestigious *Money* have studied the treatment of women by this male-dominated industry. So has the U.S. mutual fund company, Oppenheimer Management Corporation. Here is a summary of what they have to say:

- Women are less likely to pay for financial advice than men are. This could be because most fee-for-service advisors attract the larger portfolios and most women aren't there yet.

- Women often don't perceive of themselves as investors. They see themselves as savers, and will often deal with banks to address their savings needs. Financial advisors need to help women overcome that perception and to help them become more investment oriented.

- Women are excellent consumers and won't buy over the phone. Cold calling is, therefore, ineffective as a way of targeting women. Seminars, on the other hand, are the most effective way to reach women. They are educational and non-threatening.
- Financial advisors must make sure that women are made to feel equal to men. Women tend to be polite so they will not complain if they are unhappy with the service or the treatment. You simply won't see them again.
- Women are four times less likely than men to change financial advisors. They are less likely to have more than one as well. Studies suggest that women are more loyal and will provide referrals at a higher rate.
- Most women don't care if their advisor is male or female. They just want someone they can trust and who will answer their questions for them.
- Fifty-seven percent of the women in the Oppenheimer study thought they were treated with less respect than men by financial planners. Fifty-four percent of the men agreed.

In September 1993, the magazine, *Working Woman*, published their survey on whether or not financial advice is sexist. A husband and wife writing team went separately to 32 different financial planners in the United States. They had identical incomes, goals and amounts to invest. They spoke with discount brokers, full service brokers, mutual fund companies and different bank branches. They spoke with both male and female advisors, though there were significantly more men than women. This is what they found:

- Essential information about women is often ignored.
- Some advisors routinely neglect retirement planning for women.
- Women often get advice that's either too risky or too conservative.
- Specific investments are touted more often to women.
- Women get friendlier, more courteous service.
- A lot of the advice given to both sexes seems based on inadequate information.

It is because of these factors that "women-only" marketing plans are born. It may sound strange, but my sincere desire is to see books and organizations which offer financial planning specifically for women eventually rendered obsolete. It will be a glorious day when women and men can understand each other's special place and common ground; when a woman won't have to seek financial advice from a woman because she has a better chance of hearing and understanding a woman's needs; when men in the financial services industry will actually talk to a woman about her goals and plans instead of asking to speak to her partner. This attitude tends to polarize women and men into opposing camps, and quite unnecessarily so. The gender of your advisor shouldn't make a difference if everyone knows the facts and acts accordingly. But let's face it, although awareness is improving, this has yet to translate into reality. Men in the industry still assume that the "women's market" is only for women to tap into. However, until everyone admits, let alone understands, the different financial needs of Canadian women, books like this and "women-only" marketing are here to stay, if, for no other reason, than to attract attention and increase awareness.

WHO DOES WHAT

You can see that it is *not* necessarily a level playing field out there. It is critical that you be aware of possible inherent biases within the financial services industry, whether these be gender, company or product biases. In most provinces, except Quebec, there is no regulation of the financial planning industry in Canada, so just about anyone can hang out a "financial planner" shingle. Referrals from associates, friends or family members are always the best

Male Advisors   *Female Advisors*

place to start. You can also check with your local chapter of the Canadian Association of Financial Planners. The national office is at Suite 510, 60 St. Clair Avenue East, Toronto, Ontario M4T 1N5. You can call them at 416-966-9928. An important point regarding the financial services community in Canada: The Association recently did a survey of its membership and found that 80 percent of its members are commissioned sales people. Also 79 percent of the Association's members are male. Don't be surprised by this when you start shopping around.

Armed with the information presented above about the industry, you will be in a better position to create your own level playing field. You can begin to look for an appropriate financial advisor. Choose an advisor who matches the level of complexity of your portfolio, finances and lifestyle. If you are just starting out, choosing an investment counsellor who specializes in port folios of $100,000 or over will be a case of overkill. If you want a partnership agreement with a split dollar buy-sell arrangement, a rookie in the insurance business is obviously not a wise choice. A point about the rookie in the business: Sometimes they will have more time to spend with you. What they do not yet know they can glean from the resources around them. Remember, it is rare that one advisor can be all things to all people.

A financial advisor or planner is a person who will identify where you are today, help you set your goals and objectives and point out any obstacles or opportunities along the way. They will provide written recommendations and will either implement them for you, if they are licensed to do so, or coordinate the implementation of your plan. Annual reviews and periodic updates are also provided. If you are just starting out, you won't require an extensive plan. Financial advisors are on staff at your bank, trust company, insurance company, and mutual fund dealer. They are paid a salary, charge a fee or are paid on commission. Be sure you have realistic expectations about what your advisor can and cannot do. One of the biggest reasons people experience dissatisfaction with their advisor is because they may not clearly understand exactly what their role is. Financial advisors do just that—advise. They are not in the business to make unfounded or unreasonable guarantees. If they do, step lively to the front door and beat a hasty retreat. You must be crystal clear on what service your advisor provides.

How often do they intend to be in contact with you? What resources can they draw upon? Is the firm they work for stable? Who is their typical client? Do they specialize in a certain clientele or product? What is their investment philosophy and approach? Is it consistent with yours?

DESIGNATIONS

There are certain designations people should have or be working toward if they are in the financial planning business. Since the financial planning business is unregulated, just about anyone can call themselves a financial planner. In reality, however, only those with the designation *Registered Financial Planner* (RFP) or *Chartered Financial Planner* (CFP) is legitimately entitled to call themselves a financial planner, though many do anyway. In the insurance industry, the equivalent designations are *Chartered Life Underwriter* and *Chartered Financial Consultant*. Financial advisors tend to be salespeople with securities licences which allow them to sell stocks and bonds or with licences to sell life insurance and mutual funds.

In a nutshell, the general rule is that a financial *advisor* tends to be a holder of registered licences that enable them to sell financial products. *Planners* might also have these licences but they have also completed courses for their Chartered Financial Planner or have taken the six-hour RFP exam. According to the Canadian Association of Financial Planners (CAFP), 40 percent of their membership have RFP or CFP designations. Other designations the CAFP recognizes are an MBA (if the specialty is tax or finance), the insurance industry's Chartered Life Underwriter (CLU) and Chartered Financial Consultant (ChFC), Chartered Accountant (CA), Certified General Accountant (CGA), Certified Management Accountant (CMA), and the securities industry's Certified Investment Manager (CIM).

No one can sell you any financial products unless they are licensed to do so. In other words, a bank representative cannot sell you a mutual fund or a mutual fund representative cannot sell you life insurance unless they have completed and passed the necessary courses and have become appropriately licensed. Financial advisors can be licensed to sell more than one type of product; for example, your life insurance agent or banker may also have a mutual funds licence.

SALES COMMISSION OR FEE-FOR-SERVICE

In addition to achieving the special designations, most planners and advisors are also licensed by the province in which they live to sell various financial products and what they offer you depends on what licences they have. There are three ways your financial advisor or planner gets paid. The first is fee-for-service. Fee-for-service people usually do not sell financial products. These people sell their financial planning services and then send you to a salesperson to implement their recommendations. The fees will vary from about $100 an hour to a percentage of your portfolio value. The minimum fee is in the $150 range for a computer-generated plan which does not include any continuing service. For a custom-developed plan, expect to pay anywhere from $500 to $5,000, depending on its complexity. Fee-for-service planners are typically used by those with larger portfolios. This type of planner is in the minority, but their presence is growing.

Another way advisors or planners are paid is exclusively through commission on the sale of financial products. Straight sales commissioned advisors generally offer free financial consultations. Upon determining your particular needs, they are then paid commission on any product they subsequently sell to you. The challenge is to be sure you aren't being sold something you don't need. This should be easy enough to do if you listen to that inner voice, or if you do some research before going to see an advisor (for example reading this book and others like it). This kind of advisor offers a wealth of information which can be gathered at no cost providing you become adept at weeding out the sales pitches from the concrete facts. Most salespeople are responsible in their claims because the ramifications are too great if they are not. There are the few bad apples who ruin it for everyone, however. These are the brokers who get sensationalized in the media headlines for stealing some poor widow's life savings or the life insurance agent who sells only whole life insurance in order to be paid the really big bucks. These have become the stereotypes and unfortunately promote the idea that brokers and agents are not trustworthy. The regulating bodies of both industries are conscious of ethics and have certain rules to discourage unethical practice. Even more so after the Stromberg Report. If any such practices occur, the regulating bodies are quick to take appropriate disciplinary action.

The third way an advisor is paid is through a combination of both commission and fee-for-services. Some fee-based planners will charge for certain services and also make a commission when they sell certain products, like mutual funds, insurance or securities.

There is no doubt that good advice is available from all types of advisors or planners. Ultimately you make the decision as to what is best for you, not your advisor. If the financial products which the advisor is recommending meet your needs, then the fact that the advisor earns a living from selling them should not be a major factor in your decision. Simply make it your business to know how your advisor or planner is paid, whether that payment can be negotiated and whether it fits within your budget. If you sense that a particular product or company is being pushed too hard, try someone else. If you are convinced that commissioned advisors will not offer you objective advice, then fee-for-service is your answer. Remember, however, that whatever type of financial advisor you choose, you will end up dealing with a commissioned salesperson at some point to purchase your mutual fund, RRSP or insurance.

THE CONCEPT OF BROKERAGE

These days, you can go to your bank and buy life insurance. You can go to your life insurance agent and buy GICs and term deposits. You can go to both and buy mutual funds. If you have securities as collateral, you can even borrow money from your stockbroker. A bank is no longer just a bank. A brokerage sells more than stocks. A life insurance agent seldom sells just life insurance. Everyone provides almost everything. The hard line that used to separate the areas of specialty for planners or advisors has notably softened. The people in the following categories all call themselves financial advisors, though each group still has a defined area of expertise. You may want to choose one advisor or a team, depending on what your needs are and what you are comfortable with.

Most people think *stock* when they hear the term *broker*. This thinking is not always accurate. There are five brokerage sectors, including life insurance, mutual funds, mortgage, deposit and, the most well known, stocks. An industry rule of thumb is that anyone who places a steady 80 percent of their business each year with the same supplier is not a true broker. Often brokers will enter into alliances with brokers in areas where they can't provide service. In April 1992 Brendan Wood International produced an extensive study of Canadian brokers called *Brokerage in Canada.* The study found that:

- Five out of 10 insurance branches now sell mutual funds.

- Except in Ontario, about one in four stockbrokerage branches now offers life insurance products to its clients.

- One in six stockbrokerage branches offers home mortgages to its clients.

- Nine out of 10 mutual fund dealers sold GICs and RRIFs in 1991.

The study also showed that the more affluent the household, the more likely it was that the money would be spread out among different financial institutions. The trend is that sales professionals are becoming general advisors on a broad range of financial needs while their firm provides specialists who act as a resource when the clients' needs are difficult to meet.

STOCKBROKERS

Most folks assume stockbrokers sell only stocks and bonds. This is also not always the case. Brokers offer a full range of financial products: stocks, bonds, mutual funds, treasury bills, mortgage-backed securities, GICs, RRSPs, RESPs, Canada Savings Bonds, options and futures. A few offer insurance advice. Stockbrokers aren't supposed to be allied with any particular company. Some companies, however, provide incentives for the brokers to push their products and certain products pay more commission than others, depending on the product's complexity and level of support required. It's exactly the same for insurance agents or brokers. You have a right to ask about the commission structure to determine the broker's objectivity.

In the past brokers were paid straight commission. However, recently there has evolved a new kind of service called a *wrap account.* Investors are charged an all-inclusive management fee for money management services, commissions and administration. A wrap account is generally targeted to high-net-worth clients with portfolios of $100,000 or more. It is a discretionary account in which the broker and the investor have determined in advance the asset mix. They then select a portfolio manager from a list in each asset class. The fees average around two to three percent. The upside to this type of account is that it gets you access to some of the best money managers in the country, those who normally only deal in the millions of dollars and manage huge sums of money for financial institutions, corporations and pension funds. Most Canadian firms don't use the term "wrap accounts," but prefer to call them "managed products."

There are also discount brokers. They are ideal for those who do not need regular contact with a full service broker or the recommendations and access to the comprehensive research of a full service broker. If you only need someone to take your order, you can save yourself lots of money on commission by going this route. These people do not offer investment advice, send out research reports or make recommendations. This type of broker is usually for the knowledgeable investor. But if you want to buy shares, say in the company where you work or in Irwin Toys for your niece, discount brokers are an option, even for the novice. They should never replace the services of a full service broker, however. You can use both. There is a designation that is becoming increasingly more popular in the securities industry, a *Certified Investment Manager.* This designation requires a two-year course that is designed to give the stockbroker a wider base of investment knowledge than just stocks and bonds. This designation will be mandatory for the securities industry in the near future. Currently there are approximately 2,000 people with this designation.

LIFE INSURANCE AGENTS

Life insurance agents are specialists in many of the areas that you will find in the bottom half of the priority pyramid. That's where the products they are generally licensed to sell fall. They sell term deposits, GICs, annuities, mutual funds, RRSPs, RRIFs, children's education plans, and all types of life, business and disability insurance. Most agents are also licensed to sell their company's mutual funds. The advice garnered from these types of advisors tends to be on the conservative side and ideal for those just starting out. If you need insurance because you are expanding a business or starting a new business with a partner, need estate planning, are starting a family, or just want to learn the basics of financial planning, a stop at your life insurance agent's office is a consideration. They also tend to be specialists in retirement income planning because of the type of products they sell. Annuities are available only from insurance companies, and insurance companies are still responsible for the bulk of the RRIF sales in this country.

Life insurance is a very tough business, so the turnover is frighteningly high. It is important to look for certain designations to determine the level of commitment your agent has to the industry. What you should look for is a *Chartered Life Underwriter* (CLU) and *Chartered Financial Consultant* (ChFC). At the very least, your agent should be working toward these designations. Also ask if your agent is a member of the *Million Dollar Round Table*. This is a prestigious achievement which is worldwide and awarded by the insurance *industry*, not by the insurance company your agent works for. Fewer than two percent in the industry will qualify. If your agent is a member of the MDRT, it shows dedication and commitment as well as an ability to do the job very well. To get into and stay in this club, the agent must meet certain sales and service requirements on an annual basis.

MUTUAL FUND SALES REPRESENTATIVES

Many companies like Trimark, Mackenzie, AGF and Bolton Tremblay don't sell directly to investors. Some, like Altamira, sell only to investors. How you buy your fund often depends on whether or not you want a financial advisor. There are four sources where you can buy mutual funds:

1. *Brokers and dealers:* Stockbrokers, mutual fund dealers or financial advisors or planners who sell funds.

2. *Direct sellers:* These are companies that sell directly to the investors, such as Altamira Management Limited, Phillips, Hager and North Limited of Vancouver, and MD Management which caters directly to doctors and their families. These are no-load funds because the companies don't use a sales force which can offer financial advice.

3. *Tied sales force:* The most well known in this category and certainly the largest is Investors Group of Winnipeg. The financial advisors working for Investors Group sell only the

house brand but have over 24 funds to choose from. Since they sell only their own company's product, definitely look for a professional designation.

4. *Financial institutions:* Banks, trust companies, insurance companies—all who have extensive branch networks are becoming a major force in selling mutual funds. Financial institutions also use a tied sales force and offer only house brands, but often have a good variety to choose from.

CHARTERED FINANCIAL PLANNERS

These people can streamline operations by drawing on the resources of other types of financial advisors and coordinating the information for you. No one knows everything, so what expertise they lack, chartered financial planners will get from other experts like accountants, lawyers and insurance specialists. In fact, insurance agents, stockbrokers and mutual fund sales representatives can have this designation or an equivalent. People with a *Chartered Financial Planner* (CFP) designation are bound by a code of ethics called the Code of Professional Ethics of the Canadian Association of Financial Planners. The *Consumer Guide to Financial Planning* put out by the Canadian Association of Financial Planners states, "While this designation does not guarantee objective advice, it is an indication that the individual has successfully completed a study program, passed examinations and is interested in a broad approach to financial affairs.... Others have been providing valuable financial planning advice for many years and have no designation." As mentioned earlier, a *Registered Financial Planner* is someone who is a member of the CAFP, has been in the financial planning business for at least two years, and has completed the educational requirements. You can have an RFP designation without the CFP designation. RFPs are frequently popular with people already in another industry such as lawyers and chartered accountants.

BANKERS

Typically, your banker's area of expertise is credit and loans. The bank can also be a valuable source of information on business plans and how to open a business. This is where you go for your day-to-day financial needs like counter service, chequing accounts, etc. However, banks are now licensing their employees to sell mutual funds. Like insurance agents, they sell their own company's products. Banks are also going after the same service features traditionally provided by stockbrokerages. This is done through the banks' relatively new private banking service and discount brokerage. Some banks now have RRSP sales professionals who call on clients and sell on a commission-only basis.

ACCOUNTANTS

This is where you go for *tax* advice. Many people depend on their accountants for *all* of their financial advice, including investing, but unless the accountant has taken specific courses or has an RFP, this may not be wise. They are *not* financial planners or professional money managers. They can, however, help you evaluate the performance of your portfolio. Use your accountant if you are setting up or expanding a business or are self-employed, have rental property, are filing tax returns, or are establishing a proper tax and estate plan. If you have a relatively simple tax return, you don't need to pay the fees of an accountant. There are bookkeepers who are less expensive and who will do a perfectly adequate job. If you are currently using your accountant for investment advice, ask what credentials they have in this area. Extensive knowledge of taxation does not necessarily mean knowledge of investing. Accountants are paid an hourly fee which is tax deductible.

LAWYERS

I find it surprising the number of people who turn to their lawyer for financial advice just because that person is a lawyer. It is assumed that because lawyers are smart enough to get themselves through law school, they *must* know about investing. Lawyers have special areas of expertise, just as doctors do. Unless their specialty is related to tax or estate planning or small business operation or the lawyer happens to be a Registered Financial Planner, a lawyer can be one of the worst places to go for financial advice. A family law lawyer is not necessarily equipped to tell you what kind of mutual fund you need. Lawyers spend years going to law school to learn about law, not money management. Go to a lawyer when you need legal help but go to a financial advisor when you need financial help. It is, however, mandatory to visit your lawyer when doing complex tax planning or to do a will and power of attorney. How do you know if you need a tax lawyer? Usually your financial advisor or accountant will tell you. Most of us don't have to consult a tax lawyer unless there is a major problem with Revenue Canada. Lawyers are paid a fee, usually hourly. If it is a big job, they will ask for a retainer which may be payable monthly.

INVESTMENT COUNSELLORS

These folks are big league. Investment counsellors rarely handle portfolios of less than $100,000, and the vast majority won't go less than $250,000. Though this sounds like a lot of money, you will likely end up using their services for your retirement portfolio after it has been accumulating for several years, or if you have inherited a lot of money or get a big severance package. They are usually paid by taking a percentage (one to three percent) of the total of your portfolio or by a set fee.

FINANCIAL PLANNING COMPUTER SOFTWARE

The market is now beginning to offer financial planning software for those who are technologically inclined. The software ranges from the more basic, like *It Figures* or Gordon Pape's *Building Wealth in the '90s*, to the more complex, high-end material that your advisor would use. The entry level software can be a wonderful place to get the basics and to develop a sense of what you need to know before going to an advisor. It will let you develop or customize your own scenarios, depending on your own views of economy, interest rates and your projected potential investment returns.

HOW DO I FIND THE RIGHT PERSON FOR ME?

You have to shop around for the best person for the job. Anything worth having requires a little work. The best place to start is with referrals. Try a referral from your accountant for a good life insurance agent or a referral from your lawyer for her broker. Ask your friends and family members if they are happy with the person they are using. Go to the many seminars and luncheons sponsored by financial planning professionals. As mentioned earlier, contact the Canadian Association of Financial Planners for their membership list.

One more note on the matter of choosing among these various financial advisors. What has kept me with the accountant, lawyer and stockbroker that I use is their patience and willingness to educate me in areas where I'm unsure. They talk in a language I'm familiar with. When I became an advisor, I was horrified to see how many women continued to use their current financial professionals even though they were unsure of what these people did or what they were talking about most of the time. I had more women come to me and say they wanted *me* to look after everything because they didn't know enough about finances and they didn't care to know. It is an advisor's responsibility not only to advise you, but to *educate* you. Under no circumstances should you ever walk into an advisor's office, dump everything on their desk, and walk away giving them free rein. My clients *always* got started with a minimum two-hour information-gathering and education session. The education process was ongoing and was the pivotal part of my practice. I made it very clear that the final responsibility for my clients' financial lives was theirs. That's the gem Elaine passed on to me.

The door to Elaine's office had been closed all morning. When it finally opened, Elaine and the top brass of the company emerged, joking and laughing. She stopped laughing when we made eye contact. She gestured to me to come into her office.

"Looks ominous, Elaine. What brings the upper echelon down to the slums?" I queried as I sat down in the chair that I had occupied so many times before.

Elaine joked, "You still don't trust anyone over the age of 30! Which, of course, is odd considering you're so firmly entrenched in that decade yourself!" "You're seriously misled if you think I trust myself," I said, grinning. "What's going on?"

Elaine braced herself and dropped the bombshell. "I've been offered a senior management position." I blinked once as the implications of her announcement sunk in. Reeling from the shock of possibly losing my mentor, I asked, "Did they take it hard when you told them you weren't interested in the job?"

Elaine grimaced as she said, "I have to take it, the offer is too good to refuse. Besides, you are well on your way. You have a passion for your work that is clear to all who know you." Elaine smiled. "The student has outgrown the teacher."

"Nice try, Elaine. Flattery will get you everywhere," I answered despondently. "What will I do without you?"

"Joanne," Elaine asked, "who has taught you the most in the last year?"

I thought about this and answered honestly, "My clients." "Bingo!" Elaine exclaimed. "Even though your technical education is ongoing, you reach a point where the really important learning comes from the experiences of the people you deal with every day, not from what you learn in books or from me. You are at that point now. The financial planning you do for your clients is an exercise not only from your head, but from your heart and soul as well. You teach people how to balance their lives by giving them the financial tools to achieve their goals."

"Balance," I mused. "You know, Elaine, creating balance is one of the greatest challenges I face in life. When I think of my mother and the millions of Canadian women who have to balance work not only at home but in the paid workforce as well, I am humbled and awed by how remarkable we women are.

"Something else I've been thinking about. Almost every man I know has a mother, sister, daughter, friend, boss or business associate whom they care for. The men in our lives need to hear the message about women's unique financial challenges just as much as the women themselves. The education process needs to include everyone, women and men, and especially our kids." I shook my head slowly and said, "There is so much work to do, my friend."

Elaine smiled at me. "I'll be helping you. I'll be doing my part from a different place, but I want you to continue carrying the message. Who knows, maybe someday you will write a book on the subject and become a world renowned, highly respected author."

"Of course," I responded smoothly. "Maybe I'll marry Mel Gibson too."

We sat in comfortable silence. I realized this was one of those moments in life called a crossroads. Saying good-bye to Elaine was going to be very hard, but much of her attitude and good sense were already instilled in me. "Elaine," I began, "at the risk of sounding maudlin, I believe that life is a series of attachments and losses. How good we are at living depends not only on how well we attach, but on how we accept loss. I am going to miss you terribly, but perhaps we are both destined for greater things."

Elaine's eyes were misty as she said, "Joanne, you were one of my hardest cases. You taught me so much about tenacity and the courage of the human spirit. Once in a while I found myself wondering if you were going to be able to stay on track. When I talk to other women who express fear or reluctance about getting financially organized, I tell them the story of a woman I know. It's your story, Joanne, and it's one of your greatest strengths. Don't be afraid to tell it—many women will recognize themselves in your story. You may be surprised to see how it will inspire women to take action. Listen, my protégé, be sure you and Mel invite me to the wedding. With you, I have discovered, anything is possible."

11

THIS THING CALLED LIFE

So you'll get mixed up of course
As you already know
You'll get mixed up with many strange birds as you go
So be sure when you step
Step with care and great tact
And remember that life
Is a great balancing act
Just never forget to be dexterous and deft
And never mix up your right foot from your left
And you will succeed
Yes you will indeed
(Ninety-eight and three quarters percent.)

-From *Oh, The Places You'll Go!*,
the last book written by Dr. Seuss before he died.
© Dr. Seuss Enterprises, L.P. Quoted by permission.

It's been a wondrous and hectic year and a half since *Balancing Act* was first released. Elaine and I still talk often, my twin nieces are growing up healthy and happy, and I spend most of my time crisscrossing Canada lecturing to audiences on women and money. Life has been a whirlwind of profound change since I became a published author and spokesperson for whatever is on my mind at the moment. To my amusement, the two most asked questions at my seminars are: 1) Did you finally buy that house? and 2) Did you ever get a date?

Well, I figured it's time to address that curiosity my readers seem to have. Not only did I get a date, I got a husband. Believe me, no one was more surprised than I to find my version of "Lance" smack in the midst of this 18-month maelstrom called my life. He wasn't Mel Gibson, as Elaine had so glibly predicted. His name is Michael and he is every bit as charming and brilliant as Mel. More so, in my totally unbiased opinion. Our story is so inspiring, or so I've been told — especially by those who are close to giving up hope of finding Mr. or Ms. Right — that I've decided to share it with you. It's a true testament to the maxim that life is what happens when you are making other plans.

Frankly, folks, you would be right in assuming that at age 38, I've been around the block once or twice. I've been perilously close to marriage but, thankfully, have always managed to narrowly escape unscathed. In retrospect, I'm sure these close encounters of the wrong kind would have ended up in divorce court. Even though eight years ago, on my 30th birthday, I had decided to become the man I wanted to marry, I still quietly yearned for a partner to build a life with. Deep inside, I wanted to share my life's richness with someone special. I was firmly established in a successful career, living my dreams in a full and active life. I was also very single and, yes, lonely. There is nothing like a different hotel room every night for weeks on end to push that loneliness to the front of your mind.

Like so many other women, I became solidly entrenched in the career track. I bought into the doctrine that women could "have it all." Interestingly, while I was going about the business of "getting it all," my biological clock began to tick insistently. The ticking was easy to ignore at first. Though persistent, it got easily buried under career distractions. My mother is fond of telling the story that since the age of four, I have been talking of and planning the time I would have babies. This has always been one of my primary goals. However, reality has a quiet way of shaping one's life without our really knowing it. I always thought I had time; I lived my life as though I did. Most of my decisions favoured the career side of the scale. At the age of 35, I left a man I was supposed to marry in part because he changed his mind and decided he didn't want children. Even at 35, I somehow had faith that the life I wanted, including partner and children, could still happen. But before I knew it, I was 38, Mr. Right was still vapourware and the alarm on that infernal biological clock went off with a vengeance. Because of my age, I had some heavy decisions to make. I was giving serious thought to adopting a baby girl from China. The idea of becoming a single parent, though terrifying, seemed quite possible. The other option, remaining childless, was untenable.

In November 1994, I was invited to go to my friend Sandy's Grey Cup party. I was amazed that Canadians *still* rally around to eat chili and drink beer and watch—essentially ignore—this silly game on TV. I don't know what surprised me more: the fact that people still observe this annual tradition or that I actually agreed to participate. In my opinion, football has the same socially redeeming value as picking your teeth in public. For a lark, I decided to go. As I was sitting there watching grown men attempt to kill each other to get possession of a small pigskin ball, my gaze wandered over to a distinguished, athletic and quiet gentleman across the room. I found out that he bore my favourite moniker in all the world: Michael. I took that as a sign. I found myself praying that none of the many women present was his girlfriend or wife. There was something compelling about this man. He didn't fall into the category of "my normal type." In fact, he seemed quite the opposite — casual, uncomplicated, very quick to smile, quietly yet undeniably confident. My "type" has always been on the uptight side, *very* complicated, brooding and overconfident. I often jokingly say that with my track record, if I find myself attracted to someone I should hightail out of the room at lightning speed. While it's true that there are many things I do well, choosing appropriate men does not top my list. They either don't want children, live in Tuktoyaktuk, like scotch with their morning orange juice or like to burn down empty buildings as a favourite past-time. It's true that each of these people improved my quality of living, if in no other way than through the wisdom I gained on our brief journeys together. All but the pyromaniac. Last I heard, he was seen skulking about the scores of empty high-rises in downtown Toronto. For some unknown reason, I also seemed to gravitate to the suave, business-suited, corporate executive type. Michael, however, was an aerospace engineer and triathlete and lived in T-shirts and jeans. Luckily for me, he didn't belong to anyone in that room. Anyone in any room for that matter. I promptly fell head over heels in love.

From the beginning, our relationship was characterized by its complete absence of fear. And by speed. On our second date, we started talking about our respective desires to settle down and start a family. On our third, we started talking about settling down and starting a family with *each other*. Even though he owned the home where he lived with two other bachelor engineer types, Michael almost immediately adopted my home as his. I often tease him by saying he came for dinner and never left. Every weekend, more and more "boy's stuff" stayed behind, invading my female space. Shaving cream, razor, a suit, some shirts and underwear, running gear and a bicycle. I knew it was getting very serious when, after one prolonged visit, he left his electric drill behind. Weekend visits were initially from Friday to Monday morning, but quickly extended to Tuesday, Wednesday — soon he was here more than there. Many other signs indicated that he was destined to be my life partner. We wanted the same things in life: family, friends, travel and balance. He was very health and fitness conscious, as I was. When two people come together later in life, the experience can often be quite jarring. People get used to their own ways of doing things. Mine and Michael's life fell in together with absolutely no effort or disruption. This was another good omen.

In early February 1995, a mere three months after we had met, Michael and I took a ski trip to Whistler, British Columbia. I'll always remember this trip because it was the point in our relationship where I started to get seriously honest. We were already committed to getting married sometime this year. Michael wanted a family and a good-sized one at that. He thought three kids would be pretty cool. Imagine the apprehension this created in my 38-year-old ovaries! He came from a large family of five boys, all of whom became engineers. (Ironically, neither of his parents can even use a screwdriver.) It was Michael's birthday, we were cosying up in our hotel room admiring the breathtaking skyline of Vancouver. We had just finished an elaborate birthday breakfast feast. I am ashamed to admit it, but I instinctively decided to exploit that wonderful intimate moment. As I was concerned about my ability to have children, I began to probe how deeply committed he was to having his own children. I told him I had concerns because of my age and because of a possible tipped womb. I asked him how he felt about reproductive technology or adoption if we ran into trouble conceiving. It turned out to be a non-issue for him. "We'll do what we can and if it's meant to be, it will happen," he responded. Talk about the right answer. I remember mentally looking skyward and nodding as I accepted this as another sign he was to be Mr. Thomas Yaccato.

Two weeks later, I found myself back in lotus-land, in the lovely community of White Rock, to do a keynote speech for a well-known brokerage firm. I was in the hotel where I was to speak, attempting to pull myself together and get ready for the evening's event after a long, gruelling flight. This would be a big one. The sponsors had had to shut down the marketing machine soon after they had started to advertise as the response to the seminar was overwhelming. They had reached the hotel's capacity of 800 people in a mere two weeks. Hundreds were turned away.

It was two hours to curtain time when I discovered I had forgotten my lipstick. I took a cab to a nearby drugstore to purchase a new one. As I wandered up and down the aisles, I found myself staring at a colourful array of home pregnancy tests. To this day, I have no idea what compelled me to buy one. Without any forethought whatsoever, I reached out and grabbed one that didn't require a morning urine sample. Till that very moment, I hadn't consciously thought I might be pregnant. True, my period was a week late, but with my travel schedule, that happened quite often.

I'll never forget how I felt preparing for the test — a combination of nervous anticipation and "Oh, what's the big deal. You know it's going to be negative anyway." A blue line meant no go, a single red line meant a good chance you're pregnant and a double red line meant "Hustle to a doctor ASAP, you're probably having triplets!" As the little stick rested comfortably in the sample, I proceeded to get ready for my rendezvous with the sponsors less than an hour away. I was a bit nervous, so actually put the test out of my mind for close to 15 minutes. As I was slipping into my pantyhose, I remembered with a start to check the little wand.

I hopped across the bathroom struggling to balance while shoving my remaining foot into the hosiery. With a nonchalant motion, I removed the wand from the sample and found myself face to face with two of the brightest red lines I had ever seen. I caught my reflection in the mirror and started to giggle as I saw my eyes and mouth gaping wide open. I reminded myself of a big, old, ugly sea bass. I promptly fell backwards on the toilet seat which was fortunately closed, blinking with complete disbelief.

There is no way to describe the onslaught of feelings that hit me in the next five minutes. I had no idea a human being was capable of feeling such a wide variety of emotions with that much intensity in such a short time. My mind kept repeating, "Impossible, impossible, impossible." The thought of Michael flashed through my mind. "Oh Lord!" I groaned. "He wants this but he did say at the right time." I could only presume that meant *after* we were married. We hadn't even set a date. As reality began to penetrate my consciousness, I started to think that this was *the* supreme sign that he was to be *the one*. Let's hope he agreed with my conclusion. A raging battle ensued in my brain: do I call him immediately or wait and tell him face to face the next day? I did what any mature, independent thinker would do. I called my mother.

Moms are hilarious. The first thing she wanted to know was why I was so harebrained that I had to wait until I was alone in a hotel room 3,000 miles from home and one hour from a major presentation before deciding to do the test. She had a point. Then she started to gush. The advent of another grandchild sent her straight into a tizzy. I've always said grandchildren are parents' rewards for not killing their children. We thought the look on Michael's face would be too good to miss so I decided to wait a day before dropping the bomb.

Incidentally, the seminar went well. As I proceeded through the slide presentation, thoughts blasted randomly to the front of my mind: "I'm bloody well pregnant!" I was momentarily thrown off guard but managed to get back in stride each time. The sponsors were none the wiser until two months later when I called and told them what had happened. They absolutely howled with laughter and delight.

Michael's reaction was as I had expected. After setting him up brilliantly by introducing a heart-to-heart discussion about how wonderful our relationship was and how we in such a short time had built a solid foundation — all of which he enthusiastically agreed with — I hit him with "I'm so glad we're in synch. *We're* pregnant." Stunned silence followed my announcement. It seemed to me to last 20 minutes; 20 seconds is probably more accurate. Slowly, a boyish grin spread across his face as he looked into what felt like my soul and said, "Neat!" I was crying as I hugged the stuffing out of him. The rest, as they say, is history. (By the way, because of my age, I had a test done that's similar to amniocentesis, called CVS. The baby is healthy and we've named her Kate. Oh, and yes, I'm seven months pregnant on the cover of this book.)

We began to plan a wedding in earnest. Those of you who have been in my shoes, remember the first trimester exhaustion? It was all I could do to keep up with work demands in between the urgent and incessant need for sleep. Then there was the matter of what I have come to call affectionately "pregnancy Alzheimer's." I've also heard it called "baby brain." With every pound I gained, I lost the corresponding amount of brain cells. Clumsiness and forgetfulness became my two new best friends. The experts say you better develop a sense of humour about it in a hurry: it gets worse as you progress. Planning a wedding, running a company and adjusting emotionally to my new life in that mental and physical state was all proving to be much too challenging. It was the first time in my life I had to throw in the towel and admit I couldn't do it all. I was feeling completely overwhelmed by the changes and had to start making some choices. Michael and I were also surprised at how quickly the expenses began to add up. We wanted a small, private affair with immediate family and a handful of close friends. Even so, we were looking at bills totalling $10–15,000. For a one-day event. Yes, I have heard it all a million times. It's supposed to be the most special day of your life, money should be no object. Women in particular have had this message drilled into their heads since they were little girls playing with "Bridal Barbie." I say enough already. Weddings are as much for the bride and groom as they are for family and friends. In fact, more so. Michael and I began to wonder: if we could choose a perfect day, what would it look like? It didn't look overly traditional. We decided to break with convention and change our plans mid-stream. We up and eloped.

It was a Sunday; we were due to visit my sister and her fiancé for the long weekend the following Friday. They live just outside Manitoulin Island in a small town in northern Ontario called Espanola. I called Lori and asked if she and John had anything special planned for that weekend. She was very excited about our visit and was bubbling over with ideas of things for us to do. I mentioned quietly that Michael and I had only one thing we really wanted to do. "Oh?" Lori queried. "What do you have in mind?"

"What about a wedding?" I asked.

"Jeez," Lori shot back. "And I thought I was a demanding houseguest!" She then went on in good Irish-Italian fashion to have an absolute fit on the telephone. She couldn't imagine anything more perfect. She and John would stand for us. To this day I am astounded at what she pulled off. My dear sister put together an entire wedding in four days. She found a non-denominational minister, a plan A and plan B location for the ceremony (plan A was outdoors), arranged the flowers, hired a photographer/videographer, and booked the most romantic room for our wedding night. There was nothing for Michael and me to do but get the marriage certificate and the wedding rings.

We woke up on our wedding day to one of the most beautiful days God could have ordered. The cloudless sky was a brilliant blue broken occasionally by the dramatic horizon of northern Ontario. The air was so fresh and clean it actually smelled foreign. Everything seemed more vivid blue and deeper green. Our approach to the day was remarkably casual. We wanted this to be a celebration that Michael and I would enjoy. We did not want to be exhausted and stressed out. In fact, our approach to our wedding day was so casual my beloved husband-to-be had overlooked bringing anything to wear that day. A half hour before we were to leave, Lori and I found Michael and John rummaging through John's closet trying to find something appropriate for Michael to wear. If I hadn't been feeling so downright calm, I would have brained him. The wedding party consisted of the four of us, the minister, and Cleaver, John's best friend and fellow physician. Cleaver was a delightful addition to our group. His business card could have read "surgeon/coroner/photographer/videographer/pianist/all round nice guy." He not only took our pictures and videographed the ceremony, he played the piano so Michael and I could have the traditional "first dance" on our wedding night. After getting ready we proceeded to Manitoulin Island which, in the native culture, is a very spiritual place. Manitou means "great spirit." As the wedding party approached our plan A destination, a breathlessly beautiful point overlooking a massive valley, the sky literally opened up and the heavens poured down on us. We were clearly not meant to have an outdoor wedding. Undaunted, we jumped back into our cars and immediately shifted to plan B. In retrospect, it was perfect enough to have been plan A. It was a native chapel sequestered in a wilderness setting beside a remote, crystal clear lake. Michael and I thought it was the most beautiful place to get married in. And get married we did.

As we took our leave of the chapel after the ceremony, I turned to take a last look at nature's bounty. I saw a sight that made me gasp and brought tears to my eyes. Across the full expanse of the lake, in full dazzling splendour, stretched a double rainbow — not one, but two, positioned one on top of the other to create a magnificent visual colour display. We stood there awestruck. Michael and I looked at each other and slowly smiled. It was a sign. This one was divinely sent especially for us.

It was the most romantic and fulfilling experience Michael and I had ever lived. Our wedding day was filled with lots of laughter; a sense of calm and peace pervaded the day. These are not the emotions I normally associate with a wedding. Here's the kicker: our picture-perfect wedding day, including the wedding night at a gorgeous lodge on an island that one could reach only by boat, cost $1,006. It's true what they say: There are lots of things money can't buy. I learned that lesson in spades on May 20, 1995.

Michael and I settled very quickly into our new lives as a married couple. I shake my head when I think of how often I said naively of marriage, "It's only a piece of paper." Don't you believe it. Something very fundamental changes when you take part in a ceremony that symbolizes lifelong commitment. One of the other changes I experienced was my perception of financial planning. Of course, even as a single person, I had thought financial planning was an essential part of life. But now that I was married with a baby on the way, certain parts of the planning process took on different dimensions.

From the moment we started living together, and especially since our dear little Katie came to us, Michael and I have come to realize that financial planning is not a static or rigid exercise. It has to be fluid and flexible to encompass the myriad changes one undergoes during one's time on earth. I brought this home dramatically to Michael one morning shortly after we got married. Intending to illustrate a point, over breakfast I killed him.

Not literally, of course, but I took him through what would happen to Kate and me should he leave this world too soon. No quicker way to jolt someone out of newly-wed bliss than to run them over with a bus. But Michael has remarkable common sense (he married me, didn't he?) and he saw the need to address these less than cheerful financial issues immediately. This meant redoing our wills and power of attorney. The moment we had signed the marriage certificate, our previous wills had become null and void. Then there was life insurance to consider now that Kate was on the way. We looked at Michael's company benefits (I'm self-employed so I have none) only to discover that his group plan wasn't nearly enough to cover what Kate would need in the event that anything happened to him. He needed to buy his own coverage anyway. There are no guarantees in the workplace today and we both felt it would be better for him to have control of his own plan. I already had my own insurance, but I needed to do some serious upgrading because of my new family responsibilities. I was reminded of this every time I looked down and couldn't see my feet. Michael got his first taste of reality about his impending family one day when, as he casually rested his hand on my protruding tummy, Kate walloped him with such force that he moved his hand away as though he had been electrocuted. The look on his face was priceless. His eyes flew wide open and his jaw dropped. "She kicked me!" he exclaimed with awe. Meanwhile, I was gasping for breath, laughing hysterically. She actually scared the daylights out of him. Now I can't get rid of him as he tries to reproduce the experience every chance he gets. He's taken to shaking my tummy to wake her up and make her mad so she'll kick. Men can be so weird.

I have the flexibility to work part-time which Michael doesn't have so I'll be Kate's primary care-giver for the first year. This means I'll lose some time in the paid labour force, so retirement planning has to be revisited. Sending Kate off to medical or engineering school (to follow Michael's family tradition of five brothers, five engineers) will have a serious price tag. We want to get an early start on this to make it as painless as possible. How different is our tax situation now that we are married? Do we need a marriage contract? Where do we want to live now that my nesting instinct has kicked into full swing? How the heck do we organize our finances? All of a sudden, our financial responsibilities had grown exponentially and we had to figure out who was doing what and how. We each had decades of doing our *own* financial planning, thinking only of our *own* needs and wants. This was not going to work in our "new economy."

ORGANIZING FAMILY FINANCES

Nothing has made me feel more "married" (read "grown up") than sitting down with Michael and reviewing each other's financial health to determine our respective fiscal responsibilities. We went through this exercise before it was even official that we were living together. All too often I have seen couples go through hell and put their relationship through unnecessary strain because they discovered *after* they moved in together he was $52,000 in debt or she had $15,000 owing on her credit card. "Whaddya mean you only earn $21,000 a year? You drive an $18,000 car!" This is not a revelation that should be taking place after you have filled the bookcase with your books. This is not to suggest for a second that someone's earning $21,000 should preclude you from moving in with or marrying them. It's not necessarily what someone makes that counts but how they manage what they make. This will speak volumes about the character of your partner. What I am suggesting is, don't wait until *after* the fact to find out the financial condition of your partner. It is just as important as their emotional, spiritual and physical condition. *All* these elements *contribute* to why you love the person. As Michael says, "It's important to know what you're getting into, *all* of it."

The fact that women now have earning power is giving them a great deal more clout in the *decision-making* process as well as in the *executing process* for everything from buying cars to investing in mutual funds. Though the pattern of money management in the household is undergoing a dramatic shift as a result of women's increased economic power, there is a downside to this new world order. American writer Anita Jones-Lee writes in her book *Women and Money,*

Studies show that men and women fight more about money than any other topic. Part of the reason, it seems, is that women are acquiring more economic resources within the marriage. Between 1967 and 1981, for example, the number of marriages increased by 6.4 million, but the number of married households in which the husband was the sole earner fell by 5.3 million. By 1981, 5.9 million wives earned more than their husbands. Heightened by the emergence of women as capable breadwinners, the battle over money rages across the dinner table, the bedroom, appearing at some period and in some guise in almost all marriages. Sometimes the battle is a subtle shift of roles and expectations: Who should pay the taxes, who should control the chequebook? For most couples, the money issue emerges during first dating — who should pay or appear to pay at dinner — and, if not addressed, it can begin a slow silent erosion of the relationship. Many couples sweep the issue of how they relate to money under the rug, postponing it for consideration after they have tackled what they view as more pressing issues. But, sooner or later, certainly after marriage, the rug gets rather lumpy, and those pesky unanswered money issues can resurface, only this time in fights and hurt feelings that seem to build over nothing.

Jones-Lee suggests you ask the following four questions to identify whether you and your partner are relating poorly about money:

1. Do you ever feel embarrassed if you have to pay for items while in public with your mate?

2. Does your mate ever feel embarrassed if you have to pay for items while he is in public with you?

3. Do you feel a need to keep up appearances by hiding your mate's inability to earn more or his inability to handle finances in any way, such as budgeting or paying for taxes?

4. Do you resent (a) consulting your mate about how to spend money you earn, or (b) your mate's failure to consult you about how he spends money he earns?

If you answered yes to any of these questions, there is a chance that you are experiencing some difficulty, consciously or unconsciously, around the issue of money and the alignment of power in your relationship. Where do these feelings of discomfort come from? They start pretty early; in fact, they generally go right back to our parents.

Life for my generation is very different from what it was for my mother's generation. These women were financially dependent on their husbands. Often, they weren't privy to the family income, and they didn't ask to be. Financial and retirement planning didn't even enter their minds as they marched up the aisle. In those days, it was the husband's job to provide and to make the financial decisions. Both my mother and Michael's mom, Jean, paid the bills but only after they were told how much money could be spent. Both women did the shopping for their families. In Jean's case, since she didn't drive, shopping was a family event. Michael's dad had to drive and since there weren't an abundance of baby-sitters, the parents packed up five boisterous boys every Friday to do the grocery shopping. Jean said, however, that discipline was not a problem. Dad had only to raise his voice once and they would all fall into line. Michael's mother is an amazing woman. When she went into labour with baby number four she stayed home to cook and serve dinner for the family before going to the hospital. Her contractions were three minutes apart. This is pretty indicative of the selfless mindset of mothers of that generation.

Mothers sent their kids to play outside at a very early age with little worry. Though there wasn't one particular person in charge, there would be countless pairs of eyes peering through gingham kitchen curtains watching out for everyone's kids. Both Michael and I remember growing up feeling that the world was our playground. *All* the mothers looked after *all* the kids because, collectively, their job was working in the home. Today, life is different. Few women have the luxury of being able to stay at home full time to look after the children. Women now bring home their own paycheques but there is still the powerful role model of our mothers influencing our attitudes.

I am part of what I call the "sandwich generation." We were told we could be anything from a supreme court judge to a garage mechanic. Yet, every day we would come home from school to a hot lunch and a mom clucking over the state of the clean clothes we were apparently wearing when we left for school that morning. The division of financial responsibility in those days was re-markably simple: Dad brought home the paycheque and mom spent it. In many families, money was never talked about. Many of us learned our money behaviour by watching mom and dad. Sociologist Carolyn Dexter says, "The critical difference in the socialization of men and women is that, despite recent advances, women are socialized primarily to occupy a family role.... Men, on the other hand, learn both economic and family roles." Even in the academic world, as my own experience demonstrates, it is taught that numbers and counting are for boys. I am convinced that this socialization process helps to explain why some women of my generation still defer the financial planning to the men in their lives.

However, women also sometimes delegate the financial re-sponsibility to the partner as a direct result of pronounced time constraints. Financial planning becomes an additional task that is deferred or passed over because there is no time to do it. For this reason, or because they lack the knowledge of or interest in financial planning, some women let their partners take over money matters completely. I get nervous when I see this hap-pen because the amount of money you control in a relationship will in large part determine your independence. As sociologist Veronica Nieura says, "The independent financial base provided by employment provides women with an increased sense of com-petence, gives women more power within the marriage and in-creases their influence in decision-making." This may well be the case for women who are working in the paid labour force, but what about women who work full time unpaid at home. Issues of power and independence can become very tricky. It becomes even more important for these women to understand their part-ner's mindset around money. For women who choose not to get directly involved, I always recommend, at the very least, having a *complete understanding* of the state of the family finances in the event disaster strikes. That includes being able to answer the who?what?where?how? question.

For the most part, however, today's women are involved in de-ciding where the money goes. There is an abundance of research in the area of money management for families, including that done by Jan Pahl, Senior Research Fellow at the University of Kent in Canterbury, England, who did an exhaustive study on money and marriage. After reviewing the research and consulting my own experience as a financial advisor, I've come to the conclusion that there are three main systems of money management that couples use. The first two are generally used by couples who have one member working at home with no income. The third method provides various options for dual income families. There are, naturally, variations on all the themes, but the following outlines the overall approaches:

1. ***The Allowance System*** — Ugh. This is a very traditional method of managing the family finances. This works when couples see themselves as having separate spheres of responsibility in financial matters. In more traditional families, like the one I was raised in, this meant dad gave mom money to which she added any income that came from her jewelry or cosmetic parties. She was then responsible for *specific* household expenditures like food and clothes for the kids. The rest of the money and the major decisions about spending that money, including big-ticket purchases like the house and car, stayed in the control of my dad, the wage-earner. This system was predominant in my mother's time but is quickly going the way of the dodo bird in today's world. It isn't in step with the new demand that work done at home should be valued. This system often held women hostage in bad marriages for financial reasons. Interestingly enough, I occasionally still come across couples, even younger ones, who still use this method.

2. ***Whole Wage or Pooling System*** — Many of my peers who have chosen to work full-time, unpaid, at home use this system. One partner, usually the one at home, is responsible for managing all the finances of the household and is also responsible for all the expenditures, except those of a personal nature. Even the savings are pooled, which means the partners are generally like-minded about their goals. Spending allowances are paid to both people. Sometimes there is a division of "who pays what bills," but the money still comes out of one central pool. This is a much more popular method than the previous generation's allowance system as it gives the person working at home more control, independence and dignity. It also acts as a way of "paying" the caregiver for the work being done in the home.

I have also seen this system used when both people are working for wages. In this case, the money is combined but often it's one partner who controls the lot. The pooling system works well if only one person is receiving wages or if both partner's wages are comparable and they are comfortable merging everything. What characteristically defines this system is the statement, "It's not my money, it's not his/her money, it's our money."

3. ***Independent Management System*** — The essential characteristics of this system are that both partners have an income and that neither has access to *all* the household funds. Each partner is responsible for *specific* expenditures and, although the determination of who does what may change over time, the principle of separate control over income and separate responsibility for expenditures is maintained. Here are four examples of how this system can work:

   - *Equal contributions*   Couples agree in advance what expenses are pooled and what are kept separate. Essentially, both people put the same amount of money in the pot to cover joint expenses but keep their own chequing accounts and savings and investment programs. This system is good for those partners who earn approximately the same amount of money.

   - *Proportionate contributions*   If one partner makes a lot less than the other or has an income that can vary dramatically from year to year, the equal contribution method can create quite a financial strain. The proportionate contribution method creates a more balanced approach by putting a certain *percentage* of each partner's income into the pool. When I was a much younger lass of 26, and sharing an address with a gentleman who earned three times what I did, this was the method we used. We took 50 percent of both of our incomes and put it into the pot to cover the household expenses. Even though my 50 percent contributed less in terms of actual cash, it still *felt* fair.

   - *Monthly reimbursement* — This is the system Michael and I use. I pay the rent each month and he pays his mortgage. We split everything else including food, entertainment and utilities. All the receipts go into a jar on top of the fridge and are added up once a month. If one has paid more than the other, a cheque is written for the difference. Though it requires a little bit of time each month (maybe six minutes, max), this system makes life pretty easy and simple. We keep our own chequing accounts and investment portfolios but consult with each other on everything. In general terms, I know what he has and he knows what I have. A variation of this method is to let one partner pay all the bills if that partner demonstrates an interest in and flair for financial organization or if the other partner just plain and simply detests the job. At the end of the month, everything is totalled up and one partner gets reimbursed for half by the other.

- *Divvying up the bills* — Pooling money can make some people feel uncomfortable. An alternative system is that each partner becomes responsible for paying *specific* bills that are reasonably equal in value on an ongoing basis. Someone pays the mortgage/rent every month while the other pays other expenses that are close in value to the mortgage or rent payment. If you are on the proportionate system, this can also work. Determine what your percentage can pay for in terms of specific bills, and pay them each month instead of putting the money into a pot and having one person do all the work of paying the bills. The divvying up system requires ongoing dialogue to be sure it remains fair.

Whatever method you choose, remember to be sure you both have money that doesn't need to be accounted for. Ellen Roseman tells the story of her mother and mother-in-law who both stayed at home to raise families. Their first taste of financial independence came when they turned 65 and started receiving their old age pensions. My mother didn't understand the importance of financial independence until she lost everything when Dad went bankrupt. When entering into a common-law relationship or marriage, the following five points should be maintained at all times. For many women, this is simply standard procedure. But for those who haven't given their financial lives much thought, take heed:

1. Always maintain an independent credit history.
2. Do not co-sign or guarantee loans unless there is a financial

benefit to *you* or you share control over the source of income being used to repay the loan. Just recently, it was reported in *The Toronto Star* that a judge severely reprimanded a bank for going aggressively after a client's wife who had guaranteed a business loan. She was a homemaker earning no income and had no input into or knowledge of her husband's business. Yet when he defaulted on the loan, the bank went after her for close to half a million dollars. The judge ruled that not only was the woman in no position to pay back the loan, but that she hadn't fully grasped what she was signing. The woman found herself having to go through the nightmare of court proceedings and having her name dragged through the media. Granted, this is an extreme example, but the basic premise holds true: don't put your money where your brain is not welcome.

3. Always maintain a separate bank account, even if you hold joint accounts. As discussed in chapter two, many people find themselves wiped out because their partners were fast off the mark in getting to the joint accounts. Aspire to keep three to six months' salary accessible in case of disaster.

4. For those women who are depending on their partners to keep them safe and dry in their retirement — don't. Plan your pension taking into account death or divorce. That's where marriage contracts, family law, proper estate planning and good solid savings principles come into play

5. Speaking of estate planning, it is essential that you and your partner get a will. As we discussed in chapter five, 8 out of 10 people left behind after the death of a partner are women. Don't let the government step in and make decisions for you because you didn't look after this vital detail.

COMPANY BENEFITS

I sometimes joke with Michael that I married him for his company benefits. Being self-employed, I was responsible for everything: medical and dental bills, retirement plans, disability and life insurance. Having access to Michael's company benefits is certainly an added bonus, though his company is not particularly generous. This is not unusual for corporate Canada today. In response to the new economic reality, benefit plans are being scaled back. Often it's a case of doing this or laying off staff. Since I have my own insurance plans and retirement savings, I will never be at the mercy of an employer. Michael quickly understood the value of this so now we only consider his company plan as gravy.

Since I had been in the insurance industry, I know only too well the cost of company benefits to the employer — huge. If you have benefits, don't take them lightly. They can be worth thousands of dollars. When I left corporate Canada, I hadn't really thought much about them until I was forced to replace them. I shudder to think how much more financially challenging life would be without company benefits when our new daughter Katie arrives. Incidentally, the difference in group plans among companies that are the same size can be dramatic. In no way should you assume that because you work for a large corporation your benefits are the best. The following is a snapshot of Michael's company plan. It typifies what a medium to large corporation might offer and may give you some insight into what to look for:

- **Supplementary Medicare** — Our whole family is fully covered for the additional costs of semi-private hospital accommodation, 80 percent of prescription drugs and 80 percent of things like private nursing care, vision and hearing care, psychological services and reasonable charges while travelling outside of Canada, up to a maximum of $100,000 for each person. (A helpful hint here — for many prescriptions, the dispensing fee represents the largest portion of the cost. To be competitive, some pharmacies have reduced these fees. It's in your best interest, therefore, to find out which pharmacies have done this. Another way to keep the dispensing fees down is to ask your doctor to prescribe a three-month supply of those drugs you take regularly, like birth control pills.) Many companies include common-law partners under their definition of spouse. A very few forward-thinking companies also include same-sex partners. For those companies that do cover same-sex couples, the benefits are usually restricted to medical and dental.

- **Dental Plan** — Michael's plan covers 80 percent of routine dental expenses, 60 percent of the cost of major dental expenses like crowns, inlays and major surgery and 50 percent of eligible orthodontic expenses up to a lifetime maximum of $1,500 for each person. The maximum benefit payable for routine and major dental expenses per person, per year is $1,200.

- **Disability Insurance** — Michael qualifies for full salary for up to 180 days. If he remains completely disabled and has applied for C/QPP, he may receive 65 percent of his salary tax-free from the long term disability plan up to age 65. Incidentally, the C/QPP definition of disability is the most stringent one out there. The only time anyone can qualify for C/QPP Disability Benefit is if there is no hope of recovery. The company also makes sure that the monthly amount received from all sources doesn't exceed 85 percent of Michael's net earnings, which is pretty standard. While we wait for the government to approve the C/QPP claim, the insurance company pays the full benefit, including the government's share, for up to 24 months. If a decision were reached in our favour, meaning Michael was considered eligible for C/QPP, the company payments must be paid back. If no decision were reached, the LTD benefit would be automatically reduced by the C/QPP amount that has been paid. All company benefits, including his pension plan, would continue while Michael was off on LTD. If Michael pays the premiums for the disability insurance, the monthly benefit he receives would be tax-free. The strict definition of disability in Michael's company policy makes it almost useless except in the most extreme case. As a result, Michael has to get privately-owned coverage for those less than extreme possibilities. The private plan can only top up his company plan; it can't replace it.

- **Life Insurance** — As Michael's beneficiary, I would receive an amount equal to twice his salary should he die. Michael's company also offers optional coverage for the spouse and children. If Michael died in an accident, the amount would be an additional two times his salary. Even the benefits booklet says these amounts are generally inadequate protection for a family and recommends coverage equal to 10 times one's annual income. I hate industry formulas like this but I found it very reassuring that the company would take a responsible approach to educating its employees about having adequate coverage. Having enough life insurance for Kate and me was one of the most important and thoughtful gestures Michael could make for us. It would allow us to grieve in Tahiti. When we met with Elaine to talk about our new life insurance requirements, she couldn't stop giggling at my expanded waistline. "All those years spent trying not to get pregnant and now look at you!" she cracked. Review chapter five to get a handle on the wacky world of life insurance.

- **Pension Plan** — Michael has been with his company for three years. According to his company plan, he will be eligible for retirement in the year 2023. Based on what he has contributed to the plan so far, his monthly retirement income would be a whopping $213, not including C/QPP, which, for obvious reasons, we don't want to include. We cracked up when we saw this. We're out shopping for that retirement villa in Italy now. If he decides to retire at age 55, he will receive 50 percent of his normal retirement pension. This amount increases 5 percent for each additional year over age 55 and by 1 percent for every year of service over 10. If he leaves the company before retirement, he will receive a deferred pension payable at age 65. Again, the benefits booklet stresses that companies are continually reviewing their pension plans and having to downscale them. It goes on to say, "With the future of government plans uncertain, it is essential that you assume ownership of your personal retirement planning." It also says very clearly that while the company intends to maintain its plan, it has the right to amend or terminate it at any time.

Many companies, including Michael's, offer a range of other benefits including:

- **Joint and Survivor Pensions** — Regardless of the type of pension plan your company offers, there is always a joint and survivor benefit designed to protect your spouse which is, at a minimum, 60 percent of the original benefit. Some companies offer 75 – 100 percent of the pension to the surviving spouse. A joint and survivor pension is optional but in order to waive it, a signature is necessary from the spouse. We will obviously take advantage of this benefit. I don't want to miss out on my $127.80 a month.

- **Group RRSPs** — Michael recognized long ago the limitations of company and government pension plans. As a result, he has been maximizing his personal RRSP contributions for years. If he keeps this up, we'll be able to afford his and hers villas. Since he's been with his current company, Michael's personal RRSP contributions have been limited since the pension adjustment has to be deducted from his contribution level. Participation in his company pension plan is mandatory and the money is locked in until he's 65. Today, more and more companies are going the more user-friendly group RRSP route. One of the biggest advantages of group RRSPs is their flexibility. First of all, you can access the funds before you're 65. Also, group RRSPs offer some choices. Most pension plans give you no say as to how the money is invested, whereas group RRSPs offer you a choice of investments. (For a more detailed discussion on the different types of company pension plans, refer to pages 209–211.

- **Supplementary Income Replacement Plan** (Maternity and Family Leave) — This tops up Unemployment Insurance benefits to a level equal to 95 percent of Michael's base salary if he goes on maternity or adoption leave. Since that's not likely to happen unless he suffers the same fate as Arnold Schwarzenegger, he can take advantage of the company's family leave program. The infuriating thing is, he needs two managers' signatures before he can do anything. He is very much at the mercy of management as to whether or not he can take family leave. It's unpaid and up to 18 weeks. Great incentive for dads to participate.

- **Educational Assistance** — Many companies encourage ongoing education that is relevant to the employee's job. Michael's company will pay the costs of career- and job-related courses, subject to management approval. You pay for the course and, if you pass, you are reimbursed.

- **Employee Stock Purchase Plan** — This enables the employee to purchase company stock through an automatic payroll deduction plan.

- **Employee Assistance Plan** — Michael's company recognizes that many problems may arise from the stress of balancing work and family, commuting, finances and other factors. This confidential program helps employees find ways to cope if the pressure builds.

- **Payroll Deduction for the Registered Retirement Savings Plan** — This benefit is self-explanatory.

- **Group Automobile and Home Insurance** — Because of the number of people involved in these plans, great discounts can often be worked out. These are definitely worth a look.

- **Employee Vehicle Lease Program** — The same principle as above applies here as well.

Another point to remember about company benefits: the premiums you pay for the company's health and dental insurance can be claimed as a medical expense for income tax purposes. The deductible amount can also be claimed as a medical expense.

MARRIAGE CONTRACTS AND COHABITATION AGREEMENTS

When I was doing financial planning for a living, I made it a point to tell all women to whom it was relevant, to be sure they had a prenuptial agreement, marriage contract or cohabitation agreement. As an incentive to propel women into action I would cite the sobering divorce statistics in this country. Nowadays, when a woman meets the man of her dreams, one of the first questions that goes through her mind is, "Is this the man I would want my children to spend every second weekend with?" A marriage contract was another issue Michael and I needed to address now that we were a married couple. Historically, these agreements helped to protect men because they owned all the assets. Michael and I were pretty evenly matched asset-wise, but I was bringing a thriving business into the partnership. In this case, all advice pointed to the soundness of getting an agreement in advance. Marriage contracts and cohabitation agreements can benefit everyone by an early mastering of the "who gets what" dance. As you have seen, Michael and I didn't have time for a prenuptial agreement; we moved straight ahead into the marriage contract. Marriage contracts are the same as prenuptial agreements except they are postnuptial. What they do, in a nutshell, is allow you to opt out of family law legislation and the Divorce Act and determine your own destiny as a couple. These agreements, however, do not enable anyone to opt out of child support responsibilities.

The bottom line is that marriage contracts or prenuptial agreements do not have to set a negative tone for your marriage. You are free to do whatever you want, whether that be split everything down the middle or give it all away. But should your marriage break down, you are not *obligated* to do anything other than what is stipulated in the agreement. I brought a company into the marriage, Michael brought a house. Now I may choose to give Michael half the company and he may give me half the house, but we don't *have* to. But had we not had a marriage contract, we would have been required to do so by law. We both have excellent earning capabilities, so we waived support obligations no matter how dramatically our financial circumstances changed. I have no responsibility for his debts nor he for mine in the event of a break-up.

The agreement does not have to be drafted by a lawyer, but it does have to be signed and witnessed. Whether a lawyer drafts the agreement or not, getting independent legal advice is essential. Furthermore, it is important to review this document whenever major life changes occur. A case in point: what would happen to me, since I've waived the right to any financial support in the event of marriage breakdown, if we decided a couple of years from now that I would stay at home to look after our family? I would have put myself in a very precarious position. Significant changes in circumstances should automatically trigger a trip to the basement filing cabinet to review all your documents, from your will to the marriage contract.

For people who live together, it is especially important to have an agreement because common-law spouses have no statutory property rights in Canada. Michael Cochrane, author of *Surviving Divorce: The Everyday Guide For Canadians*, says this about common-law spouses, "If they do not marry, the only property they are entitled to when they leave is their own property." This is contrary to what most people think. Like a marriage contract, a cohabitation agreement predetermines what happens to assets in the event one of you dies or you separate. I strongly recommend getting good legal advice before you embark down the aisle or decide to share the same address with someone.

WILLS AND POWER OF ATTORNEY

Our meeting with the lawyer who specializes in wills, power of attorney and marriage contracts got off to a rousing start. Michael is above average in handling his financial affairs but he is distinctly human in other areas. The lawyer began by asking him pertinent details about his estate. Her first question was, "Where is the deed to the house?" This was met with a blank stare and a sheepish grin. He took a stab in the dark, "Uh, in the basement?" In jest, I threw him a look which suggested that he might meet his maker earlier than expected if he made me go through the basement of his house to find his important papers. The basement was a tumbled collection of windsurfers, racing bikes, golf clubs, camping gear, hockey equipment, downhill and cross country skis, roller blades, skateboards, miscellaneous car parts, abandoned stereo equipment, old furniture and motorcycle equipment. Oh, did I mention that Michael had a tenant with a 100-pound Heinz 57 living in the basement as well? He got the point. In very short order, we gave each other a list including the location and description of each other's investments, insurance policies, bank accounts, credit card numbers, medical card and driver's licence numbers.

The task of dividing our assets and choosing who would get what could have been somewhat unsettling; however, it proved to be an experience that brought us even closer together. Michael and I discovered that we were remarkably in synch. We easily agreed on who would raise our children, when the children would start receiving the money from our estate and in what form (this is called setting up a trust), and who was to be our executor and power of attorney.

We also agreed on the importance of ensuring that our children's claim to our assets was protected from the greedy paws of their ex-spouses. This is a standard clause to include in your will as it excludes your children's partners from a legal claim to your estate. Though Michael and I sometimes winced at certain scenarios, we forged ahead with quick dispatch and felt very grown up about the whole thing. Discovering we were of like minds on all these issues helped to establish a solid foundation to our life-long partnership.

One interesting subject brought up by the lawyer was how to deal with illegitimate children in the will. We were told we needed to decide whether any children born outside of our matrimonial union would get a share of the estate. My comments to Michael regarding this sort of extracurricular activity cannot be printed here since this is a family book. One assumes that this clause applies more to the rich and famous who often have to deal with people popping up out of nowhere claiming to be their son or daughter. We were surprised, therefore, to see this is a standard clause in all wills now regardless of your station in life.

On another matter, it was highly recommended that I get a separate will for my company, Women and Money Inc. The company shares were treated as my secondary estate as opposed to my primary estate, which consisted of my personal assets. Our lawyer advised me that it is always wise to treat company and personal assets separately in two different wills. It makes the process of transition after death significantly easier.

Because our status had changed upon marriage, Michael and I also needed to redo our power of attorney. Because of the change in Ontario's law in April 1995, we now signed off on two documents — one for the management of property and the second for personal care. We made sure to do this at the same time as we did our wills. Review chapter 5 for an in-depth treatment of wills and power of attorney.

RETIREMENT PLANNING

I often hear from people all over the country complaining about the difficulty of putting money away for retirement. I've now discovered first hand how planning for retirement can quickly take a back seat to other pressing and apparently more immediate issues such as setting up an education fund and getting more life insurance as well as things like furnishing a nursery and finding a suitable place to call home. This shocked me as I have spent a good part of my adult life educating women on the vital importance of taking care of their own retirement. Nothing like a good dose of life to make you more balanced in your perspective. Though the importance of beginning to save for retirement no later than 30 still holds true, I've come to appreciate how married and family life can make that more difficult than when you are single. Michael and I are thankful that we maximized our RRSPs over the years. We will continue to do so every year but we may now be faced with having to borrow for our RRSPs for the first time. I am also finding out first hand the importance of having spousal RRSPs as an option since I'll lose income and my RRSP contribution level will drop significantly while I'm home with Kate. Because we covered retirement planning extensively in chapter seven, there is only one other thing I'd like to add from this new perspective of mine — I've officially joined the ranks of that large group of Canadians who wonder how the hell are we going to do it all? I finally get what everyone has been complaining about.....

OUR QUANTUM OF SOLACE

Owning my own home has now become paramount. Nothing like pregnancy hormones to kick in that nesting instinct. You will remember from chapter eight that I never believed I could own my own home unless I married into one. It seemed like a financial goal that was completely out of reach. I got over this defeatist thinking and set things in motion to have my own home, regardless of my marital status, by the time I turned 40. When Michael and I first started getting serious and I found out he was a homeowner, I smiled wryly to myself at the irony. "Can you believe it?" I thought "I'll end up marrying into that house after all."

Michael realized a tidy profit when he sold his first home so he gave little thought to the potential investment downside of home ownership when he bought his second, a perfectly lovely bungalow on a huge lot. This was in 1990 as the market was beginning its long, seemingly endless descent into the pit. Like so many others at this time, Michael thought he had bought safely past the market's peak of the 80s, never imagining the correction was going to be as prolonged and severe as it was. Though a wonderfully charming place, Michael's house is in Mississauga, quite a distance from both our offices and our friends. The location is for us, in a word, terrible. The house is also half the size of the house that I rented in a beautiful, well-established neighbourhood near Toronto's city centre. All these considerations began to mean something when we tried to decide where we were going to live after Kate was born. We couldn't justify continuing to pay the expensive rent where we were and besides, my nesting instinct had kicked into high gear. Michael had two boarders living at his house, but he still carried a large part of the financial obligation. After serious deliberation that lasted 12 seconds as to whether or not I could become a "Mississauga Mom," we decided to sell his property. Most of my money went right back into my business so the idea was to take what equity we could from his house and buy our own quantum of solace. Sounds like a plan, right? Wrong. Reality intervened and blew apart the pink cloud. I learned volumes from this experience.

Michael enlisted the services of a real estate agent he had used in the past. In what seemed no time at all, the house had been on the market for two months without an offer and it had been listed for a lot less than Michael had paid for it. Certainly events like pregnancy, a wedding, running a company and so forth had a great deal to do with our inability to stay on top of this project, although you should never take on the task of selling a house unless you are prepared to put some work into it. Never leave yourself exclusively at the mercy of your agent.

We decided to drop the price further, but one month later, we still had not a single bite. I called the agent and gave him until noon the next day to be at our house with a full report. This is the kind of service you should receive as a matter of course. But after almost three months, this would be the first report from our agent and the first time he and I would meet face to face. Needless to say, after our meeting, this gentleman felt considerably more motivated. In the current climate, the house was still priced too high which sickened us because our asking price was dramatically lower than the original cost. We dropped the price again, our hopes for a proper down payment for a new house dropping with it.

A month later, even at the new reduced price, the house still had not moved. Guess what, folks, I'm now a Mississauga Mom. When our lease came due, we decided not to try and carry two places. Baby costs including child care, settled that discussion in a hurry. We will try to sell again next year, probably with better results now that the place has furniture and a family living in it.

The tough part of all this is not only the hard-earned cash one loses, but the lost opportunity for investment. This is one of the most important lessons in house buying. *Don't buy your principal residence as an investment but be sure to have an investor's eye when you buy it.* Your house is the same as any investment, like stock or mutual funds. You have no idea what the conditions will be like one month from now, let alone five years. For too long, people have believed real estate to be absolutely reliable.

Our parents told us there was nothing more secure than bricks and mortar. That may have been the case in their generation, but it surely isn't today. We have postponed buying a new home for a while, but we plan on diving right back in as soon as we can sell this house without losing our shirts and blouses. I've discovered something important, however, about this growing nesting sense of mine — it seems to be satisfied simply with owning our own half-finished basement and creaky stairs. It has very little to do with an annualized net rate of return of six or eight percent.

THE MORAL OF THE STORY

It's been four weeks since I wrote the above story. What transpired between then and now can only be described as fantastic. My mom began to accuse us of making up the whole thing.

A couple of weeks after taking down the "For Sale" sign on the house in Mississauga, Michael and I went away to our family's cottage for a well-deserved holiday. We were blissfully decompressing from city life and the pressures of attempting to sell that albatross called a home when the phone rang. It was our real estate agent. He had an offer from a couple who *really* wanted the house. So much so, they came in almost $25,000 less than our lowest asking price. I was laughing so hard that when I could finally breathe again, I called and left the agent with the message: "Go pound sand." He called back two hours later saying they had increased their offer by $20,000. Michael and I were in a real dilemma. We had made our minds up to move to Mississauga but here was an opportunity to bail out, albeit with the slimmest margin imaginable. We took a pass. A decision was a decision, and for our own sanity we needed to stick by it. Besides, it gave us very little time to find another place to live since we had already given notice at our rented home in Toronto. We chalked it up to a great adrenaline hit in an otherwise coma-like holiday.

When we returned home, Michael and I started the psychological process of reacclimatizing to suburban life and rolled up our sleeves to enthusiastically attack the house renovations. There was much to do to rid the place of the "three bachelor engineers" mode of decorating and cleaning. Michael and his brothers are very handy so we decided to do most of the work ourselves. In short order, I found myself suffering as my new-found husband vanished many evenings and weekends to swing hammers and paint brushes to get the house ready for his new family. My mother's voice kept running through my mind: "You have a family now, Joanne. Sacrifice is something you better learn to do in a hurry." So, I suffered in silence.

The first Saturday morning after our return from the cottage, Michael was playing around the front yard of the Mississauga house when a car pulled up in the driveway. A man got out and asked if the house was still for sale. He had heard from the neighbours across the street that it had been on the market. It was, according to him, exactly what he was looking for. Michael told him it had been off the market a few weeks now but he'd talk to his partner about it. Later that evening, he came in the front door, grinning like a Cheshire cat as he made his announcement. I couldn't believe it. There seemed to be more activity around that infernal house now than there had been when we had it listed. Because this would be a private sale, there would be no agent commission fees to pay so our profit margin would improve somewhat. We thought about it that night and decided to pursue it with the guy the next day. Michael called him only to find out he had put in an offer on another house the evening before. We told him to feel free to call us if his offer didn't go through. We had been through all this just the week before so we didn't really allow our hopes to rise. Again, we chalked it up to another of life's many adventures. Michael and his brother Pat returned to ripping ugly panelling from the basement walls.

But the story was far from over. We thankfully developed a cavalier sense of humour around the whole house issue and even stopped telling our friends about what was going on. It had the makings of a world-class ping pong match. Michael had gone out of town on business for a couple of days a week or so later. I was spending a quiet night at home staring, wide-eyed with disbelief at my now inconceivably huge belly when the phone rang. It was our real estate agent, apologizing profusely for disturbing us again but this time he had a couple who *desperately* wanted our house. Where the heck were these people before the sign came down? I wondered to myself. This time the offer was exactly what we wanted. As I hung up the phone, I began to giggle. Move over X-Files, this story is getting stranger by the minute, I thought. I called Michael in Boston and I'm sure the ensuing howl could be heard for miles around. After a brief discussion that involved God's unusual sense of humour, we decided to go for it. I called the agent back, told him we wouldn't go a penny below the asking price and also got him to reduce his commission by one percent. He came back later that night with $1,000 more than we asked for. The conditions for sale were very standard: the buyers had preapproved financing so it was really just a question of the home inspection. Incidentally, you should never consider a purchase of this magnitude without doing a home inspection. They're in the $300 range and could save you thousands later. The real estate agent wanted to come by the next day with the signed offer. We made the appointment for one o'clock. It looked like everything was a go.

The next morning while I was having breakfast, the phone rang. It was Len, the private sale guy. His deal had fallen through. He wanted to known if we would still be interested in selling our house. When I told him we had an offer on the table and that the agent was on his way over to have it signed, he began to make a very compelling case about making a perfectly legitimate deal without having to pay virtually thousands of dollars of commission. Since he had not been introduced to the house in any way through the efforts of our agent and the house had been off the market for several weeks, his words seemed to make a certain amount of sense. But Len needed to see the house one more time. While he dashed off to get a last look about, I called Michael in Boston again, and filled him in on the latest development. This time all he did was sigh heavily. I, however, was beginning to lose it. I could not for the life of me figure out what lesson Michael and I were to take from this experience, which could only be described as patently absurd. I kept my mother updated with the situation. It got to the point when she would hear my voice on the phone and say, "What in heaven's name is going on now?" I wouldn't even get a hello!

While Len was taking his last look at the house, I began to feel a little guilty about the real estate agent. Though he had done very little to sell the house earlier, he seemed to have become inspired after we yanked it off the market. But the thought of the thousands and thousands of dollars that would end up in our pocket instead of the agent's, pushed guilt right out. Had this agent worked hard (or even a little, frankly) to move the house, the battle in my mind would not have been so intense. But as always, good prevails and all works out in the end. Len called back two hours later saying he was uncomfortable making a decision that fast. (Picky, picky. As if a couple of hours isn't enough to decide to spend a few hundred thousand dollars.) If *our* deal fell through, he said, we should call him back.

I signed the deal with the real estate agent that afternoon. As of this morning, the financing and home inspection has been approved and that god-forsaken house that tortured us for so long has been officially sold and is out of our hands. The other good news is I've got my husband back. We have such a short time before our lives change profoundly, and we try to enjoy every quiet moment that we can. People keep telling us it will be twenty years before we have another moment like that.

Selling the house so unexpectedly has left me with another sobering new reality. I'm seven months pregnant and homeless. My good friend Peter Volpé teases me about being "Joanne Thomas Yaccato of no fixed address." Michael and I have exactly one-and-a-half months to find a new place to live. We'll likely rent for the short term, until Kate bursts onto the scene, then decide where we want to locate permanently.

Gentle readers, when I figure out what we were supposed to have learned from all of this I'll let you know. But for now, please forgive me. I'm a bit busy perusing the classifieds.....

SEPARATION AND DIVORCE

It is impossible to give this topic the time and attention it deserves in the limited confines of this book. How to deal with the emotional devastation, how to protect yourself and your children, becoming a single parent, how to find a good lawyer, the division of family property, pension plans, tax consequences, support issues, child custody — these are just a few of the issues you will face. If you are about to join the three out of 10 Canadians whose marriage is ending, there are three books you should read:

- *Surviving Divorce: The Everyday Guide For Canadians* by Toronto lawyer Michael Cochrane. Mandatory reading.

- *Taking Care of Tomorrow: The Canadian Money Book For Prime Time Women* also covers coping with the financial realities of separation and divorce.
- *Ellen Roseman's Money Guide For Modern Families* dedicates a good portion to covering these topics.

MONEY MANAGEMENT FOR YOUR CHILDREN

Educating children in money matters should be a matter of course, just like teaching them the facts of life or how to drive. Kids who don't learn to manage money have a way of showing up later on their parents' doorstep. You need only ask mine. Done in the right way, teaching your children about money can be a wonderful experience for both of you. Many young people will reach adulthood in an unforgiving economy and brutal job market and will be living with the burden of providing social programs for the baby boomers. Teaching them money management skills is the kindest thing you can do.

One approach is to have your children manage their own bank account and their allowance. Some experts say that an allowance shouldn't be tied to doing chores; it should be used strictly as a tool to teach children about savings and budgeting. Also, with this approach they don't learn that the only reason to do things around the house is for the money. I agree absolutely. Making beds and doing dishes are a fundamental part of family life. However, if they want to earn extra money, doing extra chores is an ideal way. Another suggestion is to give your teenager a larger allowance, say an amount monthly instead of weekly, and give them a freer rein on spending. They will learn the fine art of budgeting in a real hurry this way. This method will only succeed if you can abide the inevitable whining that will come the first few times it doesn't work. Patience and ear plugs will be essential. It is vital that kids understand the consequences of their actions. They need to learn the art of setting goals and be allowed to feel the elation of success and the depths of defeat.

Teach them the principles of comparison shopping when you go to buy groceries and involve them in your next car purchase. As they get older, try to educate them as well as you can about the world of marketing and advertising. Use the Saturday morning cartoon advertising blitz as an example of how companies target young children. Then show them how advertising changes on weekday afternoons to get to the women's market. Notice how Saturday afternoon sports go right after dad's money, and so on. This way you can instill in your child both a good understanding of and a healthy dose of cynicism toward the ads they are bombarded with on TV.

As for investing, my favourite technique is to catch their interest in the stock market by giving them a stock in something they can identify with, like McDonald's or Irwin Toys (Irwin is Canadian). These make great birthday or "welcome to the world" gifts. Get the children involved in the decision-making process and explain the inner workings of the market in a way that is applicable to their lives. I had a friend who did this with some McDonald's stock that I had given to her daughter. A stock split gave my friend an opportunity to teach her child even more about how things worked. Don't for a second think that this stuff is over the child's head. Remember, they are the ones teaching you the difference between RAM and ROM. (For the technological Luddites, these are computer terms.) Remember, your children learn much about life through what you do. Role modelling is a powerful influence on your kids. Make sure your own house is clean. You never know what messages are being sent to your children.

A case in point. A couple of years ago, I spent a week with my twin nieces, then five years old, who, incidentally, have been getting a financial education from me since they were three. We were sitting around the dining room table after lunch one day gravely discussing why green trucks drive faster than blue ones. One of my nieces claimed she was going to "pay cash" for a green truck just like Auntie Jo's when she grew up. (I drive a green jeep.)

I became curious. Heaven knows where she had picked up the term "pay cash." I didn't imagine she even knew what it meant. My brother, the father of these bright and talented children, was roaming about doing whatever. He overheard our chatter and came into the dining room to listen in. I decided to test the children's financial literacy. "OK girls," I began, "if Auntie Jo gave you a loony right now, what would you do with it?"

Leaning against the china cabinet with his arms folded across his chest, my brother looked on with decided interest. If the twins are anything like we used to be, his facial expression read, we are about to hear a litany of the multitude of freezies, licorice, sweet tarts and chocolate bars they were going to buy. My nieces didn't miss a beat. There was not even a slight hesitation. With absolutely no prompting, they said, "We'd put it in our piggy bank until we grew up."

My brother and I looked at each other. A knowing and relieved smile spread across our faces. All was well with the world.

SAVING FOR THEIR EDUCATION

Today a student pays on average $7,500 a year for tuition, room and board for post-secondary education. If your daughter decides to get a law degree or an MBA, you are looking at closer to $45,000. That's now. Imagine 10 years from now. It is not unreasonable to expect to pay a minimum of $20,000 a year for basic post-secondary education. The cost of educating your children is spiralling well beyond the rate of inflation as the government is forced to unload some of it's responsibilities. Schools are having to increase tuition dramatically to make up for the loss of this government money.

RESPS

There are a couple of options for saving for your child's education. The most well-known is the Registered Education Savings Plan (RESP). The two largest RESPs are the Canadian Scholarship Trust and the University Scholarships of Canada. The interest in these plans accumulates tax-sheltered but the contributions are not tax deductible. The major downside to these plans is that if your child chooses not to attend an accredited university or college, the interest you accumulated in the plan is lost and all you get back is the principal. Thirty percent of parents drop out of these plans and 40 percent of the children don't go on to university, at least not under the restrictions of the plan. These scholarships dictate that the child must utilize the income in the plan before age 25. Under these circumstances, the income is taxable in the hands of the child, not you. RESPs work on a pooled-resource concept. The interest you don't receive goes to the school of designation or to the Receiver-General. If the account lies dormant for five years after the termination date, then the interest automatically goes to the Receiver-General. There have been some recent improvements to RESPs. You can now have as many beneficiaries as you want as long as they are blood relatives, like a niece or nephew. So if my daughter goes to Europe after high school and decides to make a living as an artist or cordon-bleu chef, let's hope my sister's daughter wants to study medicine at Dalhousie University.

SELF-DIRECTED RESPS

As with a conventional RESP, you may only contribute $1,500 a year to a maximum of $31,500 for each child, but these plans offer a flexibility the others lack. A parent can choose the investment, for example a mutual fund, that the education fund goes into. These plans can be open for 25 years. If the child chooses not to go to an accredited educational institution, the parents themselves can use the money for university. If the plan isn't used within that 25-year time frame, the parents can decide which institution the interest goes to. You won't receive a charitable tax credit for this so-called donation as you would have had you made the donation yourself, however. These plans still have that glaring limitation of lost interest if no one chooses to go to an accredited post-secondary institution. As an aside, the charitable tax credit, once gifts hit $200, will give you a combined federal–provincial tax credit of 47 percent in Ontario. (It's similar in most of the provinces.) The tax credit on donations under the threshold is 27 percent. *Ellen Roseman's Money Guide For Modern Families* lists some excellent questions to ask about RESPs when meeting with a sales representative to compare plans:

1. How much do I pay to set up a pooled plan and keep it going? The enrollment fees are deducted from payments in the early years and are not refunded. But one plan, Heritage Scholarship Trust, gives back enrollment fees at maturity. You may also face annual depository fees (about $7.50 to $10.00) and annual administration fees (about 0.5 percent of the total fund).

2. If I buy mutual fund units, what are the costs? Funds sold through a commissioned sales force usually have either an upfront fee (deducted from the initial contributions) or a deferred sales charge (deducted from the redemption proceeds, often at a higher value). Find out if there are fees to switch from one mutual fund to another. How much is the management-ex-

pense ratio, the amount deducted from the fund assets each year to pay for portfolio advisory services and other costs? Depending on the type of fund, the management-expense ratio ranges from 1 to 2.5 percent a year. Is there an account set-up fee, an annual trustee fee or a charge for withdrawals and change of beneficiaries?

3. What are the eligibility requirements? Find out what educational institutions qualify for the plan. Most cover colleges and universities outside Canada, but some have restrictions on non-academic programs. Would a two-year community college course qualify, or a one-year trade school course? What happens if the child takes a one-year break after finishing high school or drops out of a post-secondary program and returns later? Some pooled plans will not pay if the child interrupts his or her studies. Does the payout depend on the child's passing the previous year? What if he or she takes summer make-up courses?

4. How much will my child receive in the second, third and possibly fourth year of studies? If the salesperson gives you projections, what future interest rates are those projections based on? Are the projections "industry averages" or actual experiences with the plan you are considering? Some plans are new and have no track record.

5. What if my child does not go to university or college? Most plans will let you transfer the funds to another family member, but the pooled plans prohibit changes beyond the age of 13 or 14. They make an exception for children with severe mental or physical problems that prevent them from taking post-secondary studies. A self-directed plan generally allows you to make changes at any time, right up to university.

6. Can I sell my RESP? If your child is not college-bound and no one else in the family is interested, it makes sense to sell the plan to someone who can use it. But if you do find a buyer, a sales price may be difficult to establish, and there may be tax implications to keep in mind. The buyer will have to factor in any tax the student pays on the money as it's withdrawn. And you, the seller, will have to pay tax on the sale proceeds. Revenue Canada has ruled that being paid to name another person's child as a RESP beneficiary constitutes a taxable capital gain.

LIFE INSURANCE SAVINGS PLANS

Life insurance companies have life insurance plans that they sell specifically for children's education. The tax-sheltered cash value of the policy is used to fund the cost of education. This cash value has no restrictions of any kind; it can be used for educa tion for your children or to buy yourself a boat. If used for the children, the money is taxed back to the student at their low tax bracket when cashed in. But remember, the cash value in the plan is based on *projections*. Make sure the interest rate being projected is reasonable. Also withdrawals and cancella tion fees can be onerous. You are also buying insurance with these plans. Be sure you are comfortable with this. Review the whole life and universal life sections of chapter five. These are precisely what insurance company education plans are. Make sure they suit your needs *specifically* as a savings tool for your child's education.

PAYING OFF YOUR MORTGAGE EARLY

Well, why not? The idea here is to eliminate your largest debt to free up cash later that can then be put aside for your child's ed- ucation. There are several ways to pay down your mortgage quickly as outlined in chapter eight. You can make prepayments, increase your payments and pay weekly. The thing to consider here is that each mortgage payment contributes to a possibly healthy tax-free return. Once the mortgage is paid off, which will ideally be a few years before your child will need the money, continue putting the same amount aside into an education fund. Since you don't have time on your side, be careful about in- vesting in higher risk investments. If you use the mortgage pay- down method and still find yourself short of cash for school, you can always borrow on the built-up equity in your house.

MUTUAL FUNDS

A stock-market-based or equity mutual fund is a great way, in fact, I would say the best way, to save for your children's edu- cation if you start early enough. This form of education savings is good because of its lack of limitations. You are not limited to the $1,500 amount each year that you may contribute, nor are you lim- ited to how the money is spent when the time comes to decide.

Since you could have 15 to 18 years to let the money accumulate, you will get the maximum benefit of compound growth. If the market swings bother you, invest in a balanced fund which generally fluctuates less, although the chances for superior growth are fewer.

By way of comparison, if you use a Canada Savings Bond, for example, to save for your child's education, all the interest it earns is attributed back to the parent. This is not the case with the capital gain you receive with mutual funds. Tax treatment of capital gains is still favourable, in spite of the elimination of the $100,000 capital gains exemption. Mutual funds still act as a significant tax deferral, since you don't pay any tax until you actually cash them in. In her book, Ellen Roseman explains that it's important to choose equity mutual funds that emphasize capital gain over income because the parents will have to pay tax on dividends or distributions from their children's equity investments. However, keep in mind that even though the attribution rules will tax you on dividends or interest, the amount is usually pretty small.

In our earlier discussion on mutual funds in chapter six, we talked about small and large cap funds. Though riskier, choose mutual funds that concentrate on smaller companies that don't pay dividends over the blue chip banks and phone companies that do. Make sure you have a good cross section of industries and countries represented in the fund so you can benefit from the superior returns one gets from diversification. The same standard applies: maintain that long-term view of a minimum of 10 years and you will generally come out in good shape. Michael and I have chosen long-term, solid-performing international funds to save for Kate's education.

Funding your child's education through equity funds involves the same principles as does your retirement planning. When your child gets closer to the age when the money will be needed, start to protect your gains by shifting into more guaranteed investments. Roseman recommends that when your child is 11 or 12, 10 percent a year should start going into money market funds, GICs and the like. Others advise starting to shift as your child moves through high school. Your financial advisor will help you pick a fund that is appropriate for your specific goals.

YOUR CHILDREN'S EARNINGS

I learned early in life that anything worth having requires a little pain and sacrifice. I saved for my own university tuition. I worked part-time from the age of 15, full-time in the summer and I put money aside into a separate account earmarked for school. My dad had his own business and he paid me to do odd jobs. My savings, plus a student loan, got me through school. Michael did the same. He got through engineering school with money earned through summer jobs and student loans. The wonderful lessons your children learn through becoming part of the process of putting themselves through school are invaluable. Michael and I plan on making sure Kate learns some of these life skills. Because the costs of education are escalating dramatically, we will be sure to give her a significant head start, but not a free ride.

CONCLUSION

Michael and I have been together for close to a year and I am amazed at the changes in our lives. My husband is bound and determined to make me a complete handyperson. Every time he comes home from Canadian Tire or Home Depot, his eyes are bright with excitement as he shows off his strange purchases. I feign enthusiasm but he knows full well by my glazed eyes that he might as well be showing me surgical tools. In all honesty, I love it. It won't hurt to become more confident with a screwdriver. Michael jokes that he has become the kind of man who goes to Canadian Tire on Saturday mornings even if he has nothing to buy. He shares his vision of Kate in her own tiny set of overalls passing him his tools as he works under the car or builds a new deck. He's got the baby jogger already picked out so he can take her on his hour-long run each day. In his mind, nothing is going to stand in the way of our daughter being anything she wants. He is a true and balanced feminist. With Michael's steadfast male influence and my highly developed feminine perspective, this little girl is going to be blessed with the most well-rounded role modelling you have ever seen!

Though I have always intuitively understood the world of women and the challenges we face trying to handle it all, I'm about to discover that balancing act for myself first hand. I pray that I will be able to balance all that is important in my life — family, career and personal time. I've had 20 years to develop a career; perhaps now is the time to dedicate a good portion of myself to my family. Michael is an enthusiastic and equal partner in child and homecare. When I'm too tired to move, he has already proven he can carry more than his fair share. Mom was so right, life is a balancing act. When I feel the pressures of my career close in around me, all I have to do is feel that kick or elbow prod from deep within and my mental, physical and emotional balance is completely restored. To have a fulfilled and enriched life, it simply has to be this way. Frankly, Kate is depending on it.

GENERAL RESOURCE DIRECTORY

FINANCIAL ASSOCIATIONS

Canadian Bankers Association
P.O. Box 348, Postal Station
Commerce Court
Toronto, Ontario
M5L 1G2
416-362-6092

Financial Women International
c/o CIBC
Commerce Court Postal Station
Toronto, Ontario
M5L 1A2
416-980-2211

Investment Dealers Association of Canada
121 King St. W., Suite 1600
Toronto, Ontario
M5H 3T9
416-364-6133

Canadian Securities Institute
121 King St. W., Suite 1550
Toronto, Ontario
M5H 3T9
416-364-9130

Investing for Women
1920 Ellesmere Road, Suite 302
Scarborough, Ontario
M1H 2V6
416-438-8787

Chartered Accountants of Canada
277 Wellington St. W.
Toronto, Ontario
M5V 3H2
416-977-3222

Canadian Institute of Actuaries
360 Albert Street, Suite 820
Ottawa, Ontario
K1R 7X7
613-236-8196

Canadian Shareowners Association
1090 University Avenue W.
P.O. Box 7337
Windsor, Ontario
N9C 4E9
519-252-1555

The Social Investment Organization
366 Adelaide St. E., Suite 443
Toronto, Ontario
M5A 3X9
416-360-6047

Institute of Canadian Bankers
1002 Sherbrooke St. West, Suite 1000
Montreal, Quebec
H3A 3M5
514-282-9480

The Trust Companies Association of Canada
335 Bay St. Suite 205
Toronto, Ontario
M5H 2R3
416-866-8842

Investors Association of Canada
26 Soho St., Suite 380
Toronto, Ontario
M5T 1Z7
416-340-1722

Canadian Tax Foundation
1 Queen St. E., Suite 1800
Toronto, Ontario
M5C 2Y2
416-863-9784

Canadian Institute of Chartered Accountants
277 Wellington Street West
Toronto, Ontario
M5V 3H2
416-977-3222

Canadian Association of Financial Planners
60 St. Clair Ave. E., Suite 510
Toronto, Ontario
M4T 1N5
416-966-9928

The Investment Funds Institute of Canada
151 Yonge St., 5th Floor
Toronto, Ontario
M5C 2W7
416-363-2158

Canada Deposit Insurance Corporation
50 O'Connor St.
P.O. Box 2340, Station D
Ottawa, Ontario
K1P 5W5
1-800-461-2342

*Women and Money Inc.
468 Queen St. East, 5th Floor
Toronto, Ontario
M5A 1T7
416-367-3677

*(See our advertisement at the back of this book for details)

CANADIAN STOCK EXCHANGES

Toronto Stock Exchange
Exchange Tower, P.O. Box 450
2 First Canadian Place
Toronto, Ontario
M5X 1J2
416-947-4700

Montreal Stock Exchange
Tour de la Bourse
800, sq. Victoria, C.P. 61, 4th Floor
Montreal, Quebec
H4Z 1A9
514-871-2424

Vancouver Stock Exchange
Stock Exchange Tower
609 Granville St., Box 10333
Vancouver, British Columbia
V7Y 1H1
604-689-3334

Alberta Stock Exchange
300-5th Ave. S.W., 21st Floor
Calgary, Alberta
T2P 3C4
403-974-7400

Winnipeg Stock Exchange
1 Lombard Place, Suite 2901
Winnipeg, Manitoba
R3B 0Y2
204-987-7070

CREDIT ASSOCIATIONS

Equifax Canada Inc.
60 Bloor Street West, Suite 1200
Toronto, Ontario
M4W 3C1
416-964-5482

Associated Credit Bureaus of Canada
80 Bloor St. W., Suite 900
Toronto, Ontario
M5S 2V1
416-969-2247

Ottawa Women's Credit Union
300 Slater St.
Ottawa, Ontario
K1P 1W8
613-233-7711

Credit Institute of Canada
5090 Explorer Drive, Suite 501
Mississauga, Ontario
L4W 3T9
905-629-9805

Credit Counselling Service of Metropolitan Toronto
27 Carleton Street, Suite 301
Toronto, Ontario
M5B 1L2
416-593-7434

INSURANCE ASSOCIATIONS

Independent Life Insurance Brokers of Canada
2175 Sheppard Ave. East, Suite 310
Willowdale, Ontario
M2J 1W8
416-491-9747

Insurance Bureau of Canada
181 University Avenue
Toronto, Ontario
M5H 3M7
416 362 2031

The Insurance Institute of Canada
18 King St. East
Toronto, Ontario
M5C 1C4
416-362-8586

Life Underwriters Association of Canada
41 Lesmill Road
Don Mills, Ontario
M3B 2T3
416-444-5251

Canadian Institute of Actuaries
360 Albert St., Suite 820
Ottawa, Ontario
K1R 7X7
613-236-8196

Canadian Life and Health Insurance Association
Suite 1700
1 Queen St. East
Toronto, Ontario
M5C 2X9
416-777-2221

PHILANTHROPY

The Canadian Centre for Philanthropy
1329 Bay Street, 2nd Floor
Toronto, Ontario
M5R 2C4
416-515-0764

Canadian Centre for Business in the Community
The Conference Board of Canada
255 Smyth Road
Ottawa, Ontario
K1H 8M7
613-526-3280

LEGAL AFFAIRS ASSOCIATIONS

The Canadian Bar Association
50 O'Connor St., Suite 902
Ottawa, Ontario
K1P 6L2
613-237-2925

Law Society of Upper Canada
130 Queen Street West
Toronto, Ontario
M5H 2N6
416-947-3300

National Association of Women and the Law
1 Nicholas St., Suite 604
Ottawa, Ontario
K1N 7B7
613-241-7570

Women's Legal Education and Action Fund
415 Yonge St., Suite 118
Toronto, Ontario
M5B 2E7
416-595-7170

REAL ESTATE ASSOCIATIONS

The Canadian Real Estate Association
320 Queen Street, Suite 2100
Ottawa, Ontario
K1R 5A3
613 237 7111

National Real Estate Service
1188 West Georgia St., 19th Floor
Vancouver, British Columbia
V6E 4M9
604-685-3474

Appraisal Institute of Canada
1111 Portage Avenue
Winnipeg, Manitoba
R3G 0S8
204-783-2224

BUSINESS ASSOCIATIONS

Canadian Professional Sales Association
145 Wellington St. W., Suite 310
Toronto, Ontario
M5J 1H8
416-408-2685

Business Development Bank
150 King St. W., Suite 100
P.O. Box 23
Toronto, Ontario
M5H 1J9
416-973-0341

Canadian Federation of Independent Business
4141 Yonge Street
Willowdale, Ontario
M2P 2A6
416-222-8022

Canadian Organization of Small Business
Ste. 102, 10010-107A Ave.
Edmonton, Alberta
T5H 4H8
403-423-2672

Consumers Association of Canada
267 O'Connor St., Suite 307
Ottawa, Ontario
K2P 1V3
613-238-2533

Democracy Watch
135 Rideau Street, 3rd Floor
P.O. Box 821, Station B
Ottawa, Ontario
K1P 5P9
613-241-5178

WOMEN'S ASSOCIATIONS

Status of Women Canada
360 Albert St., Suite 700
Ottawa, Ontario
K1A 1C3

National Action Committee on The Status of Women
234 Eglinton Ave. E., Suite 203
Toronto, Ontario
M4P 1K5
416-932-1718

Canadian Association of Women Executives and
Entrepreneurs
81 McLennan Ave.
Toronto, Ontario
M4T 2H4
416-482-2933

Canadian Federation of Business and
Professional Women's Clubs
56 Sparks Street, Suite 308
Ottawa, Ontario
K1P 5A9
613-234-7619

Canadian Association of Insurance Women
c/o United Canadian Shares Limited
1601 Church Avenue
Winnipeg, Manitoba
R2X 1G9
204-632-9331

Centre for Women in Business
Mount Saint Vincent University
Halifax, Nova Scotia
B3M 2J6
902-457-6449

Women Entrepreneurs of Canada
390 Bay Street, Suite 1200
Toronto, Ontario
M5H 2Y2
916-860-1125

Women-Focused Entrepreneurial Training
Federal Business Development Bank
800 Victoria Square
P.O. Box 335
Montreal, Quebec
514-283-5904

Women's World Finance/Cape Breton Association
Canadian Affiliate of Women's World Banking
P.O. Box 1142
54 Prince Street
Sydney, Nova Scotia
B1P 6J7
902-562-1772

PROVINCIAL WOMEN'S DIRECTORATES

British Columbia Ministry of Women's Equality
756 Fort Street
Victoria, British Columbia
V8V 1X4
604-387-0413

Alberta Women's Secretariat
Kensington Place, 8th Floor
10011-109th Street
Edmonton, Alberta
T5J 3S8
403-422-4927

Saskatchewan Women's Secretariat
3rd Floor
1914 Hamilton Street
Regina, Saskatchewan
S4P 4V4
306-787-1548

Manitoba Women's Directorate
100-175 Carlton Street
Winnipeg, Manitoba
R3C 3H9
204-945-3476

Women's Advisory–Government of North West Territories
Post Office Box 1320
Government of North West Territories
Yellowknife, North West Territories
X1A 2L9
403-920-3106

Yukon Women's Directorate
Post Office Box 2703
Whitehorse, Yukon
Y1A 2C6
403-667-3030

Ontario Women's Directorate
2 Carlton Street
12th Floor
Toronto, Ontario
M5B 2M9
416-314-0300

Secrétariat à la Condition Féminine
875, Grande Allée Est
2e Etage
Quebec, Quebec
G1R 4Y8
418-643-9052

New Brunswick Women's Directorate
Centennial Building
Room 413, King Street
Fredericton, New Brunswick
E3B 5H1
506-453-2143

Nova Scotia Department of Human Resources–Women's
Directorate
Post Office Box 943
Halifax, Nova Scotia
B3J 2V9
902-424-5820

Prince Edward Island Women's Secretariat
Post Office Box 2000
Charlottetown, Prince Edward Island
C1A 7N8
902-368-5570

Newfoundland Women's Policy Office
Executive Council
4th Floor, Confederation Building
St. John's, Newfoundland
A1B 4J6
709-729-5098

CYBERSPACE RESOURCES*

Aliza Sherman's Cybergirl page (http://www.interport.net/~asherman/) has links to resources on domestic violence, breast cancer and sites about and by women.

Amy Goodloe's site (http://www.best.com/~agoodloe/home.html) has many links to pages by and for women; she also runs several free women-only e-mail lists, including **internet-women-help** and **internet-women-info**. For details, e-mail majordomo@best.com and in the message space put only *info internet-women-info* or *info internet-women-help*.

For worldwide women's activism, check **WomensNet** (http://www.igc.apc.org/womensnet/).

Voices of Women World has articles and interviews (http://www.voiceofwomen.com).

Women's Wire, an on-line service based in San Mateo, Calif., focuses on content for women. For information, call 1-800-210-8998.

For details on **Systers**, a private discussion list for women in computer fields, send e-mail to systers-admin@systers.org with the word *subscribe* in the subject line.

For feminist resources, check the **English Server at Carnegie Mellon** University (http://english-www.hss.cmu.edu/Feminism.html) or the **University of Maryland's Women's Studies** database, (http://www.inform.umd.edu:8080/EdRes/Topic/WomensStudies/).

For surveys with **findings on women and their habits on-line**, check Interactive Publishing Alert (http://www.netcreations.com/ipa/), Georgia Tech (http://www.cc.gatech.edu/gvu/user (underline) surveys/) and Matrix Information and Directory Services, (http://www.mids.org).

* Copyright 1995, USA TODAY. Reprinted with permission.

ENDNOTES

CHAPTER ONE

[1] "Women everywhere still trail in wages, power, UN reports," John Stackhouse, *The Globe and Mail.* August, 1995.

[2] *Ibid.*

[3] Shelly Phipps, "Social Policy and the Family," *Canadian Public Policy,* XX1, no. 1, March 1995.

CHAPTER TWO

[4] Wendy Cuthbert, "Collection agencies will help in debt dilemmas," *The Financial Post,* August 19, 1993.

[5] Anthony Kirby, "Check credit rating to save embarrassment," *The Globe and Mail,* November 15, 1991.

[6] *Ibid.*

[7] Edith Morber, "Credit card costs," Consumer and Corporate Affairs Bulletin #25146, June 1993.

[8] Frances Cerra Whittlesey, "Why Women Pay More," Center for Study of Responsive Law, 1993.

CHAPTER FOUR

[9] Robert Kerton, quoted by Janice Turner in "Sex discrimination in the marketplace," *The Toronto Star,* January 3, 1992.

[10] "Why do female consumers often pay more than men do?" *The Toronto Star,* January 3, 1992.

[11] Ian Ayres, "Fair Driving: Gender and Race Discrimination in Retail Car Negotiations," *Harvard Law Review,* vol. 104, February 1991.

[12] "Gypped by Gender," NY Department of Consumer Affairs, 1992.

[13] Deborah Kolb, "Is It Her Voice or Her Place That Makes a Difference? A Consideration of Gender Issues in Negotiations," Industrial Relations Centre, Queen's University, 1992.

[14] Frances Cerra Whittlesey, op. cit.

CHAPTER FIVE

[15] The Trust Companies Association of Canada National Survey, Angus Reid Group and Consumer Line Omnibus, 1992.

[16] William P.G. Allen, *The Estate Planning Handbook* (Toronto: The Carswell Company, 1985).

[17] D. Molloy, M.D., "The Living Will—A Physician's Perspective," The Canadian Bar Association, 1991.

[18] "Disability Insurance: Where Will The Money Come From If You're Disabled?" Canadian Life and Health Association, 1992.

[19] DAWN speech, 1991.

CHAPTER SIX

[20] "Opportunities in the Mutual Funds Market," Brendan Wood International, September 1993.

CHAPTER SEVEN

[21] Financial Affairs, Multiple Retirement Services, Issue #8.

[22] Hubert Frenken, "Women and RRSPs," in *Perspectives on Labour and Income* (Ottawa: Statistics Canada) Winter 1991, Vol. 3, No. 4, page 8.

[23] *Canadian Retirement Income Social Security Programs*, Report of the Task Force on Social Security Financing: Canadian Institute of Actuaries, November 1993.

[24] Hubert Frenken and Karen Maser, "Employer-sponsored pension plans—who is covered?," in *Perspectives on Labour and Income* (Ottawa: Statistics Canada) Winter 1992, Vol. 4, No. 4.

[25] Hubert Frenken and Karen Maser, "RRSPs—new rules, new growth," in *Perspectives on Labour and Income* (Ottawa: Statistics Canada) Winter 1993, Vol. 5, No. 4.

CHAPTER NINE

[26] Elaine Wyatt, *The Money Companion* (Toronto: Penguin Books, 1991) The Financial Times Personal Finance Library, page 56.

27 "Expanding Our Horizons," The Canadian Advisory Council on The Status of Women, 1993.

28 *Tax Facts: What Every Woman Should Know*, The Canadian Advisory Council on The Status of Women, 1993.

29 "Women and Taxation," Fair Tax Commission, 1992.

30 *Ibid.*

31 *Ibid.*

INDEX

Women and Money Inc. is a research and education company. Our mandate is to educate women about money and financial institutions about women. Using a variety of educational tools, we elevate women's financial literacy and the awareness of the economic realities facing women today. These tools include the Canadian best-seller *Balancing Act: A Canadian Woman's Financial Success Guide*, written by our president, Joanne Thomas Yaccato, and the groundbreaking *Closing the Gender Gap* series of workshops, seminars and keynote speeches. Whether you are an individual seeking information about women and money, or a financial institution seeking education about the women's market, Women and Money Inc. has the resources.

Balancing Act: A Canadian Woman's Financial Success Guide is available in bookstores across Canada. Women and Money Inc. offers corporate rates for orders of 10 or more. For more information about our services or to order *Balancing Act* in bulk, or to hire Joanne as a keynote speaker, please contact:

Women and Money Inc.
468 Queen Street East
5th Floor
Toronto, Ontario
M5A 1T7
Tel.: (416) 367-3677
Fax: (416) 367-1591
Internet: Women@ibm.net